POWERFUL ENVIRONMENTS FOR PROMOTING
DEEP CONCEPTUAL AND STRATEGIC LEARNING

STUDIA PAEDAGOGICA

New Series
41

Editorial Board
Prof. Dr. E. De Corte (Chairman)
Prof. Dr. A. De Munter
Prof. Dr. M. Depaepe
Prof. Dr. B. Maes
Prof. Dr. G. Vandemeulebroecke

Powerful environments for promoting deep conceptual and strategic learning

Edited by
L. Verschaffel, E. De Corte, G. Kanselaar
and M. Valcke

Leuven University Press
2005

Uitgegeven met de steun van de
K.U.Leuven Commissie voor Publicaties

© 2005 Universitaire Pers Leuven / Leuven University Press /
Presses Universitaires de Louvain
Blijde-Inkomststraat 5, B-3000 Leuven

All rights reserved. Except in those cases expressly determined by law, no part of this publication may be multiplied, saved in an automated datafile or made public in any way whatsoever without the express prior written consent of the publishers.

ISBN 90 5867 469 X

D / 2005 / 1869 / 77

NUR: 847

Table of Contents

Introduction   9

Part I: General perspectives   17

1. **The problem of knowledge in the design of learning environments**   19
   S. Vosniadou
   University of Athens, Greece

2. **On learning environments that foster subject- matter competence**   29
   A.H. Schoenfeld
   University of California, Berkeley, USA

3. **Engagement in learning: Designing learning environments that are really used**   45
   T. de Jong
   University of Twente, The Netherlands

Part II: Promoting deep conceptual and strategic learning in mathematics   61

4. **Does social interaction influence 3-year-old children's tendency to focus on numerosity? A quasi-experimental study in day care**   63
   M.M. Hannula, A. Mattinen, and E. Lehtinen
   University of Turku, Finland

5. **Using mathematical symbols at the beginning of the arithmetical and algebraic learning**   81
   A. Fagnant, J. Vlassis, and M. Crahay
   Université de Liège, Belgium

6. **Collaboration in small group mathematics problem solving: A case study**   97
   G.H.J. Seegers and D.J. Hoek
   University of Leiden, The Netherlands; Open University of the Netherlands

7. **Remedying secondary school students' illusion of linearity: Developing and evaluating a powerful learning environment**   115
   W. Van Dooren, D. De Bock, A. Hessels, D. Janssens, and L. Verschaffel
   University of Leuven, Belgium

8. **Improving procedural transfer in mathematics with interactive animations**   133
   P. Gerjets, K. Scheiter, and R. Catrambone
   Knowledge Media Research Center, Germany

9. **Teaching percentages in the primary school: A four country comparative study**   147
   F. Depaepe, E. De Corte, P. Op 't Eynde and L. Verschaffel
   University of Leuven, Belgium

Part III: Promoting deep conceptual and strategic learning in other major curricular domains   173

10. **Teaching-learning environments and student learning in electronic engineering**   175
    N. Entwistle, J. Nisbet, and A. Bromage
    University of Edinburgh, UK

11. **Learner control over information presentation in powerful electronic learning environments used in physics education**   199
    L. Kester, P.A. Kirschner, and G. Corbalán-Pérez
    Open University of the Netherlands

12. **The impact of external graphical representations in different knowledge domains: Is there a domain specific effect?**   213
    K. De Westelinck and M. Valcke
    University of Ghent, Belgium

13. **Using representational tools to support historical reasoning in CSCL**   233
    G. Kanselaar, C. van Boxtel, and J. van Drie
    University of Utrecht, The Netherlands

List of Contributors   257

Introduction

Introduction

Over the past two decades a substantial amount of research has been reported relating to the development and evaluation of powerful learning environments for the acquisition in students of worthwhile educational objectives focussing on conceptual understanding, higher-order cognitive and metacognitive skills, and self-regulated learning. This research has been mainly undertaken from three distinct, but related perspectives in the study of learning and instruction, namely instructional psychology, instructional technology, and instructional design. Against this background, a Research Network was initiated in 2002 with the aim of interactively contributing to the advancement of theory and methodology relating to the design, implementation, and evaluation of powerful learning environments. This network, which is coordinated by the Leuven Center for Instructional Psychology and Technology and funded for a five-year period by the Flemish Fund for Scientific Research, involves 14 European research teams, most of which have contributed to this book.

This volume is based on the plenary lectures and working sessions during the Research Network's third workshop, which was held from September 30 until October 2, 2004 in Hof Lanchals, Brugge (Belgium). The theme of the workshop was "Designing powerful learning environments to promote deep conceptual and strategic learning in major curricular domains". This topic was addressed in different ways (theoretically, empirically, methodologically), at different levels (primary, secondary, or higher education, including teacher education), in different subject-matter domains (mathematics, physics, social sciences...), and from the distinct disciplinary perspectives reflected in the network (instructional psychology, instructional design, or instructional technology).

Part I of the volume consists of three chapters that present general perspectives on the central theme of the workshop. It starts with a critical reflection on the cognitive apprenticeship model of learning and instruction by Stella Vosniadou. The next chapter is a contribution of Alan Schoenfeld, who was the invited scholar from outside the network for this workshop. The learning environments described by Schoenfeld are clearly apprenticeship-like, but do not at all neglect the subject-matter aspect of learning and teaching. One of the major elements of Schoenfeld's learning environments, namely the importance of interaction in a "community of learners" is echoed in the third chapter of Part I written by Ton de Jong. In Part II six studies are reported wherein novel learning environments for elementary and secondary mathematics education were designed, implemented and evaluated. In Part III of the volume another set of four investigations is presented relating to the design, implementation and evaluation of powerful learning environments in other subject-matter domains, namely physics, history, and the social sciences.

Part I

In the first chapter Vosniadou examines critically a framework that has had substantial impact over the past 15 years on research relating to the design and evaluation of powerful learning environments, namely the *cognitive apprenticeship* metaphor. While acknowledging that this framework has contributed relevant ideas and guidelines for instruction of cognitive skills, she argues that cognitive apprenticeship has depressed the role of knowledge. And, acquiring competence in the different disciplines requires the learning of significant domain-specific knowledge. The author then shows that it is possible to design learning environments that maintain the benefits of the cognitive apprenticeship approach to learning and instruction, and that combine them with the acquisition of deep conceptual domain knowledge. The chapter ends with the presentation of principles for developing such learning environments, such as: focusing on key concepts in curriculum domains, empirically based sequencing of the learning of concepts, addressing students' entrenched presuppositions, stimulating metaconceptual awareness, and using models and external representations to clarify scientific explanations.

Schoenfeld's contribution starts from the observation that acquiring competence in the different disciplines involves besides the learning of subject matter also the development and mastery of habits of mind. A key question is then, how does one create learning environments that foster these aspects of domain competence? The main argument of this chapter is that a central notion with regard to learning, both in and out of school, is that of *community of practice*: learning takes place when one interacts actively and purposefully with a group of people engaged in a particular body of work. Schoenfeld documents and illustrates this basic idea by reflecting on various attempts to create such learning communities, especially his own courses relating to mathematical problem solving, but also Brown and Campione's work on "Fostering a Community of Learners", and Scardamalia and Bereiter's research on knowledge building and the "Knowledge Forum". In all these projects, the goal was rich and purposeful interaction; in some, technology was used to facilitate such interactions. The author argues that despite differences in grade level (ranging from elementary through graduate school) and subject-matter domains (ranging over mathematics, literature, history, and the life sciences), there are strong commonalities in assumptions and practices across those environments.

In the last chapter of Part I De Jong starts from the observation that contemporary students are accustomed to fast, multi-faceted, interactive, and socially entrenched information. Consequently, they expect their universities and schools to reflect these characteristics in the learning environments they are immersed in. Curriculum-embedded, collaborative discovery learning environments may answer this need by offering students a mainly self-directed "experience" instead of direct instruction. In designing these experiential environments several considerations are important. First, engagement of learners should be stimulated, for example, by giving them a "role" or by letting them play an element in the environment. Second, realistic contexts should be used that cross the boundaries of traditional curri-cular topics (physics, chemistry, mathematics, biology, or even language, management etc.). Third, collaboration with others learners should be a central aspect of the learning experience. Fourth, learners should be offered means to express their knowledge and be given opportunities to share this knowledge with others learners. Finally, the learning experience should help students to stretch their boundaries by offering cognitive tools that support the learning process. In this chapter these design principles are documented and illustrated on the basis of several learning systems, namely ZAP ("Zeer Actieve Psychologie"; in English "Very Active Psychology"), a series of short interactive programs in the domain of psychology; KMQuest, a game to learn about Knowledge Management; and Co-Lab, a learning environment for collaborative inquiry in science.

Part II

The goal of study by Hannula, Mattinen, and Lehtinen was to investigate whether it is possible to enhance 3-year-old children's tendency to Spontaneously FOcus on Numerosity (SFON), and thus start children's deliberate practice in early mathematical skills. Participants were 3-year-old children in Finnish day care. The SFON scores and cardinality-related skills of the experimental group of 17 children were compared to the corresponding results of the control group. The results show an experimental effect on SFON tendency and subsequent development in cardinality-related skills from pre-test to delayed post-test in the children with some initial SFON tendency in the experimental group. Moreover, social interaction had an effect on children's SFON tendency.

The chapter by Fagnant, Vlassis, and Crahay focuses on symbolizing activities in mathematics education. In mathematics, by contrast with other sciences, objects cannot be grasped by perceptual means. Access to them is only possible with the help of symbolic representations of objects under consideration. Consequently, it can be said that the use of symbols is intrinsically bound to mathematical knowledge. Several authors currently consider symbolizing activities as integral to mathematical reasoning rather than an external aid to it. Symbolizing and meaning making are mutually constitutive and emerge together. By contrast, in the traditional view of instruction, teachers give ready-made symbols, explain what they mean and how they are to be used. In the French Community of Belgium, this kind of approach is still current in mathematics. In this chapter two empirical studies are discussed that aimed at analysing symbolizing activities at two different school levels. The first research concerns addition and subtraction in words problems in grades 1 and 2, whereas the second one focuses on elementary algebraic operations in grades 8 and 9. In these two cases, data were collected through individual interviews. Both studies show that traditional approach leads students to an inefficient use of mathematical symbols. In the first study, it was observed that students develop superficial strategies based on key words. The second one also shows that students apply superficial procedures; these are based on an erroneous and inflexible use of algebraic symbols (e.g., the minus sign) leading them to an inability to recognize the structure of algebraic operations.

The focus of the study by Seegers and Hoek is on how teacher's coaching style may support students working on mathematics problems in small groups. As an additional element the graphic calculator (GC) is integrated in the solving process. Instructional activities included modeling problem solving, stimulating reflection, and giving feedback on the process of collaboration. These activities reflect the twofold goal of the study: to model the process of problem solving and to improve the process of collaboration. These activities were developed and implemented in a cyclical process in collaboration with the teachers that participated in the study. Implementing these activities, observational data, field notes and teacher interviews were used to evaluate their effects. In a next cycle, adapted or alternative activities were developed and implemented. Teachers changed their coaching style during collaborative work from giving content-related feedback to process-oriented feedback. These changes went together with a higher level of student discourse and a more investigative approach towards problem solving supported by the graphic calculator.

Already at a very young age, children experience the wide applicability and intrinsic simplicity of linear/proportional relations. In primary and secondary school mathematics education, moreover, extensive attention is paid to this type of relations. In the long run, students develop the misbelief that each relation can be quantified as proportional, which is called the "illusion of linearity". The best-known example of misconceptions originating from such a "synthetic model of linearity" in students is the misbelief that if a geometrical figure enlarges $\underline{k}$ times, its area and/or volume become $\underline{k}$ times larger too. The chapter by Van Dooren, De Bock, Hessels, Janssens, and Verschaffel discusses a teaching experiment aimed at remedying this misbelief in 8th graders. Ten experimental lessons were developed in order to obtain a conceptual change in these students. The learning results were tested by means of a pre-test-post-test-retention test design with an experimental group and a control group. Students in the control group did not evolve in their problem-solving behaviour. In the experimental group, the intervention was successful: there was a drastic decrease in students' automatic use of proportional strategies for solving non-proportional geometry problems. Nevertheless, some students continued to reason proportionally for all types of problems, while others suddenly started to apply non-proportional strategies to proportional problems too. Whereas the linearity illusion was broken in most students, this did not always result in a deep conceptual understanding of proportional and non-proportional situations and relations.

In the experiment described in the next chapter, Gerjets, Scheiter, and Catrambone investigated the effects of different kinds of computer-based visualizations on the acquisition of problem-solving skills in the domain of probability theory. Learners received either purely text-based worked examples, text plus an instruction to mentally imagine the examples' contents, or they could retrieve either static pictures or concrete animations that depicted the problem statement and the problem states achieved by applying a specific solution step. It could be shown that frequently using static pictures or imagining the examples' contents both improved problem-solving performance on isomorphic problems. However, there were no positive effects of using animations. Rather, the frequent use of animations led to substantial increases in learning time, while it slightly decreased performance at the same time. Thus, the use of concrete animations to visualize solution procedures was more harming than helpful for conveying problem-solving skills.

The last chapter of Part II by Depaepe, De Corte, Verschaffel, and Op 't Eynde outlines a small-scale video based, comparative study of the teaching of mathematics in four European countries that is part of the METE-project (Mathematics Education and Traditions in Europe). The study makes an attempt to partly overcome a number of constraints of previous comparative video studies. It aims at a comparison of mathematics education in the upper primary school (grades 5 and 6) and the lower secondary school (grades 7 and 8) in Flanders, England, Hungary and Spain. The study compares for each country a sequence of four or five lessons within a certain mathematical domain: percentages and polygons in the upper primary school, and polygons and linear equations in the lower secondary school. This chapter focuses on the percentage part of this comparative study.

Part III

In the first chapter of Part III, Entwistle, Nisbet, and Bromage present early findings from the ETL project, a national study in Britain which is investigating teaching and learning across five contrasting subject areas in higher education. The focus here is on electronic engineering and, in particular on analogue electronics. Staff in six course units has collaborated with the researchers to enable data to be collected from their students, and in four of the units changes were made on the basis of the evidence presented to them. The effects of these "collaborative initiatives" were investigated using data obtained from the following year groups derived from questionnaires and interviews with both students and staff. On this basis, a clearer idea has been developed about the nature of teaching and learning in the subject with implications for ways of enhancing the teaching-learning environments provided for students in future.

Modern curricula make use of powerful electronic learning environments to facilitate complex skill acquisition. Such environments contain realistic problems and varied information resources. Kester, Kirschner, and Corbalán-Pérez zoom in on learner control over information presentation and the acquisition of complex cognitive skills during problem solving in powerful electronic learning environments. Giving novices in a domain control over the presentation of necessary information can facilitate self-regulated learning and lead to higher learning outcomes, but is also problematic for two reasons. Domain novices have difficulty in both determining their information requirements to solve a problem and in acting upon their information requirements (i.e., choosing and using the right information at the right time). Two types of support to help domain novices to properly interact with the information resources are proposed: limited learner control and supported learner control. Limited learner control pre-structures and pre-orders the available information which has beneficial effects on learning, but can also present the wrong information at the wrong time which could hamper learning. Supported learner control combines the best of both worlds by allowing for self-regulated learning and by providing support for self-regulated learning by pre-structuring the information sources and offers conceptual and procedural support to enable even domain novices to become self-regulated learners.

Through a series of three studies De Westelinck and Valcke question the generalizability of Mayer's cognitive theory of multimedia learning (CTML) to the knowledge domain of the social sciences. The first research builds on the assumption that this knowledge domain differs in the way instructional designers are able to develop adequate depictive external graphical representations. Earlier CTML-research is mostly carried out in the field of the natural sciences where the external graphical representations are depictive in nature and/or where the representations can be developed from an existing or acquired iconic sign system. The research results reveal that studying this type of representations does not result in higher test performance and does not result in lower levels of cognitive load. The second research builds on these former results and questions under which condition the performance on retention and transfer test can increase. Therefore the new principle activation is added to the research design. Results show that the performance on the retention and transfer test is higher when the learner is active, i.e., develops his/her own external graphical representations. Developing external graphical representations beholds different individual representations because every individual makes his or her external graphical representations. These differences make out the starting point of the third research which tries to answer the question about the types of external graphical representations the learners/participants make.

In order to make progress in the design of powerful learning environments that are able to provoke and support high level historical reasoning, it is necessary to know more about important components, modes and specific problems of reasoning within the domain of history. Reasoning reflects a transformation of knowledge and information and is constructed during the encounter with a problem or a question. Kanselaar, Van Boxtel, and Van Drie present a model of historical reasoning with six important components. The study investigates the effects of the joint construction of external representations on the collaborative process. By providing representational guidance, the study aimed at promoting co-elaborated and domain-specific reasoning. Three representational formats, namely an argumentative diagram, an argument list and a matrix, were compared with a control group. Sixty-five student pairs from pre-university education collaborated on a historical writing task in a CSCL environment. The analyses included analyses of interaction processes in the chat, the quality of the co-constructed representation, the quality of the essay and the scores on the individual post-test. The results indicate that each representational format has its own affordances and constraints. For example, Matrix users talk more about historical changes, whereas Diagram users focus more on the balance in their argumentation. However, this did not result in differences in the quality of historical reasoning in the essay, nor in outcomes on the post-test.

This book could not have been produced without the help and support of several people. First we would like to thank Geraldine Clarebout, Karine Dens, Joke Torbeyns, Wim Van Dooren and Bartel Wilms for their indispensable organizational, technical and administrative support in the preparation and realization of the workshop of which this book is an outcome. We also thank Betty Vanden Bavière for her immense assistance in preparing the final manuscript of this volume. Finally, we are also indepted to the Fund for Scientific Research, Flanders, which provided substantial financial support to organize this workshop.

March 2005

Lieven Verschaffel
Erik De Corte
Gellof Kanselaar
Martin Valcke

Part I
General perspectives

Chapter 1

The problem of knowledge in the design of learning environments

Stella Vosniadou

1   Introduction

In an insightful discussion of the reasons why educational research is at present not "very influential, useful, and well funded," Burkhardt and Schoenfeld (2003, p. 3) argue that by employing an *engineering approach* educational researchers would be in a position to better link research to practice and thus make educational research more credible. In contrast to the *humanistic approach*, which is based on critical argumentation and reflection of ideas, and the *scientific approach*, which is based on empirical results, the *engineering approach* to research is concerned with practical impact – "to use existing knowledge and insights to produce new and high quality solutions to practical problems – to create new materials, devices, products, etc." (p. 5).

In this chapter, I will examine a metaphor that has played an important role in guiding the engineering type of research that aims at designing powerful learning environments, namely the *cognitive apprenticeship* metaphor. I will argue that this metaphor has provided important guidelines for teaching cognitive skills, but that it has downgraded the problem of knowledge. Learning and the development of expertise in curricular domains require the construction of significant domain knowledge. I will show that it is possible to keep the advantages of the cognitive apprentice metaphor without ignoring the development of knowledge and that serious knowledge building efforts require more attention to be paid on the design of research-based, developmentally appropriate curricula for the different subject-matter domains.

2   The cognitive apprenticeship metaphor

The cognitive apprenticeship metaphor has been introduced in the design of learning environments to address the problem of authenticity and to avoid the creation of inert knowledge. Collins, Brown, and Duguid (1989) have argued that many school activities are not meaningful because they are not connected in some manifest way with the world outside school, and because students do not understand why they are doing them. Lack of meaningfulness can be a source of inert knowledge because it makes it difficult for students to understand the relevance of what they have learned and thus, to transfer knowledge and skills to out of school situations. In apprenticeship teaching the meaningfulness of tasks is guaranteed by the very nature of the activity since the learning task usually involves practical skills embedded in their social and functional context.

Traditional apprenticeship aims at teaching the practical skills of a craft, such as tailoring, basket weaving, etc. The apprentice has access to a model or several models of masters who practice the skill in authentic contexts. By focusing on observing the specific methods masters use to carry out tasks in a domain and through continuous feedback and coaching, the apprentice slowly learns to execute the whole skill. According to Collins, Brown, and Newman (1989), apprentices use a variety of methods to facilitate learning, but of those, observation is particularly important because it helps the learner create a conceptual model of the task that guides initial efforts to imitate it and provides an interpretive structure for making sense of feedback and corrections from the master on the road towards autonomous execution.

Cognitive apprenticeship is different from traditional apprenticeship in that its aim is not to teach a practical/physical skill, but the cognitive and metacognitive skills experts use to handle complex tasks. Unlike physical skills, which are external and thus readily available, cognitive skills are internal and lack transparency. The purpose of cognitive apprenticeship is to externalize and bring out in the open the cognitive, internal, processes used by experts in a domain, thus making it possible for students to use the methods of traditional apprenticeship, methods such as observation, coaching, and modeling, in view of learning those processes.

Learning environments designed from the cognitive apprenticeship point of view focus on the teaching of expert skills. For example, Collins, Brown, and Newman (1989) propose three kinds of strategies/skills that students must learn. These are local inquiry learning strategies, control strategies, and heuristic strategies. Local inquiry learning strategies include all learning how to learn types of strategies, while control strategies are the kind of strategies that help students manage their problem solving, such as deciding what to do when one is stuck with a problem he/she cannot solve or selecting the most appropriate of various possible strategies for the solution of a given problem. Heuristic strategies are important because they can provide effective techniques for accomplishing complex tasks. Heuristic "tricks of the trade" are usually acquired by experts tacitly and are considered difficult to be taught explicitly.

As mentioned earlier, in cognitive apprenticeship the teacher must find ways to bring the internal cognitive skills out in the open where the students can observe and practice them. In doing so, the teacher needs to pay attention to the sequence in which these skills must be acquired – for example, simple skills should precede complex skills, and global skills should precede local skills.

Cognitive apprenticeship has been very successful in guiding the design of learning environments that teach thinking skills. Good examples of this are Palincsar and Brown's "reciprocal teaching" (Palincsar & Brown, 1984), and Schoenfeld's method for teaching mathematical problem solving (Schoenfeld, 1985). Another example, is the kind of educational software developed to teach metacognitive skills, such as Barbara White's SCI-WISE or Inquiry Island (see White, Shimoda, & Frederiksen, 1999). These teaching methods/learning environments succeed in producing situations where the cognitive skills become externalized and explicit and where strategies are modeled for self-correction and self-monitoring.

Unfortunately, cognitive apprenticeship has not been able to deal with the very problem of authenticity that it set out to solve in the first place. This is because in cognitive apprenticeship the tasks and problems do not arise from the demands of culturally authentic and socially shared activities in the context of the workplace as in traditional apprenticeship. According to Collins, Brown, and Newman (1989) "cognitive apprenticeship must find a way to create a culture of expert practice for students to participate in and aspire to, as well as device meaningful benchmarks and incentives for progress" (p. 459).

One solution to this problem is to propose that the purpose of schools is to enculturate students into the cultures of the subject-matter areas they are taught in school, i.e., into the culture of mathematicians, physicists, writers, historians, etc. This is a road that some researchers have taken. But, as Brown, Ash, Rutherford, Nakagawa, Gordon, and Campione (1993) correctly note, this is a rather romantic suggestion. Practitioners of these subject domains do not usually populate schools, particularly when we are referring to primary and secondary education. History teachers or mathematics teachers are not usually practicing historians or mathematicians Thus, cognitive apprenticeship maybe an authentic activity for graduate school students – and it is indeed the main means whereby our graduate students become trained – but not for younger students, let alone those who attend primary school.

Another solution proposed by Ann Brown and her colleagues (Brown et al., 1993; Brown, 1992; Brown & Campione, 1990), is that schools should be communities where students learn to learn and that teachers should model intentional learning and self-motivated scholarship. "If successful, graduates of such communities would be prepared as lifelong learners who have learned how to learn in many domains. We aim to produce a breed of "intelligent novices" (Brown, Bransford, Ferrara, & Campione, 1983), students who, although they may not possess the background knowledge needed in a new field, know how to go about gaining that knowledge. These learning experts would be better prepared to be inducted into the practitioner culture of their choosing; they would also have the background to select among several alternative practitioner cultures, rather than being tied to the one to which they were initially indentured, as in the case of traditional apprenticeships."

Such a solution to the problem of authenticity, however, may lead the cognitive apprenticeship metaphor in the direction of focusing on expert practices and ignoring both the problem of authenticity and the problem of knowledge. Is it really possible to create intelligent novices in the Brown et al. (1993) sense? Expertise consists not only of expert practices but also of a body of well-defined knowledge. When an apprentice becomes a tailor or a shoe-maker, she/he acquires the related skills and cultural practices together with the related domain knowledge and belief systems that go with the trade or discipline in question, as they have accumulated over the years in the culture. Cognitive apprenticeship becomes empty when its purpose is to practice cognitive skills in the absence of substantial knowledge building, and where the domain knowledge is secondary to the skills to be learned. By focusing only on the process and by not paying sufficient attention to knowledge building, the cognitive apprenticeship metaphor runs into the danger of emptying schooling of one of its most important purposes, the construction of knowledge. This turns to be a rather interesting conclusion in view of recent movements towards a knowledge-based society, a society in which the main wealth-producing work is knowledge.

3 Situated cognition and the problem of knowledge

According to Bereiter (1997) situativity theory and the cognitive apprenticeship metaphor have failed to provide a cogent idea of the point of schooling and a new educational vision exactly because they have not been able to adequately address the problem of knowledge. The difficulty according to Bereiter (1997) is the confusion in situativity theory between process and product when the product of the activity is knowledge. As he argues, when the work of a community of practice is that of manufacturing paint, there is no problem in separating the manufacturing process from the product, i.e., paint. The process of manufacturing paint is a situated activity embedded in the relevant contexts and cultural practices, but the product paint is not. Paint itself is not situated. It can be used in many different situations and for many purposes.

One can make the same argument about knowledge as the product of a situated activity. Bereiter (1997) argues that in school situations knowledge products are created that are different from the knowledge implicit in the processes that produce them. This argument is difficult to understand because unlike the previous situation where the product is paint, in the situation of schooling the product is knowledge. But, as Bereiter correctly states, the results of knowledge construction do not have to be seen as something entirely internal to the minds of individual children (as in cognitive accounts) or internal to the distributed cognition of the classroom (as in sociocultural accounts). Students produce knowledge objects (ideas, explanations, conjectures, theories) and so on that can be written up and communicated inside and outside the classroom. Bereiter and Scardamalia (1989, 1993, see also Scardamalia, Bereiter, & Lamon, 1994) focus on the tangible knowledge objects students produce through the use of electronic media and make these objects the focus of their knowledge-building environments.

While I completely agree with Bereiter's argument for knowledge building, I think that focusing only on students' products is not adequate by itself to solve the problem of knowledge. Our culture has produced important knowledge objects (science, mathematics, history, etc.) that are tangible and can be communicated, taught and learned. Unlike practical skills and trades where knowledge and skills are intrinsically interconnected and where the product is something different, like a costume or a shoe, the knowledge that has been produced by science and mathematics, history and literature is not necessarily interconnected with the skills that produced it. The objective knowledge products in the form of theories and artifacts produced by our culture can be taught to individuals who do not plan necessarily to be practicing historians, scientists, etc.

The theories produced as a result of scientific activity are like the paint previously mentioned. They are the products of a creative manufacturing process - produced through the situated practices of scientists, but nevertheless, with an objective reality. They are products, divorced from the processes that produced them. Just like paint, but also much more than paint, they can be used in different situations for different purposes by different people. They can be used by engineers and architects, by computer scientists and artists, among others, to produce technological artifacts that change our objective reality and the very culture within which scientific activity takes place. It is difficult to understand arguments claiming that the knowledge products of scientists and mathematicians cannot be taught to students at school, for the purpose of preparing these students to participate in their culture as informed citizens. Here, I agree completely with Brown et al. (1993) when they say that the purpose of schooling is not to apprentice children in the traditional academic disciplines but to create informed consumers, interpreters, and critics of science, history and mathematics, at least at the level of basic education.

To summarize, in order to create learning environments for deep conceptual knowledge and strategies we need to couple cognitive apprenticeship with carefully designed curricula for the teaching of knowledge in the subject-matter domains. Only then we can achieve substantial gains in conceptual understanding. In the pages that follow I will outline some principles for the design of learning environments that focus on the development of knowledge and skills in science, based on our experimental work (Vosniadou, Ioannides, Dimitrakopoulou, & Papademetriou, 2001).

4   The design of research-based curricula in science

The finding that the understanding of science concepts and explanations is a difficult and time-consuming affair calls for a reconsideration of current decisions regarding the breadth of coverage of the curriculum in science education. It may be more profitable to design curricula that focus on the deep exploration and understanding of a few, key concepts in one subject-matter area rather than curricula that cover a great deal of material in a superficial way. This latter strategy is likely to lead students to logical incoherence and misconceptions. It tends to encourage the casual memorization of facts, and does not develop the analytic skills necessary for conceptual change and the development of new representations. It also makes teachers very anxious about covering all the material with the result that not enough attention is paid to what students actually understand.

The design of curricula needs to be based on the results of detailed empirical investigations that provide information about the way students acquire information in a given subject-matter area. Usually the concepts that comprise a subject-matter area have a relational structure that influences their order of acquisition. For example, research has shown that students need some information about gravity in order to understand how people can live all around a spherical earth, on the outside, without "falling down". Furthermore, an understanding of the spherical shape of the earth and of where people live on the earth, is a necessary requirement for understanding explanations of the day/night cycle, and so on. These findings need to be taken into consideration when designing curricula.

Special attention must be paid so that the information included in the curricula addresses students' prior ideas and beliefs. Research has shown that strong beliefs such as that force, heat or weight are properties of objects, that space is organized in the directions of up and down, that unsupported objects fall in a downward direction, and so on, exert tremendous influence on the way students interpret new information often becoming the cause of persistent misconceptions.

In science instruction counterintuitive information is often introduced as a fact which the students are "told" (also see Bransford, 1989). For example, in astronomy, students are commonly told that "the earth rotates around its axis" or that "the sun is much bigger than the earth", or that "the sun is a star", without an explanation of how it is possible for the earth to move when we do not feel any such movement, how it is possible for the sun to be much bigger than the earth when in fact it appears to be much smaller, and how it is possible for the sun to be a star when stars appear in the sky only at night, have a different shape than the sun, are much smaller, and so on.

It is important when designing science instruction and curricula to distinguish new information that is consistent with prior knowledge from new information that runs contrary to prior knowledge. When the new information is consistent with prior knowledge, it can be incorporated easily into existing conceptual structures. This type of information is most likely to be understood even if it is presented as a fact without any further explication. However, when the new information runs contrary to existing conceptual structures, simply presenting the new information as a fact may not be adequate. In this situation students seem to have two courses of action available to them. One is simply to add the new fact to their existing conceptual structures. If they do this, it will result in internally inconsistent and fragmented knowledge. The other is to distort the new fact to make it consistent with what they already know. In this case, the result will probably be a synthetic model, otherwise known as misconception. In order for the counterintuitive information to be understood, students must be given adequate explanations, and many times additional information, not entirely obvious at the beginning. It is particularly, in these kinds of situating where instruction that follows the cognitive apprenticeship metaphor can be most useful.

The situations where new information cannot be simply told, but has to be explained, present an excellent case where the teacher can introduce experiments in the classroom and teach the students cognitive skills such as systematic observation, data gathering, hypothesis testing, etc. For example, in our experimental classrooms on observational astronomy, we had students do systematic observations of helium balloons slowly disappearing in the sky in order to understand how distance and the perception of size are related, before giving them facts about the size of the moon, sun, stars, etc. In these situations students can learn the necessary cognitive skills while they also try to understand challenging ideas.

Another area where cognitive apprenticeship can be particularly useful is in teaching metacognitive skills. Although students are relatively good interpreters of their everyday experiences, they do not seem to be aware of the explanatory frameworks they have constructed and of the presuppositions that constrain them. Even when they start to achieve this metaconceptual awareness they do not understand that their explanations are hypotheses that can be subjected to experimentation and falsification. Therefore, their explanations remain implicit and tacit. Lack of metaconceptual awareness of this sort prevents students from questioning their prior knowledge and facilitates the assimilation of new information into existing conceptual structures. This type of assimilatory activity seems to form the basis for the creation of misconceptions and lies at the root of the surface inconsistency so commonly observed in students' reasoning.

To help students increase their metaconceptual awareness, it is necessary to create learning environments that make it possible for them to express their representations and beliefs. This can be done in environments that facilitate group discussion and the verbal expression of ideas. It is also important to create learning environments that make it pos-sible for students to express their internal representations of phenomena, to compare them with those of others. Such activities may be time-consuming but they are important for ensuring that students become aware of what they know and what they need to learn. In this area, teaching methods such as *reciprocal teaching* (Palincsar & Brown, 1984) or computer-based environments such as SCI-WISE (White et al., 1999) can be proven to be particularly useful.

One of the problems of traditional instruction is that it moves students very quickly from memorizing and applying formal quantitative laws into problem-solving situations without teaching them the qualitative models that scientists themselves use to support their reasoning (Nersessian, 1992, 1995). Models and external representations can be used to clarify aspects of a scientific explanation that are not apparent when the explanation is given in a linguistic or mathematical way. The visual qualities of a model are useful in making an explanation better understood and more easily memorized (Mayer, 1993).

5 Conclusions

The adoption of the engineering approach in the design of learning environments has been a positive move in the direction of linking educational research to practice. However, the design of learning environments has been guided so far by the cognitive apprenticeship metaphor which has downgraded the problem of knowledge. The cognitive apprenticeship metaphor has provided important guidelines about how to teach cognitive skills. If cognitive apprenticeship could be used together with a set of another guideline about how to design curricula and teach subject-matter knowledge, we would have a better framework to provide the design of learning environments.

References

Bereiter, C. (1997). Situated cognition and how to overcome it. In D. Kirshner & J.A. Whitson (Eds.), *Situated cognition. Social, semiotic, and psychological perspectives* (pp. 281-300). Hillsdale, NJ: Erlbaum.

Bereiter, C., & Scardamalia, M. (1989). International learning as a goal of instruction. In L. B. Resnick (Eds.), *Knowing, learning, and instruction: Essays in honor of Robert Glaser* (pp. 361-392). Hillsdale, NJ: Erlbaum.

Bereiter, C., & Scardamalia, M. (1993). *Surpassing ourselves: An inquiry into the nature and implications of expertise.* La Salle, IL: Open Court.

Bransford, J. (1989). Why wisdom cannot be told. In S. Vosniadou & A. Ortony (Eds.), *Similarity and analogical reasoning*, New York, NY: Cambridge University Press.
Brown, A.L. (1992). Design experiments: Theoretical and methodological challenges in creating complex interventions in classroom settings. *Journal of the Learning Sciences, 2,* 141-178.
Brown, A.L., Ash, D., Rutherford, M., Nakagawa, K., Gordon, A., & Campione, J. C. (1993). Distributed expertise in the classroom. In G. Salomon (Ed.), *Distributed cognitions: Psychological and educational considerations.* Cambridge: Cambridge University Press.
Brown, A.L., Bransford, J.D., Ferrara, R.A., & Campione, J.C., (1983). Learning, remembering and understanding. In J. H. Flavell & E.M. Markman (Eds.), *Handbook of child psychology: Vol. 3. Cognitive development* (4th ed., pp. 77-166). New York: Wiley.
Brown, A.L., & Campione, J.C. (1990). Communities of learning and thinking, or A context by any other name. *Human Development, 21,* 108-126.
Burkhardt, H., & Schoenfeld, A.H. (2003). Improving educational research: Toward a more useful, more influential, and better funded enterprise. *Educational Researcher, 32*(9), 3-14.
Collins, A., Brown, J. S., & Duguid, P. (1989). Debating the situation: A rejoinder to Palincsar and Wineburg. *Educational Researcher, 18*(4), 10-12, 62.
Collins, A., Brown, J.S., & Newman, S.E. (1989). Cognitive apprenticeship: Teaching the crafts of reading, writing, and mathematics. In L.B. Resnick (Ed.), *Knowing, learning, and instruction: Essays in honor of Robert Glaser.* Hillsdale, NJ: Erlbaum.
Mayer, R. E. (1993). Illustrations that instruct. In R. Glaser (Ed.), *Advances in instructional psychology.* Hillsdale, NJ: Erlbaum.
Nersessian, N. J. (1992). How do scientists think? Capturing the dynamics of conceptual change in science. In R. N. Gierre (Ed.), *Cognitive models of science* (pp. 3-44). Minneapolis, MN: University of Minnesota Press.
Nersessian, N. J. (1995). Constructive modeling in creating scientific understanding. *Science Education, 4,* 203-226.
Palincsar, A.S., & Brown, A. L. (1984). Reciprocal teaching of comprehension-fostering and monitoring activities. *Cognition and Instruction, 1,* 117-175.
Scardamalia, M., Bereiter, C., & Lamon, M. (1994). The CSILE project: Trying to bring the classroom into world 3. In K. McGilly (Ed.), *Classroom lessons: Integrating cognitive theory & classroom practice* (pp. 201-228). Cambridge, MA: MIT Press.
Schoenfeld, A. H. (1985). *Mathematical problem solving.* New York: Academic Press.
Vosniadou, S., Ioannides, C., Dimitrakopoulou, A., & Papademetriou, E., (2001). Designing learning environments to promote conceptual change in science. *Learning and Instruction, 11,* 421-429.
White, B. Y., Shimoda, T.A., & Frederiksen, J.R. (1999). Enabling students to construct theories of collaborative inquiry and reflective learning: Computer support for metacognitive development. *International Journal of Artificial Intelligence in Education 10,* 151-182.

Chapter 2

On learning environments that foster subject-matter competence

Alan H. Schoenfeld

1 Introduction

For nearly two decades there has been a consensus among researchers in mathematics education regarding the fundamental dimensions of mathematical competency: the knowledge base; problem solving strategies; monitoring and self-regulation; beliefs and dispositions regarding the subject and oneself. There is a plausible argument that those same dimensions are central to performance in all academic domains.

The question is, how does one create learning environments that foster all of these aspects of domain competence? A central notion with regard to learning, both in and out of school, is that of *community of practice*. The idea is that learning across all the dimensions identified above takes place when one interacts actively and purposefully with a group of people engaged in a particular body of work. One way to think about "designing powerful learning environments to promote deep conceptual and strategic learning in major curricular domains" is to think about designing learning communities in particular ways – shaping the communities so that they provide the affordances along all of the dimensions discussed above.

In this chapter I reflect on various attempts to create powerful learning communities – my problem solving courses; a Ph.D. program at Berkeley grounded in the notion of "cognitive apprenticeship"; Brown and Campione's work on "Fostering a Community of learners"; and Scardamalia and Bereiter's work on knowledge building and the "Knowledge Forum." In all, the goal was rich and purposeful interaction; in some, technology was used to facilitate such interactions. I argue that despite differences in grade level (the instructional programs range from elementary school through graduate school) and subject matter (topics examined in these courses range over the life sciences, history, literature, and mathematics), there are strong commonalities in assumptions and practices across those environments. They are:
- Disciplines offer distinctive and powerful forms of sense-making.
- Such sense-making includes knowledge, values, ways of seeing, and habits of mind.
- These come to life for individuals via membership in rich, thriving intellectual communities.

- The learning environments discussed in this chapter are successful because they are self-consciously designed to foster interactions that support all of the above.
- Technology, if and when it is used, should be in the service of the above.

I argue that those who wish to design rich and productive learning environments would do well to attend to these issues.

2 My basic thesis

The thesis underlying this chapter is that academic (and other) disciplines offer distinctive forms of sense-making. That is, each discipline has its own norms and types of learning and doing; and each provides ways of seeing and understanding.[1]

It follows that learning is not simply about mastery of subject matter. "Learning to think mathematically" (or like a physicist, or historian, or...) involves mastering the tools of the trade, of course – but it also involves developing the habits of mind of those who engage in the discipline.

This observation is crucial. Habits of mind are developed and/or shaped in *communities,* through consistent patterns of interaction. Thus:

> The character of the learning community in shaping students' values, perspectives, habits of mind, and knowledge is of utmost importance.

In what follows I shall give a series of examples taken from various learning environments – the most extensive examples coming from my problem solving courses, which I have taught for almost 30 years. In those examples I shall try to convey the flavor of community discussions, rather than an exposition of content knowledge. Full detail on the courses, and the theo-retical notions underlying them, may be found in Schoenfeld (1985, 1992).

3 Case 1: My course in mathematical problem solving

In this section of the chapter I discuss some examples of discussions in my course in mathematical problem solving. These serve as the basis for a discussion of the purposes of the course – and what I really teach.

---

[1] I am going to assume that this assumption is unproblematic. I am, for example, a decent mathematician and a relatively good problem solver. Yet I am at best mediocre at physics, which has different habits of mind. Conversely, some of my physicist friends are not very good at formal mathematics. That there are disciplinary patterns of thinking and behavior is a commonplace – "lawyer jokes" or jokes about any profession are grounded in stereotypes about intellectual practices common to members of that profession.

Alan H. Schoenfeld

3.1 Example 1: The Magic Square Problem

The following problem is given the first day of my problem solving course.

Can you place the numbers 1, 2, 3, 4, 5, 6, 7, 8, and 9 in the box to the right, so that when you are all done, the sum of each row, each column, and each diagonal is the same? This is called a magic square.

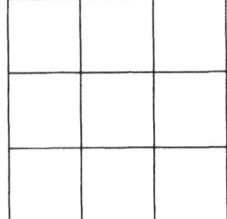

I have the students work in groups. Typically, all the groups will arrive at a solution in about 5 minutes. (They almost always solve the problem by trial and error, making some lucky guesses along the way.)

I ask the students to give me a solution, and they do. Then I ask, "Are we done?" They always answer "yes." That is because, in traditional mathematics classrooms, there is a simple and universal routine:
1. the teacher poses a problem;
2. the students work on it;
3. a solution is presented and worked on until it is correct;
4. the class moves on to another problem.

Hence my students expect me to "declare victory" and move on. But, this exchange is only the beginning.

I proceed by saying (something like): "No, we're not done. We've only solved the problem one way. Is there another way to solve it?" and I may mention at that point that there are books on famous results in mathematics, like the Pythagorean theorem, which present dozens upon dozens of different solutions. "Getting the answer" is only part of doing mathematics; coming up with alternative solutions and making connections are equally important.

Having made this point, I begin to focus on some mathematical habits of mind. In their solutions, students had ultimately made some good guesses. Could we be more systematic about solving the problem? In particular, I introduce the notion of *subgoals*. Is there a piece of information that would help us solve the problem?

Yes, they agree, it would be good to know what the sum of each row, column, and diagonal should be; and it would be good to know which number goes in the center.

This provides the opportunity to engage in another standard mathematical problem solving strategy, working backwards. What if we had a solution? What would it look like? Imagine we had a solution to the magic square – but that the numbers were illegible. It would look something like this:

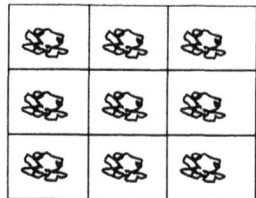

where none of the figures can be read. BUT, we know that the sum of each column is the same. If we call that sum S, then the sum of all three columns is 3S:

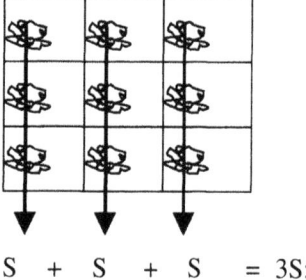

S + S + S = 3S;

And, since the three arrows altogether go through each square once, each of the digits from 1 through 9 is counted once. Hence

3 S = 1 + 2 + 3 + 4 + 5 + 6 + 7 + 8 + 9 = 45, so s = 15.

Now we know for certain that the sum of each row, column, and diagonal is 15. One could resort to "trial and error." But we can also use this information, and use the strategy of *working forwards*. Each sum has to add up to fifteen. Which sets of three digits add up to fifteen?

When I ask this question students typically generate random triples of numbers that add up to fifteen. This makes it impossible to keep track of what they have tried, and to know when they are done (that is, when they have generated all the possible triples that add up to 15). This provides the opportunity for a conversation about the value of taking a systematic, structured approach to problems. That said, we generate all the triples (in increasing order):

(1,5,9); (1,6,8); (2,4,9); (2,5, 8); (2,6,7); (3,4,8); (3,5,7); (4,5,6).

We now return to the question of which number goes in the center. A student observes that the center square is involved in four sums. When we look at the list of triples, we see that only one number, 5, appears in four triples. Thus, 5 must go in the center![2] Similarly, each corner cell of the square is involved in three sums, each "side cell" only twice. When we observe that each of the even numbers 2, 4, 6, and 8 appears in the list three times, and each of the odd numbers 1, 3, 7, and 9 appears in the list only twice, it becomes obvious that even numbers must go in the corners, odd numbers in the sides. Once this has been discovered, it is easy to fill in the magic square.

At this point the class has found all the ways of thinking about the original problem that I know. Having exhausted the solution space, I ask: "OK, are we done?" They respond "yes," and I respond "no." They have found multiple solutions, but all they have done is to solve my problem – they have not made it their own yet. Are there extensions? Generalizations? No mathematician stops with a solution; the question is, is this the most powerful solution? Are there other ways to think about the phenomena in this problem? Is this problem an instance of something more general? And so on. The class and I begin to explore the problem space.

– What if we began with the numbers 3, 4, 5, 6, 7, 8, 9, 10, and 11 instead of the digits from 1 through 9? Or 23 through 31? Or 1, 3, 5, 7, 9, 11, 13, 15, and 17?
– The sum of each row, column, and diagonal in this case was 15. Can we find a magic square where each sum is 87? 88?
– Can we find 4x4 magic squares? 5x5? And so on.

This simple problem, which the students had solved in five minutes, is worth at minimum an hour's conversation. If the students get involved, extensions and generalizations can occupy them for weeks and months. (There is a large literature on magic squares.) And, there is much to learn from it. Among the lessons potentially learned from this one problem are the following:

– Various strategies (establishing subgoals; working forwards; working backwards; considering extreme cases; and more)
– The value of being organized
– The importance of multiple solutions
– The importance of abstracting and generalizing.

3.2 Example 2: A problem with numbers

Here is another problem my students and I discuss early in the course.

---

[2] Another line of argument students have come up with is to look at *extreme values*. They ask, can 9 go in the center? The answer is no, because 8 has to go somewhere – and the triple that includes 8 and 9 adds up to more than 15. The same line of argument, once discovered, eliminates 6,7, and 8. The "mirror" of this argument is that 1 can not go in the center, because the triple that includes 1 and 2 could not add up to 15. Similar reasoning excludes 2,3, and 4. Only 5 is left for the center.

"Take any three-digit number and write it down twice, to make a six-digit number. (For example, the three-digit number 789 gives us the six-digit number 789,789.) I'll bet you $1.00 that the six-digit number you've just written down can be divided by 7, without leaving a remainder.

"OK, so I was lucky. Here's a chance to make your money back. Take the quotient that resulted from the division you just performed. I'll bet you $5.00 that quotient can be divided by 11, without leaving a remainder.

"OK, OK, so I was very lucky. Now you can clean up. I'll bet you $25.00 that the quotient of the division by 11 can be divided by 13, without leaving a remainder?

"Well, you can't win 'em all. But, you don't have to pay me if you can explain why this works."

By the time my students have begun to work on this problem, they understand that multiple solutions to problems are valued. Here are some of the issues we discuss:

What do you observe when you perform the three divisions as asked?

When we have looked at a few examples, it becomes clear that the process ends up producing the number we stared with. That is, the number 269 produces the number 269,269 – which, when divided by a bunch of other numbers, yields 269 again.

So, $\left(\frac{269,269}{x}\right) = 269$. Thus $269x = 269,269$, or $x = 1001$.

Now, how do you check a division? By multiplication!

```
      269
   x 1001
      269
   269000
   269269
```

Aha! And, there is nothing special about 269; this works for any three-digit number.

What does it mean to divide by 7, 11, and 13?

This seems like a trivial question, but it has meaning. What does it mean to divide by 2 and 5? You are dividing by 10. So, dividing by 7, 11, and 13 is dividing by $7 \times 11 \times 13 = 1001$. Now you can follow through as above.

What does the number abc,abc really stand for?

I note that we tend to take base 10 notation for granted. What is the number we write as 269, 269? That is shorthand – the real number is
$200,000 + 60,000 + 9,000 + 200 + 60 + 9$.
An arbitrary 3-digit number abc,abc is also written in shorthand:

abc,abc =
   100,000a + 10,000b + 1,000c + 100a + 10b + c =
   100100a + 10010b + 1001c =
   1001 x (100a + 10b + c) =
   1001 x (abc) =
   7 x 11 x 13 x (abc)
Thus abc,abc is divisible by 7, 11, and 13 – and the quotient will be the original number.

Finally, what if you try simple cases and look for a pattern?

Many years ago a student noted that one problem solving approach I had suggested was "If you don't have any good ideas, try some simple cases and look for a pattern." The simplest 3-digit number she knew of was 001. She tried that, and got
   001 yields 001,001 – which is 7 x 11 x 13 x 001
   002 yields 002,002 – which is 7 x 11 x 13 x 002
   003 yields 003,003 – which is 7 x 11 x 13 x 003
   004 yields 004,004 – which is 7 x 11 x 13 x 004...
by which time the pattern was completely obvious to her.

Let me again summarize the lessons potentially learned from this one problem:
– Various strategies (working forwards, working backwards, looking for patterns...)
– The importance of multiple solutions
– The importance of abstracting and generalizing
– Beginning confidence that the students can master mathematics on their own...

At some point during the solution of this problem, I ask if we are done. A student sighs in mock resignation: "We're *never* done!" A few weeks later, another student asks me: "Why haven't you been asking us if we're done?" The answer is that I have no need to: the class has begun to seek multiple solutions and generalizations by itself, so I no longer need to goad them into it.

3.3 Example 3: Who gets to say which mathematics is correct?

At the beginning of the course, I ask for student volunteers to present solutions up at the board. Invariably, they start writing their solutions on the board and then turn to me for confirmation. But, I refuse to validate the solution: "I'm sure the class is capable of saying whether what you've said is correct. Folks, what do you think?" The class then argues its way to a conclusion. By the end of the first week of class, students anticipate my behavior. A student will start to write on the board, turn to me, and then turn away: "I know, I know: Folks, what do you think?" I am very explicit about this behavior. The point is that most of the time, students are quite capable of judging the correctness of mathematical arguments within their realm.

One of the best moments in my problem solving course occurred after a long discussion of the "concrete wheel" problem, borrowed from Andy diSessa. Here is a discussion of the problem, drawn from Schoenfeld, 1994:

> *The problem*: You are sitting in a room at ground level, facing a floor-to-ceiling window which is twenty feet square. A huge solid concrete wheel, 100 miles in diameter, is rolling down the street and is about to pass right in front of the window, from left to right. The center of the wheel is moving to the right at 100 miles per hour. What does the view look like, from inside the room, as the wheel passes by? (See Figure 1)

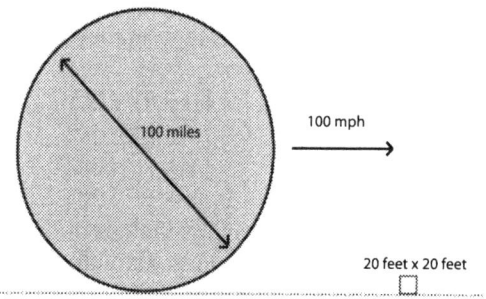

Fig. 1. The situation described in the concrete wheel problem

This problem tends to provoke immediate and widely divergent intuitive reactions. That year, as often happens, students made the following conjectures:
a) The room will go (almost) instantaneously dark as the wheel first passes the window. It will stay dark for a short while and go (almost) instantaneously light as the wheel leaves.
b) Same as (a), but the room stays dark for a relatively long time.
c) The room darkens slowly, as though a large window shade was being pulled more or less:

  i) horizontally from left to right, as follows;

  ii) diagonally from the upper left corner as follows;

iii) or vertically downward as follows.

The room then stays dark for a short/long period of time, after which it lightens in a way complementary to the way it darkened.

The class broke into groups to work on the problem. One group argued for one conjecture, while a second group argued for another. There was an intense discussion, with the rest of the class following the conversation. Finally one group prevailed. As is my habit, I made my usual comment: "O.K., you seem to have done as much with this as you can. Shall I try to pull things together?" One of the students replied "Don't bother. We got it." The class agreed.

One might think of this event as being trivial – the students simply indicated that they had understood the material. Or, one might see their rejection of my offer to pull things together as being rude. But either view misses the significance of the event. What counts here is that the classroom was functioning as a mathematical community. Various points of view were advanced and defended mathematically. The arguments in favor of different positions were made on solid mathematical grounds and ultimately the correct view prevailed, for good reason. One could ask for no better at a meeting of professional mathematicians. Even more importantly, the locus of mathematical authority had shifted from what it was at the beginning of the course. From the student's point of view, I was no longer needed as an authority figure to provide external *certification* of results. They judged the argument's correctness on their own. This was *their* mathematics. They had ownership of it, not only in the motivational sense, but also in the deep epistemological sense that characterizes true mathematical knowing and understanding.

3.4 Summary discussion of examples 1, 2, and 3

Let me summarize what I try to teach in my problem solving course. On the one hand, the course is aimed directly at the aspects of thinking and problem solving discussed in Schoenfeld (1985; 1992):
– the knowledge base;
– heuristic strategies;
– monitoring and self-regulation;
– productive beliefs;
– mathematical practices.

On the other hand, I work equally hard to help the student develop what has been called a "mathematical disposition," aspects of which include:

independence; confidence; the tendency to be analytic; to value mathematical thinking; to abstract and generalize; to see mathematics as a sense-making activity and to engage in it accordingly.

I hope it is clear from the examples given above that the primary mechanism for this last set of "dispositions" is social. That is, my students develop these dispositions via participation in a very specialized community of practice.

4 Case 2: The EMST Ph.D. program in education

By design, the Education in Mathematics, Science, and Technology (EMST) Ph.D. program at the University of California, Berkeley is an "Apprenticeship Environment" in which students become researchers by means of structured participation in a research community. For an extended discussion of this environment, see Schoenfeld (1999).

As I write this chapter, I am in the middle of teaching my course "the nature of mathematical thinking and problem solving," which is taken by many first-year Ph.D. students. A cornerstone of the course is a research project, in which students are expected to analyze some mathematical behavior. What they analyze varies according to the students' interests. One student this term is analyzing the strategies employed by people as they play poker. Another set up an experiment to look for gender differences in small-group interactions. A third is looking at how sensibly students with different degrees of mathematical knowledge use the tools of a computer algebra system to solve problems.

None of the students felt that they were ready to do research – and they were right! In having the students start early, we are following a maxim I borrowed from my friend and colleague Hugh Bukhardt: "fail early, fail often." The assumption is that no matter how well read a student might be, the student will make a wide range of mistakes when first conducting empirical work. Hence it is unwise to wait until the student has passed Ph.D. qualifying examinations before having the student do empirical work – the student should start early, and learn some valuable lessons. Among those lessons:
– experiments do not often turn out the way you expect;
– issues of methodology are thorny, and need careful attention;
– making sense of empirical phenomena often calls for the construction of analytical schemes consistent with the forms of data gathered.

My students have begun to learn these lessons. Last week they "reported out" to the class. The student who thought that she would see gender differences in groups said that she saw none – but, that as groups worked on problems, she found that some constructed powerful representations that helped them, and others did not. She is now analyzing the student work with an eye toward the use of representations. It goes without saying that her work will have many rough edges, and will be nowhere near publishable – but, she will have learned many important lessons from her project, including how to "live" with data until you have begun to make sense of them.

Courses like the one just described are typical in our program. They are one of many mechanisms by which students in our program engage with research ideas. For example, we have students produce research projects over the summer following their first year. Often these projects are based in course projects; the student considers the course project to be a pilot, and goes about putting together a more structured study. Often these projects are flawed – but differently, and often more subtly. The same process is repeated the second year, both in courses and in a "second year project."

All of our students belong to faculty members' research groups, and they are actively involved, from early on, in the conduct of research. Some research groups are "agenda driven:" there is a set of tasks to be done, and people pitch in. Beginners usually start with small tasks, and as they become more competent, take on more responsibility. Some groups have more "emergent" agendas; they are structured to serve students' current needs. In one of my research groups, for example, group members (including me) sign up for help on a weekly basis. The person might have:
– written a paper, and want comments;
– collected some data and need help thinking through them;
– prepared a dissertation proposal;
– prepared a talk to be given elsewhere;
or have any of a number of other things he or she wants to share with the group. Typically new students start out by watching as more experienced researchers present work and make comments. Soon they feel comfortable making comments. Before long they realize that the environment is supportive, and they bring their own work in for comment. This past week, for example, two first-year students who are working on projects for my "nature of mathematical thinking and problem solving" course brought in videotapes for the group to discuss. The group discussions helped to shape the ways they will think about the project for my course.

To sum things up in a nutshell, our students live in an environment where people engage in research all the time, and others are expected to share in it. As a result, the values of the research community are transparent. What counts as good research? It is one thing to read about research, quite another to participate in the discussion and refinement of studies on an ongoing basis. How does one justify a claim? The research group makes it clear what it considers to be adequate evidence, and whether one has met the standard. Here too, the central mechanism for learning is membership in a community of practice. (Productive) Habits of mind are shaped by (productive) interactions with others.

5 Case 3: Brown and Campione's "Fostering a Community of Learners" (FCL)

Brown and Campione's work on "Fostering a Community of Learners" (Brown, 1992; Brown, Campione, Webber, & McGilley, 1992; Brown & Campione, 1996) represents one of a small number of exemplars of carefully designed learning environments that focus both on the importance of subject matter and on learning as an inherently social activity. Brown and Campione's FCL work, which has been undertaken in biology, history, literature, and mathematics, has at its core the following set of ideas:
- The disciplines themselves are ways of making sense of phenomena.
- Learning a discipline involves learning prototypical or paradigmatic ways of sense-making in that discipline as well as coming to grips with a substantial body of domain-specific knowledge.
- Classroom activities must foster active engagement with the content and processes of the discipline, with students developing and testing ideas in ways consistent with the paradigms of the disciplines they study. Learning involves membership in intellectual communities, where ideas are developed and shared collaboratively. (Schoenfeld, 2004, p. 239).

While a great deal of attention has been given to particular techniques such as "jigsawing," which are employed in FCL classrooms, such techniques are simply mechanisms to get at the underlying principles of FCL. In FCL classrooms, students conduct (sometimes individual, sometimes collaborative) investigations of various sorts. They engage in the codification of and reflection on what has been investigated. There are communal activities involving active communication and critique, both orally and in writing, of what has been learned.

Details aside, the "basic system" of FCL is given in Figure 2.

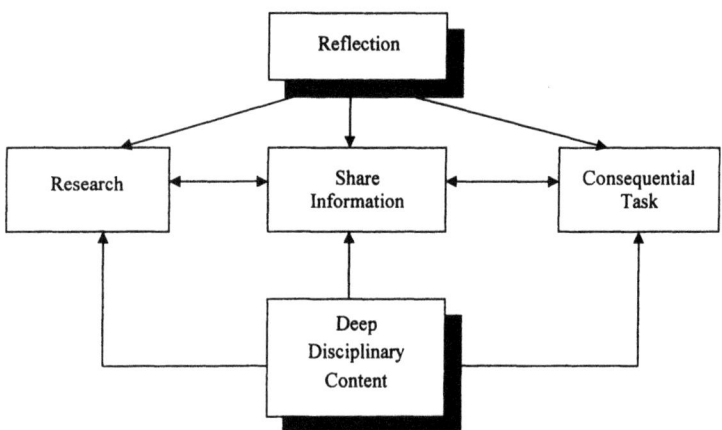

Fig. 2. Community of learners: The basic system (Brown & Campione, 1996, p. 293)

A fundamental premise of Brown and Campione's design work is that students should learn about important subject matter ("deep disciplinary content") by engaging in extended discipline-related projects in substantial ways. Often they do this by engaging in collaborative projects, where they set out to address a question or issue whose resolution requires the application of substantial domain knowledge (a "consequential task"). Addressing the question calls for research to find relevant information; sharing the results of that research with others and comparing information discovered; and reflecting collaboratively on the adequacy of the information and the state of the project. FCL classrooms employ various activity structures designed to support students in these endeavors.

Student research is structured in various ways: through participation structures for reading and studying, "guided viewing" and "guided writing," consulting experts, and peer- and across-age teaching and research. There are, analogously, structured mechanisms for the sharing of information with others: the "jigsaw" procedure, in which groups of students become knowledgeable about particular knowledge and then are reconstituted in different groups to share knowledge; cross-talk, "majoring," help-seeking, and "exhibitions." These information-sharing activities take place in a goal-oriented context. All of this work takes place in what Brown & Campione call "a metacognitive environment," a community in which interactions are geared toward these specific goals:
– active, strategic nature of learning;
– self-regulation and other-regulation for common good;
– autocriticism, comprehension monitoring;
– effort after meaning, search for understanding;
– atmosphere of wondering, querying, worrying knowledge;
– reflective practices (Brown & Campione, 1996, p. 318).

To end by emphasizing what should be obvious: it is no accident that Brown and Campione focus on the idea of a *community* of learners. For both theoretical and pragmatic reasons, the habits of mind that Brown and Campione wish to help students develop – both the discipline-specific knowledge and strategies, and the more general dispositions toward learning – are best developed in communities whose ongoing interactions support that development.

6   Case 4: Scardamalia and Bereiter's CSILE/The "Knowledge Forum"

A second notable family of learning environments is those created by Carl Bereiter and Marlene Scardamalia, first under the name of CSILE (Computer-Supported Intentional Learning Environments) and later under the name of the "Knowledge Forum" (Bereiter & Scardamalia, 1989; Scardamalia, 2002).

In contrast with FCL, Knowledge Forum learning environments have technology at their core: the technology is explicitly designed to foster student interactions focusing on significant content matter. But in many ways, the underlying principles are the same. In many ways (save for technology) the discussion that follows applies to all of the educational efforts discussed in this chapter.

Let us start with goals: "The challenge addressed by Knowledge Forum and knowledge building pedagogy is to engage students in the collaborative solution of knowledge problems, in such a way that responsibility for the success of the effort is shared by the students and teacher instead of being borne by the teacher alone." (Scardamalia, 2002, p. 76.)

In an extended discussion focusing on the "socio-cognitive and technological determinants of knowledge building," Scardamalia characterizes key features of knowledge forum communities and the technological support structure underlying them. Some aspects of those communities are as follows.

Real ideas, authentic problems. Like the other environments discussed in this chapter, Scardamalia and Bereiter have students focus on substantial, meaningful tasks. The technology is used to support communal interactions.

Improvable ideas. All ideas are treated as improvable, and the community works collectively to make its thinking as good as possible. This is a matter of habits of mind, and of the construction of "safe" environments where it is comfortable for people to put out ideas, refine them, and sometimes abandon them.

Idea diversity. Multiple perspectives and connections between them are valued and encouraged.

"Rise above." Self-conscious efforts are made to "see the forest for the trees," to generalize and abstract.

Epistemic agency. "Participants set forth their ideas and negotiate a fit between personal ideas and ideas of others, using contrasts to spark and sustain knowledge advancement rather than depending on others to chart that course for them. They deal with problems of goals, motivation, evaluation, and long-range planning that are normally left to teachers or managers." (Scardamalia, 2002, p. 78)

Community knowledge, collective responsibility. A shared goal is contributing to the overall enterprise (the knowledge of the group), not simply achieving as an individual. One is both an individual and a member of the community; one has responsibilities to oneself and the community.

The list goes on. Other features of the environment – *democratizing knowledge, symmetric knowledge advancement, pervasive knowledge building, constructive use of authoritative sources, knowledge building discourse,* and *embedded and transformative assessments* – are all organized in ways that contribute to the community's effectiveness. In short, this is a community with a technological backbone – but the emphasis is on the notion of community, with the technology serving as a facilitating medium.

7 Some "bottom lines" in conclusion

Scardamalia and Bereiter's work using the "Knowledge Forum" has been conducted at a range of grade levels, from elementary through high school. The same is true of Brown and Campione's work on "Fostering a Community of Learners" (see, e.g., the March-April 2004 special issue of the *Journal of Curriculum Studies*.) My mathematics problem solving courses have been taught at the undergraduate level. And, the EMST environment is a Ph.D. program whose goal it is to produce educational researchers. Yet, there is a strong commonality among all of these learning environments. The following premises undergird all of the efforts discussed in this paper:
– Disciplines offer distinctive and powerful forms of sense-making.
– Such sense-making includes knowledge, values, ways of seeing, and habits of mind.
– These come to life for individuals via membership in rich, thriving intellectual communities.
– The learning environments discussed in this paper are successful because they are self-consciously designed to foster interactions that support all of the above.
– Technology, if and when it is used, should be in the service of the above.

As the range of examples indicates, details of implementation can and must vary according to the population of students, the topics being studied, and the available technological infrastructure. However, anyone who wishes to design a learning environment that fosters the development of subject matter competence would do well to attend to these premises.

References

Bereiter, C., & Scardamalia, M. (1989). Intentional learning as a goal of instruction. In L. B. Resnick (Ed.), *Knowing, learning, and instruction: Essays in honor of Robert Glaser* (pp. 361-392). Hillsdale, NJ: Erlbaum.

Brown, A. L. (1992). Design experiments: Theoretical and methodological challenges in creating complex interventions in classroom settings. *Journal of the Learning Sciences, 2*, 141-178.

Brown, A., Campione, J., Webber, L., & McGilley, K. (1992). Interactive learning environments – A new look at learning and assessment. In B. R. Gifford & M. C. O'Connor (Eds.), *Changing assessments: Alternative views of aptitude, achievement, and instruction* (pp. 121-211). Boston: Kluwer Academic Publishers.

Brown, A., & Campione, J. (1996). Psychological theory and the design of innovative learning environments: On procedures, principles, and systems. In L. Schauble & R. Glaser (Eds.), *Innovations in learning: New environments for education* (pp. 289-325). Mahwah, NJ: Erlbaum.

Journal of Curriculum Studies. (March-April 2004) Special issue devoted for "Fostering Communities of Teachers as Learners." Volume 36, Number 2.

Scardamalia, M. (2002). Collective cognitive responsibility for the advancement of knowledge. In B. Smith (Ed.), *Liberal education in a knowledge society* (pp. 67-98). Chicago: Open Court.

Schoenfeld, A. H. (1985). *Mathematical problem solving.* Orlando, FL: Academic Press.

Schoenfeld, A. H. (1992). Learning to think mathematically: Problem solving, metacognition, and sense-making in mathematics. In D. Grouws (Ed.), *Handbook for research on mathematics teaching and learning* (pp. 334-370). New York: MacMillan.

Schoenfeld, A. H. (1994). Reflections on doing and teaching mathematics. In A. Schoenfeld (Ed.), *Mathematical thinking and problem solving* (pp. 53-70). Hillsdale, NJ: Erlbaum.

Schoenfeld, A. H. (1999). The core, the canon, and the development of research skills: Issues in the preparation of education researchers. In. E. Lagemann & L. Shulman (Eds.), *Issues in education research: Problems and possibilities* (pp. 166-202). New York: Jossey-Bass.

Schoenfeld, A. H. (2004). Multiple learning communities: Students, teachers, instructional designers, and researchers. *Journal of Curriculum Studies, 36,* 237-255.

Chapter 3

Engagement in learning:
Designing learning environments that are really used

Ton de Jong

1 Introduction

The world is changing and changing fast. Contemporary students live in a world full of impressions, fast changing viewpoints, information everywhere, zapping information, play and joy etc. They use facilities such as MSN, on-line gaming, and SMS. They expect a constant access to information, mostly in a social context. At the same time we see drastic changes in learning environments, moving them to rich, multi-media, collaborative, and individualised environments. Though starting from different angles, these two developments seem to come together. Modern learning environments such as WISE (Slotta, 2004), BGuILE (Reiser et al., 2001), or BioLogica (Hickey, Kindfield, Horwitz, & Christie, 2003) combine all kinds of opportunities to learn and communicate in a facilitative setting. In these learning environments, specific design measures are taken to foster learning. Recently, two reviews have appeared in which design guidelines for complex powerful learning environments with an inquiry character are discussed (Linn, Bell, & Davis, 2004; Quintana et al., 2004). These design guidelines help to a) increase the engagement of learners, b) realise the situatedness of learning, c) improve the quality of collaboration in learning, d) enable students to express their knowledge, e) give students the opportunity to engage in key learning processes. In this chapter these principles are illustrated with three learning environments: ZAP (Hulshof, Eysink, Loyens, & de Jong, in press), Co-Lab (van Joolingen, de Jong, Lazonder, Savelsbergh, & Manlove, 2005) and KM Quest (Leemkuil, de Jong, de Hoog, & Christoph, 2003). These environments were developed under the coordination of the Department of Instructional Technology at the University of Twente, the Netherlands. This chapter presents a short

---

Part of this work was partially supported by European Community under the Information Society Technology (IST) RTD programme, contracts IST-1999-13078 and IST-2000-25035. The author is solely responsible for the content of this (chapter). It does not represent the opinion of the European Community, and the European Community is not responsible for any use that might be made of data appearing therein. Another part of this work has been sponsored by Stichting SURF, Utrecht, The Netherlands.

overview of these three environments using the design guidelines presented above. The chapter ends with some considerations as to how these environments are designed so that they are used in practice.

2 ZAP, KM Quest, and Co-Lab, examples of non-traditional Technology Enhanced Learning environments

ZAP, KM Quest, and Co-Lab are three learning environments of very different kinds. ZAP is a series of short modules in the domain of psychology in which learners experience a psychological phenomenon, act like psychological discoverers, or are subjects in a psychological experiment. KM Quest is an internet-based collaborative game for learning principles and processes of knowledge management. Co-Lab is a collaborative learning environment for guided discovery learning by groups of students in integrated science topics. All learning environments are based on an inquiry learning approach and try to engage the learner actively in the learning process.

2.1 ZAP

ZAP (in Dutch: Zeer Actieve Psychologie, in English "Very Interactive Psychology") is a series, currently around 55, of short interactive programs in the field of psychology. ZAPs intend to engage students in psychology by having them experience, discover, or experiment with psychological phenomena. In *experiencing* phenomena students see how psychological phenomena work. For example, they perform a reasoning task (e.g., with syllogisms or the Wason selection task) or a problem solving task (e.g., the missionaries and cannibals problem), or experience a visual phenomenon (e.g., the Ponzo illusion). In *discovering* phenomena students are placed in the role of an experimenter who carries out an experiment with human or animal subjects. For example, students can play Pavlov and carry out conditioning experiments with a virtual dog, or perform tests with a virtual split brain person. In *experimenting* with phenomena, students are themselves subjects in an experiment, for example in mental rotation or memory experiments. In all cases, students see the outcomes of their own activities: their responses as subject in an experiment; the resulting actions of the virtual human or animal as a consequence of their actions as a discoverer; or the outcomes of their experiences with a phenomenon. Figure 1 shows an example of a feedback screen after a student has made a judgement in the Ponzo illusion task. In this task the student has to judge the length of a line and make it the same length as a line that is positioned higher. Due to the "triangle" lines an illusion of depth is suggested that leads the subjects to make the bottom line too long. Removing all lines but the two horizontal lines after having tried to make the two lines equal in length makes this very clear to students, and because it is based on their own actions, the experience really touches them. For experimenting ZAPs (i.e., ZAPs where the student is subject in an experiment) a special feature is offered, the so-called monitor, in which individual outcomes for a specific experiment can be aggregated for a group of students. Instead of individual outcomes, data aggregated over a sample of subjects are shown, as is normally the case in psychological experiments.

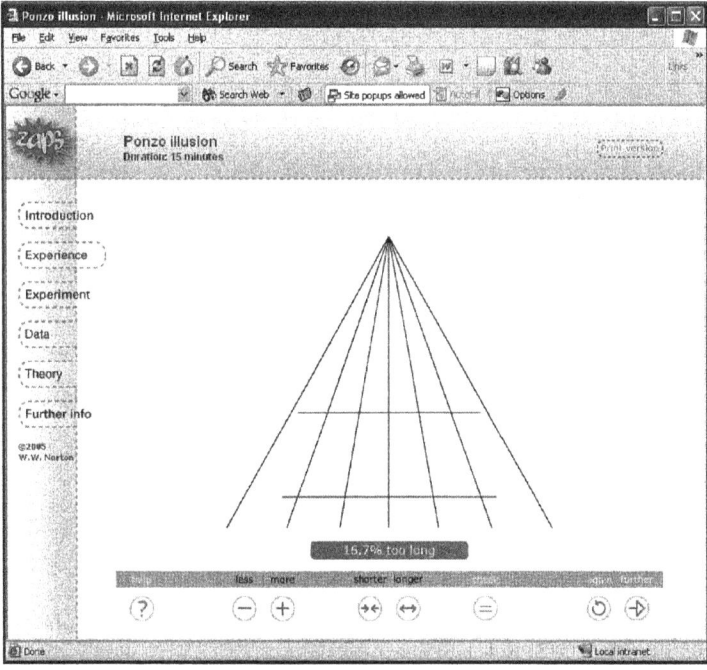

Fig. 1. A ZAP screen showing an example of the feedback that a student receives in the Ponzo visual illusion task.

The overall design of all ZAPs is the same. Students start with a short introduction that gives a real world context for the phenomenon that is treated. The student then goes to the experience, experiment, or discovery. Data are presented without delay and are immediately visible for the students. Only after that is theory presented to explain the phenomenon and to frame the student's own data. Finally, a further information section may place the phenomenon in a broader context. Figure 2 shows an example of an introductory text; it gives students just enough information to do the activity, in this case an experiment on the FAN effect. This effect is based on the assumption that memory is built up from nodes of concepts and links between them. Once a concept is stimulated, the activity is spread to all other nodes (concepts) that are linked to the stimulated concept. However, the total activity is assumed to be the same, which means that the more you know, the less activity linked concepts will receive. This has the effect that when you know more about a topic it might take longer to retrieve a related concept or fact from memory. The general structure of a ZAP is also shown to the left in the figure.

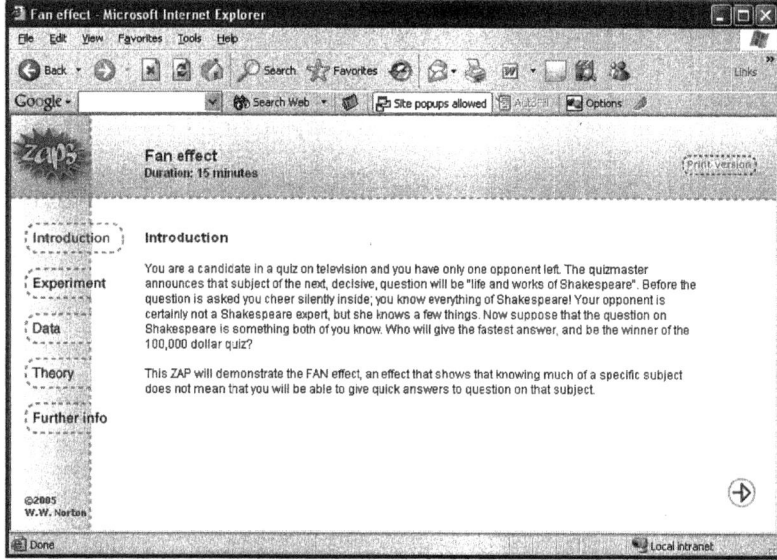

Fig. 2. Example of the structure of a ZAP and of an introductory screen.

2.2 KM Quest

KM Quest is a game for learning about Knowledge Management (for a more detailed description see Leemkuil et al., 2003). In designing KM Quest, we have used the following general description of games: Games are (competitive) situated (learning) environments based on a set of rules and/or an underlying model, in which some goal state must be reached under certain constraints. Games are situated in a specific context that makes them more or less realistic, appealing and motivating for the players. Important elements that are related to the situatedness of games are validity/fidelity, complexity, risk, uncertainty, surprise, unexpected events, role-play, access to information, and the representational form of the game (Leemkuil & de Jong, 2004). The KM Quest simulation game is situated in the context of a fictitious large organisation, "Coltec", a manufacturer of adhesives, coatings, etc.. An underlying business model is used to generate dynamic information about the behaviour of a large set of business and knowledge variables. The simulation game is played by three players who share the role of the same knowledge manager, and who collaboratively have the task of improving the efficacy of the knowledge household of the company. This is not an aim in itself, but it is related to objectives for the management of the company in general. Players play their role for three consecutive years in the life span of the company. Basically, in the game, players can inspect the status of business process indicators and knowledge management process indicators; they can also ask for additional information, install a measurement system, and implement knowledge management interventions to try to change the behaviour of the business simulation. To trigger activities from the players and to make sure that players are confronted with different types of knowledge management problems, the players are confronted with an unexpected event that could affect the knowledge household of the company. Players have to decide if and how they want to react to these events, generated from a pool of around 50 events. Figure 3 shows the main interface of KM Quest, which was designed to make the learner feel immersed in the situation, sitting behind a desk as a knowledge manager. The bookshelf contains books that present an overview of what has been done over the different quarters (the game is played in sections of "quarters") of the game and that give access to background information. The newspaper signals the unexpected events, and the whiteboard the current state of the company. To perform a knowledge management action, learners click on the computer on the desk and then enter the knowledge mana-gement process. Here they see worksheets dedicated to specific know-ledge management processes; an example of such a worksheet is given in Figure 4.

In KM Quest, the learning scenario is divided into two main phases: a training phase and a playing phase. There are, as well, two additional phases: one to introduce the learning environment, and one for reflection and debriefing. The environment uses a multitude of instructional facilities, most of them based on a cognitive apprenticeship model (Brown, Collins, & Duguid, 1989): opportunities for practicing problem-solving strategies, just-in-time information presentation, collaboration tools (shared forms and chat functions), prompts and supports for articulation/explicitation, monitoring of progress, a reflection and debriefing function and advanced visualisation of game outcomes.

The knowledge management model is the normative model that prescribes 'good' knowledge management practice. As a procedure, it consists of a sequence of phases and steps, with decision points and results. These phases are: a *focus phase* in which learners (knowledge managers) decide which aspects of knowledge management in the company they will focus their attention on and how they will set their targets; an *organization phase*, in which the current situation in the company is assessed and alternatives for action are considered; an *implementation phase* in which the specific knowledge management actions are made concrete; and a *monitoring phase*, in which the development of business and knowledge management variables

Fig. 3. KM Quest virtual office.

over time can be followed. These phases again are made up of several knowledge management activities, and for each activity a dedicated (and shared) worksheet is made available. This worksheet helps the students to work on the activity in a structured way. Figure 4 presents an example of a shared worksheet as part of the overall KM process model. In this example, students have to indicate (in the "Focus phase" as indicated in the diagram at the top left of the inner screen) what properties of knowledge domains they will focus on during the knowledge management process.

With regard to collaboration issues, special attention is given to the use of shared worksheets and workspace (and activity) awareness, meaning, for example, that learners know who is present, are informed by an email alert when others have been working in the environment, and where others are in the workspace. Learners can "call" each other and a learner may invite other users to the worksheet on which he or she is currently working. If the other learner accepts this invitation, he or she is automatically "tele-transported" to the place where the invitation originated. Visualisation of the variables in the business model is based on an analysis of the properties and scales of the indicators. A broad range of visualisations is defined, including bar charts, line graphs, numbers, pie charts, icons etc. Colour is widely used to support the interpretation of the information.

Designing learning environments that are really used 51

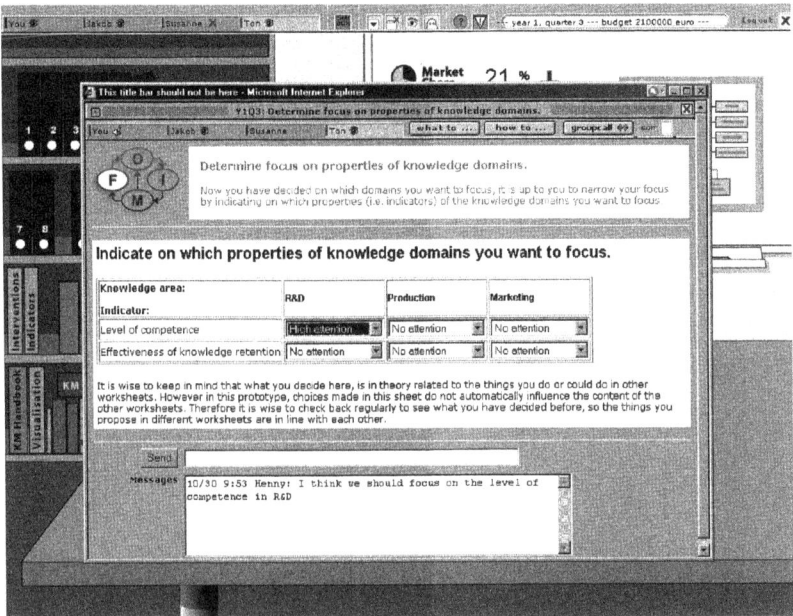

Fig. 4. Example of a process worksheet.

2.3 Co-Lab

Co-Lab is an environment for collaborative inquiry learning in science domains (van Joolingen et al., 2005). The Co-Lab environment consists of "buildings" that each represent one larger topic from science (e.g., a "greenhouse effect" building). Each building contains floors that refer to a specific subtopic within the overall theme of the building (e.g., a "black sphere" floor in the "greenhouse effect building"). These subtopics can be more applied but also be very basic specific science topics. Each floor has a similar lay-out and is composed of a "hall", a "lab room", a "theory room", and a "meeting room". Figure 5 shows an overall view of a floor within a Co-lab building. In Co-Lab a group of three learners work collaboratively. In the hall they find a general assignment (a mission statement) for the particular floor and some other general tools. In the lab room, learners can collect data by running simulations, operating remote laboratories, or inspecting (remote) databases. Learners use the information from the lab room to create models with the use of a modelling tool in the theory room. With the help of this modelling tool, learners can smoothly and gradually move from qualitative to quantitative modelling. The outcome of the self created model can be compared with the outcomes of the experiments in the lab room. In the meeting room, learners plan and monitor their work with the help of a so-called process coordinator. This process coordinator helps students organize and plan their work in phases, organize their data, generate reports, etc. In each of the rooms there is a set of cognitive tools to support the learners for the activities that can be performed in that particular room. Further, the environment has a chat, shared whiteboards, a control management tool (taking care of the learner's control in the environment and showing learners who is in control at a given time), and a repository where learners can save models, outcomes of simulations, etc.

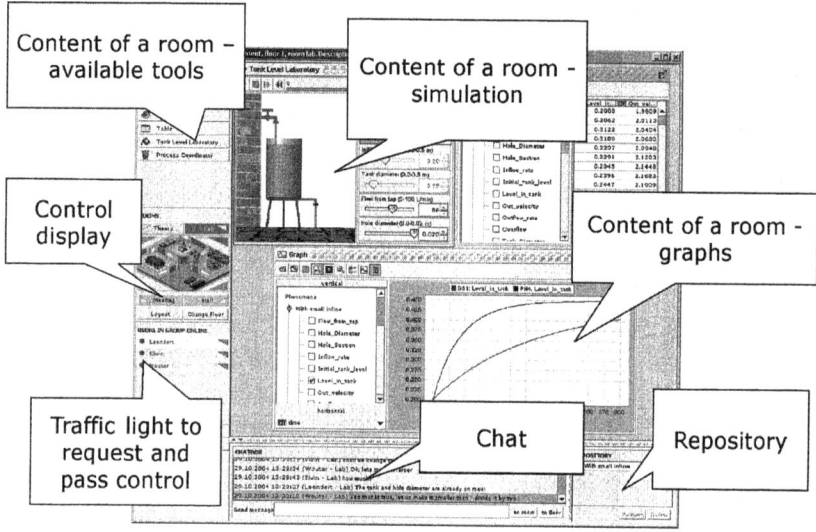

Fig. 5. Interface of a Co-Lab "floor".

3 Engagement

All three environments discussed in the previous sections give learners a specific role to ensure their engagement in the learning process. In ZAP, learners can have three roles: experiencing a phenomenon, being the scientific discoverer, or being a subject in an experiment. In all three cases, student engagement is enhanced because students see the results and data from their own personal activities and not, as is the usual case, from experiments or experiences by others. In KM Quest, learners have the role of a knowledge manager in a company, and they share this role with two other learners. The interface as depicted in Figure 3 tries to enhance this feeling; by sitting behind the desk, the illusion of a real job is being created. In addition, what learners can do makes them feel like a knowledge manager. For example, they can implement specific knowledge management measures and see how these actions affect the state of the company, in both its business and its knowledge management variables. In Co-Lab the learner is placed in the

Designing learning environments that are really used 53

role of a scientist, which is seen as an important way to stimulate student engagement (Dunbar, 2001). In Co-Lab, students are in the driver's seat and determine which experiments are done. To emphasize this role, the "meeting room" was designed. In this room, students discuss the planning of their actions in Co-Lab and they prepare and write a scientific report as the outcome of their experimentation, in this way mimicking a group of researchers preparing a scientific publication.

4 Situatedness

Of the three environments mentioned, KM Quest has the clearest view of situatedness. This whole system mimics a real company. The company used is what is a called a "product leadership" company. This is a company that attracts customers by offering high quality, specialised products. The application partner in the project in which KM Quest was developed, Airbus Industries, is an example of such a company. The engineers from Airbus who were piloting and evaluating the system were therefore confronted with a fictitious company that from a structural point of view was the same as their own company. The type of action the learners can take in KM Quest as knowledge management actions are also realistic actions; the events that appear are events that may occur in reality too, and the model that drives the game and renders values for knowledge management and business variables is tuned so that it gives realistic outputs.

In Co-Lab there is a double type of situatedness. First, the lab situation that is depicted more or less resembles the way a real laboratory might look. The different rooms are rooms that might be present in a real laboratory; for example, a meeting room was introduced to give the collaborating students the idea that they could really sit and work together. The second type of situatedness concerns the topics that need to be investigated. In Co-Lab, there are currently two "real life" topic buildings, namely a greenhouse effect building and a water management building. These larger topics were chosen to enhance student motivation and to offer a perspective within which the also basic science subtopics can be addressed.

In ZAP, finally, the experiences and experiments are similar to the ones really used in laboratories. Of course, laboratories are not real life, but they offer the students a good view of realistic experimental psychology. Moreover, all ZAPs start with an example from everyday life to make students aware of the context in which the psychological phenomenon may function (see Figure 2).

5 Collaboration

The ZAP system does not provide students with direct collaboration facilities, but Co-Lab and KM Quest have collaboration as their starting point. In Co-Lab and KM Quest, students have chats at their disposal for communication; in both of these environments there is a distinction between a general chat and specific chats that are dedicated to a specific element in the environment. In KM Quest these specific chats are related to the specific knowledge management activities and their associated worksheets. An example of a specific chat can be seen in Figure 4. The chat depicted at the bottom of the screen is associated with the worksheet that helps students to focus on properties of the knowledge domain. In Co-Lab, general and dedicated chats are also used. There is a general chat that is always present; besides that, every room in Co-Lab has its specific chat. This relates the specific Co-Lab activities such as experimenting, modelling etc. with a particular chat. This division (general and specific chat) helps students organise their communication and relate it to specific activities.

Apart from the verbal communication issue as reflected in chats, students in KM Quest and Co-Lab share elements. In KM Quest learners share sets of worksheets that are associated with different activities in the KM process. Choices have to be made, data have to be entered, and KM actions have to be selected on these forms. These shared worksheets can in some cases be filled in by a single student, but in other cases a vote by the three students is needed to make a decision. For example, the decision to implement a knowledge management action (e.g., send personnel to a course, install an intranet, etc.) is taken by voting. Another specific aspect in the collaboration between learners in KM Quest is the location of the learners. At one moment in time they can be at several places in the system performing different KM activities. However, when students need to communicate on a specific topic they often need to be together to see the same shared worksheet, and sometimes it is difficult to "find" each other. For this, the "group call" button was created. A student wanting other students to join her or him may press the group call button, which generates an invitation to the other two learners to join the first student. When they accept and click the invitation they are automatically "tele-transported" to the place in the system where the inviting learner was. In Figure 4, in the inner window, a group call button is visible.

In Co-Lab, sharing elements is regulated through a system of control. This system takes care of the fact that some interactive elements in the environment cannot be under control by more than one student at the same time. For example, it is not possible for two learners to edit the same model synchronously. Control is indicated by the "traffic sign" as seen in Figure 5. The student who has control has the "green light"; the other two students have a "red light" and can only observe what the student in control is doing. A student seeking control over a tool may send a request to the one who is in control, who can then hand over control. Not all tools, however, have this form of "strong control". In "weak control" tools there is no regulation of control, so that all students may at the same time try to take control. In a number of cases the view the tool is synchronized. This means that all students see the same content at the same time. Finally, there are elements in Co-Lab where there is no control at all: students may browse through background information as they wish, and they do not necessarily see the same content at the same time.

6 Expression

When students can express their ideas in an artefact, understanding of a domain is further enhanced (Löhner, van Joolingen, & Savelsbergh, 2003; Penner, 2001; Vreman-de Olde & de Jong, 2004). Co-Lab provides students with specific facilities to express their view of the domain; by designing a model, students can try to explain what they have observed in a simulation or remote laboratory. In Co-Lab students use system dynamics modelling (Steed, 1992) to construct and evaluate models. After having constructed models, the students can run them and compare the outcome of their models to the outcome of the experiments they have done with the simulations or with the remote laboratories. Overall, modelling is not an easy task for learners. To help them in this process Co-Lab provides the students with specific facilities to specify relations between variables. Specifying relations in a model can be done in several ways: graphically, quantitatively, and qualitatively. For the qualitative mode, students do not need knowledge about mathematical relations; they simply pick a type of relation from a set of pre-defined relations. The graphical mode of specifying a relation still works qualitatively, but here students can draw the type of relation themselves. For the quantitative mode, finally, students have to specify the relation in the form of a mathematical formula. Models created in a qualitative way can also be run and they provide output. Further, the Co-Lab tools ensure a smooth transition to quantitative models. Figure 6 shows how a variable in Co-Lab can be specified in, going from left to right, the quantitative (mathematical) way, the qualitative manner, and the graphical approach.

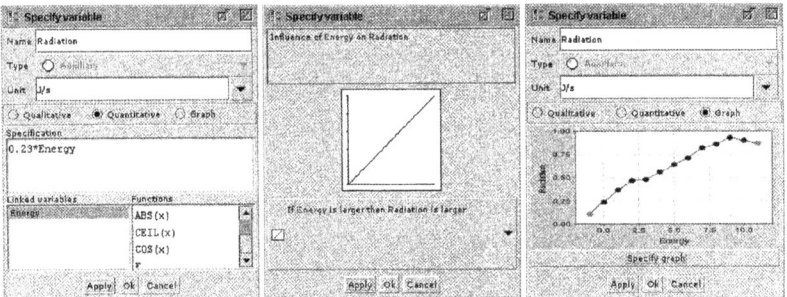

Fig. 6. Specifying a relation between variables in Co-Lab.

7 Cognitive tools

Learning environments such as the ones sketched above put high cognitive demands on learners. They have to engage in a diversity of effortful learning processes and orchestrate these into a balanced learning trajectory. Cognitive tools are those elements in the learning environment that are designed to support or scaffold a specific learning process. Overviews of cognitive tools in the context of inquiry learning can be found in de Jong and van Joolingen (1998), Linn et al. (2004), Quintana et al. (2004), and de Jong (in press).

An example of a cognitive tool in ZAP is the "reference data" function. With this function, students can compare the outcomes of their own experiment with data that come from experiments with large groups. This helps them put their own actions into perspective and make abstractions from their data.

An example of a cognitive tool in KM Quest is the so-called *Advisor*, which monitors the state of the business and knowledge management model. The *Advisor* warns the group of learners that they are "in danger" if one of the key indicators approaches a critical value. In a similar way it signals when there is a certain fixed discrepancy between the desired value and the current value of an indicator that is related to the objectives the players have set during the game. The *Advisor* also presents a list of proper interventions (see Figure 7).

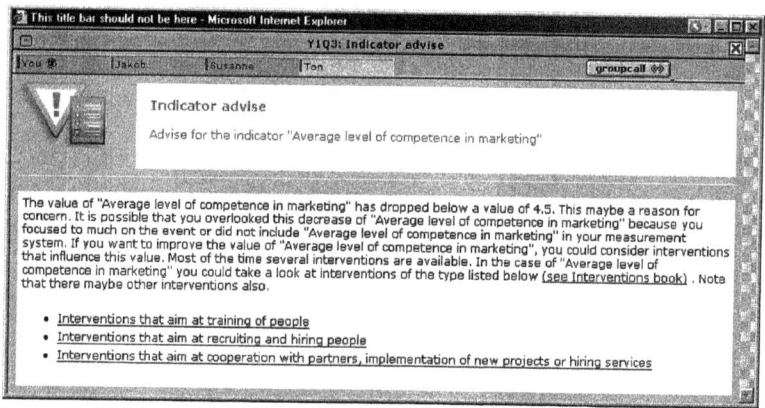

Fig. 7. *Example of feedback from the Advisor.*

One of the main cognitive tools in Co-Lab is the *Process Coordinator*. In this process coordinator, learners are supported in their planning, monitoring, and reporting activities. The *Process Coordinator* presents an overview of goals and subgoals, gives students the possibility of adding their own goals and including their notes and results so these can constantly be monitored, and generates from this overview a draft report that students can hand in after their experimentation.

8 Engagement of students: Designing environments that are really used

The common denominator of ZAP, KM Quest, and Co-Lab is that students produce results that are based on their own, experimental results (ZAP), behaviour of the company (KM Quest), or models that can be executed (Co-Lab). This sense of ownership or engagement, is, in our view, an important aspect of the success of use of the environments. This success is reflected in the actual use of these programs. ZAPs are now used in almost all Dutch (and some Belgian) universities (who can use the Dutch versions on-line for free) and a commercial English version is published by an American publisher (W.W. Norton). KM Quest is in use at several institutions of higher education throughout Europe and has been taken over by a large publisher who distributes it for the higher education sector in the Netherlands (Wolters-Noordhoff). Co-Lab is not used commercially as yet; the first version of the product was finished in 2004, and needs more development and content to be successfully launched.

All three products have also been extensively developed in cooperation with users. During the development of ZAPs, prototype versions were extensively evaluated. First-year psychology students evaluated the usability of the different components of a number of ZAPs in collective and individual sessions. They were asked questions about their layout and content, and general comments were collected. Based on this evaluation, improvements were made to the textual components, and revisions were made to the acti-vity component. In an experimental evaluation, ZAPs were compared to plain text without the interactive component (Hulshof et al., in press). At first sight, there was an advantage for the textual version, but students in the ZAP condition appeared to have a better retention than students in the textual version. There was even a tendency for students in the ZAP condition to improve their retention over time. During the development of Co-Lab and KM Quest larger formative studies with learners (and teachers) have been undertaken, and the results from these studies have been used to improve the products. To enable these evaluations, early prototypes of all three systems were built, and users were confronted with these systems in order to gather their views and requirements. In this way, our work followed what Burkhardt and Schoenfeld (2003) have called the "engineering approach". In this approach, research takes place around the launching of a product and all research is not necessarily done before the product is delivered. This may lead to products for which all aspects may not be underpinned by scientific evaluations, but it facilitates the development of products that are really used.

References

Brown, J. S., Collins, A., & Duguid, P. (1989). Situated cognition and the culture of learning. *Educational Researcher, 18*, 32-42.

Burkhardt, H., & Schoenfeld, A. (2003). Improving educational research: Toward a more useful, more influential, and better-funded enterprise. *Educational Researcher, 32(9)*, 3-14.

de Jong, T. (in press). The guided discovery principle in multimedia learning. In R. E. Mayer (Ed.), *Cambridge handbook of multimedia learning*. Cambridge, UK: Cambridge University Press.

de Jong, T., & van Joolingen, W. R. (1998). Scientific discovery learning with computer simulations of conceptual domains. *Review of Educational Research, 68*, 179-202.

Dunbar, K. (2001). What scientific thinking reveals about the nature of cognition. In K. Crowley, C. D. Schunn, & T. Okada (Eds.), *Designing for science: Implications from everyday, classroom, and professional settings* (pp. 115-140). Mahwah, NJ: Lawrence Erlbaum Associates.

Hickey, D. T., Kindfield, A. C. H., Horwitz, P., & Christie, M. A. T. (2003). Integrating curriculum, instruction, assessment, and evaluation in a technology-supported genetics learning environment. *American Educational Research Journal, 40*, 495-538.

Hulshof, C. D., Eysink, T. H. S., Loyens, S., & de Jong, T. (in press). ZAPs: Using interactive programs for learning psychology. *Interactive Learning Environments*.

Leemkuil, H., & de Jong, T. (2004). Games. In P. Kirschner (Ed.), *ICT in het onderwijs: The next generation* (pp. 43-64). Alphen aan de Rijn: Samsom.

Leemkuil, H., de Jong, T., de Hoog, R., & Christoph, N. (2003). KM Quest: A collaborative internet-based simulation game. *Simulation & Gaming, 34*, 89-111.

Linn, M. C., Bell, P., & Davis, E. A. (2004). Specific design principles: Elaborating the scaffolded knowledge integration framework. In M. Linn, E. A. Davis, & P. Bell (Eds.), *Internet environments for science education*. Mahwah, NJ: Lawrence Erlbaum Associates.

Löhner, S., van Joolingen, W. R., & Savelsbergh, E. R. (2003). The effect of external representation on constructing computer models of complex phenomena. *Instructional Science, 31*, 395-418.

Penner, D. E. (2001). Cognition, computers, and synthetic science: Building knowledge and meaning through modelling. *Review of Research in Education, 25*, 1-37.

Quintana, C., Reiser, B. J., Davis, E. A., Krajcik, J., Fretz, E., Duncan, R. G., et al. (2004). A scaffolding design framework for software to support science inquiry. *The Journal of the Learning Sciences, 13*, 337-387.

Reiser, B. J., Tabak, I., Sandoval, W. A., Smith, B., Steinmuller, F., & Leone, T. J. (2001). BGuILE: Strategic and conceptual scaffolds for scientific inquiry in biology classrooms. In S. M. Carver & D. Klahr (Eds.), *Cognition and instruction: Twenty five years of progress* (pp. 263-305). Mahwah, NJ: Lawrence Erlbaum Associates.

Slotta, J. (2004). The web-based inquiry science environment (WISE): Scaffolding knowledge integration in the science classroom. In M. Linn, E. A. Davis, & P. Bell (Eds.), *Internet environments for science education* (pp. 203-233). Mahwah, NJ: Lawrence Erlbaum Associates.

Steed, M. (1992). Stella, A simulation construction kit: Cognitive process and educational implications. *Journal of Computers in Mathematics and Science Teaching, 11*, 39-52.

van Joolingen, W. R., de Jong, T., Lazonder, A. W., Savelsbergh, E., & Manlove, S. (2005). Co-Lab: Research and development of an on-line learning environment for collaborative scientific discovery learning. *Computers in Human Behavior, 21,* 671-688.

Vreman-de Olde, C., & de Jong, T. (2004). Student-generated assignments about electrical circuits in a computer simulation. *International Journal of Science Education, 26,* 859-873.

Part II
Promoting deep conceptual and strategic learning in mathematics

Chapter 4

Does social interaction influence 3-year-old children's tendency to focus on numerosity?

A quasi-experimental study in day care

Minna M. Hannula, Aino Mattinen, and Erno Lehtinen

1 Introduction

The goal of this study was to investigate whether it is possible to enhance 3-year-old children's tendency to spontaneously focus on numerosity, and thus promote children's deliberate practice in recognising and producing small numbers of objects or incidents in their everyday surroundings in day care. This study was motivated by the earlier studies of Hannula and Lehtinen (2001; 2004; in press) and Hannula, Räsänen and Lehtinen (2005). These longitudinal studies showed remarkable individual differences in children's Spontaneous FOcusing on Numerosity (SFON), some stability in this SFON tendency across time and across different contexts, and a clear positive relationship between SFON tendency and the development of early mathematical skills from the age of 3 to 7 years. The children with a strong tendency to focus on numerosity in novel tasks were better at verbal counting skills and their range for rapid recognition of small numbers of objects without counting (i.e., subitizing) was larger than the children who did not focus on numerosity (Hannula et al., 2005).

1.1 Spontaneous focusing on numerosity

Hannula and Lehtinen (2001; 2004; in press) demonstrated that a separate intentional process of focusing on the aspect of numerosity is dissociable from enumeration skills in 3 – 7 –year-old children. In these studies, it was shown that many children failed in test tasks measuring spontaneous focusing on numerosity in particular because they did not focus on the numeric aspects of the situations. After being guided to pay attention to numerosity, all the children were successful in similar tasks, showing that

---

We wish to warmly thank the personnel of the seven day-care centres in Turku for their valuable help in conducting this study, the parents for their positive reactions on our study, and especially the children for their genuine, enthusiastic participation.

they had the mathematical skills required for the SFON tasks. In agreement with Sophian's (1998) views, Hannula and Lehtinen (2004; in press) concluded, that during the childhood years, conceptual and procedural advances in enumeration enable and facilitate the child's tendency to focus on numerosity, which in turn, leads to the child's own practice in utilizing numerosity in a variety of situations, which in turn develops enumeration skills further. Thus, SFON is an important factor in the acquisition of cultural tools of numeracy; it is by no means self-evident that, in natural social situations, all children would as equally easily notice the number of objects, and utilize this information in action. This leads to considerable differences in children's practice with quantitative skills. Correspondingly, Ericsson and Lehman (1996) have shown that experts are capable of "seeing" multiple possibilities to practice their skills in everyday situations, and this has been an essential part of their development from a very early age. In the same way, we assume that children's own spontaneous focusing on numerosity frequently leads them to perceive different numbers of objects or events in their surroundings, and thus they get practice in recognising and producing numerosity. This, in turn, develops their enumeration skills in several ways: not only broadening the enumeration range, but also, along with more developed enumeration skills, a larger and larger quantity may appear as a possible subject for enumeration. Moreover, knowledge about the use of enumeration means in different tasks will increase with practice, so the child may tend to focus more on numerosity in new more demanding tasks. Interesting question follows from these findings showing the significance of the child's spontaneous practice in the area of early mathematical skills. Could SFON tendency be affected by means of social interaction in the early phases of cardinality development?

1.2 Possibilities of influencing 3-year-old children's SFON tendency

In principle, studies on the development of both early mathematical and attentional skills indicate that 3-year-old children might have a great potential to learn to focus their attention on the aspect of number in addition to other culturally-valued relevant aspects. First, 3-year-old children already have the basic abilities for individuating objects, forming one-to-one correspondences between objects, and non-verbally recognising very small cardinal values of the sets (Hannula & Lehtinen, 2001; Mix, 2002; Wynn, 1990, 1992b). These early number recognition skills, functioning with very small numbers make focusing on the exact number, in principle, possible. Second, 3-year-old children's higher order attentional processes are sufficiently developed to enable voluntary goal-directed processes such as selective attending to goal-relevant aspects of the situation (for reviews, see, Ruff & Rothbar, 1996; Tomasello et al., in press).

1.3 Early mathematical development

Knowledge of exact cardinal values and the number words related to these cardinal values, as well as utilizing skills for numerical aspects in action develop during early childhood years (for a review, see Mix, Huttenlocher, & Levine, 2002). In the development of cardinality a child gradually moves from the innate, preverbal perceptual ability to individuate and discriminate small numbers of objects to the ability to represent exact cardinal values for oneness, twoness, and possibly threeness non-verbally in action (Mix et al., 2002). According to Spelke (2003), the role of language, especially verbal number words and language related to enumeration enable the transition to more developed number representations. Children learn the meanings of words by relating the words to their pre-existing concepts, which are made explicit by their core knowledge systems (Spelke, 2003). According to Karmiloff-Smith (1995), the number-relevant information available to young children is implicit in procedures for processing environmental input. The components of that knowledge subsequently become explicitly defined by the process of redescription. Redescription is the process by which children's representations become more manipulable and flexible, allowing conscious access to knowledge. Focusing attention on the exact number of objects or incidents in one's surroundings, i.e., the attentional process enabling the utilization of the preattentional subitizing mechanism for quantification, is an essential skill to be learnt before the child can utilize his or her innate mechanisms efficiently for utilizing quantification in his or her action (Hannula et al., 2005). Wynn's longitudinal study (1992b) shows how children learn the cardinal meanings of "one, two and three" in a piecemeal fashion. Some 3-year-olds already possess the first cardinal number words, and have some skills in the verbal counting of objects. However, most of them can not yet determine the cardinality of a larger set of objects by verbal counting (Wynn, 1992b).

A major step in early mathematical development is to learn to use counting to determine the cardinality of a set of objects or incidents. A great deal of this development occurs around 3 to 3.5 years of age (Fuson, 1988; Wynn, 1992b). Determination of the cardinality of a set and counting are at first separate and different situations for children, but they are gradually connected when children understand that counting is not an isolated activity, but has the goal of determinating the cardinal value of the set (Bermejo, Morales, & deOsuna, 2004; Fuson, 1988). The child's first attempts to use counting for the determination of cardinality of a set are of great diagnostic importance, and a visible sign of developing concepts and skills (Goldin-Meadow, Alibali, & Church, 1993). The remarkably slow development of cardinality and counting skills (e.g., Fuson, 1988; Wynn, 1990) could be explained by the major differences in preverbal and verbal counting systems (Wynn, 1992a, 1992b), and the need for lots of practice in acquiring cardinality recognition skills. In the study of Hannula and Lehtinen (2001), it was found that those children whose tendency to focus on numerosity was very strong at the age of 3 showed better development of their cardinality recognition skills in the period from 3 to 4 years of age. The period beginning from the age of three years might be the time when children's spontaneous practice in enumeration should be triggered. In this study, we explore whether social interaction has an effect on children's SFON tendency, which in turn would enhance children's cardinality-related development.

1.4 The role of social interaction in focusing on relevant aspects

The purpose of the current study was to explore the possibility of promoting 3-year-old children's ways of perceiving their surroundings so that they would focus their attention on the aspect of number. Social interaction and the aid of more experienced members of society are crucial for the development of higher order processes in self-regulation, especially the controlling of attention (Gauvain, 2001; Ruff & Rothbart, 1996). Gauvain (2001) describes how the social context affords children structured opportunities to practice, refine, and extend their cognitive skills. Participation in shared activities requires and also develops understanding of the intentions of others, cultural learning, motivation to share psychological states with others, and specific forms of cognitive representations for shared actions (Tomasello et al., in press). Gleissner, Meltzoff, and Bekkering (2000) have shown that 3-year-old children already code human behaviour and imitate it on the basis of hierarchically organised goals, which gives them the opportunity to focus on relevant and more abstract aspects of the actions observed. The joint processes of children and adults direct children's attention to relevant aspects of tasks, and help children to acquire the culturally-based numerical tools necessary for living in a society. These joint processes also help children to understand the purposes of the tasks and certain cognitive strategies embedded in a variety of everyday activities (Gauvain, 2001; Mix, 2002).

On the basis of an intensive case study, Mix (2002) presents evidence of how a wide range of socially and linguistically mediated numerically meaningful activities in everyday family life emphasize conceptual growth in early mathematical development. Correspondingly, Lobato and her colleagues have shown that the social and physical aspects of a certain situation can support children's attention toward particular mathematical properties rather than others in mathematics lessons (Lobato, 2003; Lobato, Ellis, & Munoz, 2003). Studies on the mathematical activities of parents and their children have shown that children's better mathematical skills are related to parents' skills in modelling mathematical thinking in everyday contexts, and in contexts involving the usual preschool material (Anderson, 1997, Blevins-Knabe & Musun-Miller, 1996; Huntsinger, Jose, Larson,

Krieg, & Shaligram, 2000; Linnell & Fluck, 2001; Saxe, Guberman, & Gearhart, 1987). Although these studies have not regarded focusing on numerosity as a separate process from other numerical skills, they provide good reason to state that socio-cultural factors might also have a role in the formation of SFON tendency.

1.5 Variation in number as a promoter of focusing on the aspect of number

Experiencing variation in the aspect of number might be one pedagogical tool to enhance the learning of early mathematical skills (Marton & Booth, 1997; Lindström, Marton, Lindahl, & Packendorff, 2002). Thus, enhancing variation in the numerical aspect of tasks could make children more aware of the aspect of numerosity. This is when their implicit knowledge about small numbers may become more explicit targets of intentional focusing. According to Marton and Booth (1997), the variation in how people experience a certain phenomenon, and the specific meaning it has for them, is the most fundamental aspect of learning. Thus, to learn something means to become capable of experiencing various aspects of a phenomenon in a certain, specific way. These different aspects (e.g., shapes, colours, or numerosity of set of objects) may appear serially, and as separate aspects to focus awareness on. An aspect which someone is focally aware of is interpreted against the background of potential variation in the aspect. Thus, "threeness" is experienced against the background of a potential variation in the aspect of number, against "twoness" and "fourness", for instance (Marton & Booth, 1997).

1.6 Aims of the study

In this study, we explored whether it is possible to influence children's SFON tendency by guiding children's attention towards the aspect of number within such a small range of numbers that children can handle. Variation in number was used as one of the ways to make the aspect of number more salient for the children. Our earlier studies have shown that a strong SFON tendency is positively associated with the development of cardinality-related skills. Thus, we also studied the effects of the SFON enhancement on the development of these mathematical skills. The day-care setting was selected as the context of the study to enhance our knowledge of how SFON tendency appears in a naturalistic, relevant learning environment of Finnish 3-year-old children. Locating the empirical study in kindergartens also made it possible for us to study whether children's SFON observed in day-care surroundings would be related to their SFON tendency measured by the SFON tasks used in our earlier studies.

2 Method

2.1 Participants

The participants were 34 3-year-old (range from 2 years 10 months to 3 years 2 months) children, who were in day care in seven Finnish urban kindergartens. The experimental group consisted of 17 children from three groups of children in three kindergartens. The control group of 17 children was selected from 24 children in four kindergartens by matching children's age, gender, SFON scores and cardinality-related skills (the number of recognised and produced numbers of objects and the level of counting attempts) and to the corresponding characteristics of the experimental group. The children were from native Finnish speaking families, and they had no developmental delays. The control group participated in typical Finnish day care without any special emphasis on promoting SFON tendency.

2.2 Design and data gathering

In the experimental group the day-care personnel provided children activities aimed to increase the children's SFON tendency during their normal day-care hours for four weeks. In the experimental and control groups the pretest was followed by the posttest at an interval of four weeks, and the delayed posttest was presented five months after the posttest. In order to measure children's general SFON tendency, a set of three different SFON tasks (or parallel versions of them) were presented at the pre-, post-, and delayed posttests. Accordingly, cardinality related skills were assessed at every measurement point and the number sequence production was tested at the delayed posttest. In addition, the day-care personnel of the experimental group gathered observational data on children's SFON manifestation during the phase of enhancement.

2.2.1 SFON tasks

Our aim was to get a reliable indicator of a child's general SFON tendency across different task contexts. This kind of indicator is aimed to capture a child's amount of focusing on numerosity, and thus the amount of practice acquired in utilising enumeration skills in his or her surroundings. To enable the measuring of children's spontaneous behaviour only novel tasks or at least tasks with novel materials and/or contexts can be used each time. Furthermore, when presenting the SFON tasks, no use can be made of any phrases which might suggest that the tasks were somehow mathematical or quantitative. In order to hinder the confounding effect of number recognition skills on the measures of SFON the SFON tasks have to include only such small numbers of items that all children should be able to handle.

Furthermore the SFON tasks must be procedurally so easy that every child is able to carry out the task.

All the child's (a) utterances including number words (e.g.,"I'll give him two berries"), (b) use of fingers to express numbers, (c) counting acts, like a whispered number word sequence and indicating acts by fingers and/or head, (d) other comments referring either to quantities or counting (e.g., "Oh, I miscounted them"), or, e) interpretation of the goal of the task as quantitative (e.g., "I gave an exactly accurate number of them"), were identified. The child was scored as focusing on numbers, if she or he produced the correct numerosity, and/or, if she or he was observed expressing any of the aforementioned (a - e) quantifying acts. The scoring was based on analyses of video-recorded task situations.

All SFON tasks included four trials, in which the numbers of objects used were 2, 2, 1, and 3, respectively. For the further analyses of pre- and posttest results only the first three trials with numbers of objects one and two were used to confirm that children had the skills required for the SFON tasks. However, due to the considerable ceiling effect of this variable, the fourth trial with number of objects being three was used to in the delayed posttest. Thus, the maximum score on individual SFON tasks was 3 at the pre- and posttests, and 4 at the delayed posttest. The SFON tasks were presented in the following order: Imitation and Selection tasks with non-disappearing items, and Imitation task with disappearing items.

Due to our interest on children's general SFON tendency across different task contexts instead of interest in SFON in specific task contexts, we used the sum score of the SFON tasks, expressed as a percentage for the further analyses. Thus the pre- and posttest SFON percentage described how many times out of all the nine presented SFON trials the child focused on numerosity. Correspondingly, the delayed posttest SFON percentage described how many times out of all the twelve presented SFON trials the child focused on numerosity.

2.2.2 Imitation task with visible items

Three versions of the imitation task were used. In the pretest the toys used were carrots and white toy-looking hares, in the posttest dogs and bones, and in the delayed posttest carrots and brown real-looking hares.

The procedure was as follows: The experimenter placed two similar hares and then a plate of 5 cm long carrots on the table in front of the child. The toys were identified, and then the experimenter said to the child, "Look what I'm doing. I'm doing this, this. Now, you do exactly what I did." While saying "this, this", the experimenter lifted two carrots, one at a time, and placed them side by side in front of the experimenter's hare. The child imitated the experimenter as well as he or she could and placed carrots in front of his or her hare. The number of carrots across the separate items was 2, 2, 1, and 3.

2.2.3 Selection task

The materials of Selection task at the pretest were pink creatures in the form of pear with either two, one or three leg(s) and five boxes, and a bag. On the covers of the boxes there were different numbers of disarranged socks. The boxes were on the table in front of the child in line from left to right arranged according to the number of socks as follows: 4, 2, 5, 1, 3. The boxes were completely covered by a table cloth at the beginning of the task. The materials for the posttest were four pictures of houses, where the numbers of openings for windows were similar to numbers of legs in the pink creatures (2, 2, 1, 3). At the delayed posttest hedgehog-looking creatures and the boxes of pictures of rubber boots were used.

The experimenter started the task by lifting a creature from her bag by saying: "This creature has a problem. The creature's legs feel terribly cold. Fortunately there are boxes of socks under the cloth." The experimenter uncovered the boxes keeping the creature in her hand, and told the child: "Give this creature, its own box of socks." After the child had given a box of socks to the creature, it was lifted to the bag "to go and put the socks on". Then the following creatures were presented.

2.2.4 Imitation with disappearing objects

The materials of the tasks at the pretest were a toy parrot, capable of swallowing, placed in front of the child on the table, and a plate of red glass berries (2 cm in diameter) placed in front of the parrot. At the posttest the materials were a bear-shaped savings box with a hole for money in the back, and a box of Finnish Marks. At the delayed posttest a toy-dog and a plate of brown "chocolates" were used. The testing procedure was similar in all the task versions.

The experimenter started the task by introducing the materials and then said: "Watch carefully what I'm doing, and then you do just like I did." The experimenter put two berries one at a time into the parrot's mouth, and they disappeared with a bumping sound into the parrot's stomach. Then the child was told: "Now you do exactly like I did". The number of berries across the separate items was 2, 2, 1, and 3.

2.3 Tasks for cardinality-related skills

Cardinality recognition and production skills were measured by a "caterpillar task" at the pre-test and delayed posttest (for a more detailed description, see Hannula & Lehtinen, 2001). The materials in the caterpillar task were ten cloth "caterpillars", with 1 - 10 legs, and a small box of socks for the caterpillars. The parallel posttest task version was called as "the pig task". The materials were sows with different numbers of teats, a small box for piglets, and small piglets. In the pig task, the child was asked to bring as many piglets as the sow could feed from the box on the opposite side of the table after being shown how the piglets can be nursed by the sow.

The child was introduced to a frame story about caterpillars needing socks before going out, and a model caterpillar with socks already on. Then the child was asked to bring the next 2-legged caterpillar as many socks as the caterpillar needed from the box on the opposite side of the table. It was carefully confirmed that the child understood the quantitative goal of the task, i.e., bringing exactly the correct number of socks to the caterpillar. The caterpillars were presented in the order 2, 1, 3, 4, 2, 5, 6, 1, 7, 8, 2, 9 and 10, where the numbers represent the number of legs of the caterpillars. The highest number, at which the child twice brought the correct number of socks to the caterpillar, determined the upper range of the child's skills on cardinality recognition. The maximum score on the task was 10.

In addition to cardinality recognition, the total number of a child's attempts to count a set of items during the task was analysed. The criterion for a counting attempt was the appearance of at least two number words, either with or without visible pointing acts, for at least two different items one after another.

2.4 Number sequence production task

At the delayed posttest the child was asked to count as far as she or he could. If the child did not understand the request, the experimenter demonstrated the task by counting to 15. The number sequence production was determined by the highest number up to which the child counted accurately in one of the two trials.

2.5 SFON enhancement

Children's attention was directed to numerosity (how many objects or incidents there were) in structured games organised by adults, as well as in everyday situations (dressing, cleaning up, and free play). The aim was to provide plenty of different tasks and situations, where 3-year-old children could focus on the numbers of objects/incidents within a range of such small numbers that they could deal with. Furthermore, children were aided in discerning the numerosity from the other features across different tasks. The personnel of the kindergartens continued carrying out some SFON enhancement activities integrated into the everyday activities in day care for about one month after the training period. Then the children were relocated to new kindergarten groups, in which no specific SFON training was offered.

All the nurses and teachers of the children in the experimental groups were supported in several ways in conducting the training. First, they were told the overall idea of the phenomenon of SFON in two lessons. Then, the second author visited the kindergartens once or twice a week giving hands-on guidance to the personnel; how to recognise and produce incidents, in which a child focuses on numerosity. The kindergartens received the package of materials for the structured games at the beginning of every training week. The personnel's focusing on children's SFON incidences was motivated by asking them to gather observational data on these incidences by tally charts located in different areas of the children's group.

The aim of the personnel was to notice and promote the moments when a child paid attention to the number of objects or incidents. Focusing on the small numbers of items (clothes, slices of bread, toys, etc.) embedded in normal everyday action, was given special emphasis. Discussions about small numbers of items, and the question "How many of something?" were used to awaken children's interest in the variation and existence of numerosity when the numbers of everyday materials were manipulated by games of giving, taking and making something. Children's attention was specifically focused to small numerosity in the range 1- 3, which they should all have been able to recognize and produce. The cardinal number words of 1-3 were used embedded in action.

There were also three different structured games including small numbers of items to enhance children's interest in focusing on numerosity. A board with changeable numbers of animals of one kind was used daily as an arena for paying joint attention to the aspect of number. The number of animals was changed according to a singing game in the morning, and many times secretly during the day. Soon the children themselves began to get interested in looking at how many animals there were on the board. The animal characters and matching contexts were fish in an aquarium, elephants in a circus, and birds on a wire. In the last week, all three contexts were used.

Two to three times a week the pairs of numerically matching pictures were shown to the children in different forms, e. g. pictures of 1, 2, or 3 ice cream balls with corresponding pictures of 1, 2, or 3 ice cream cones. The children were asked to match the pictures on the basis of numerical correspondence.

Furthermore, every child was provided with a structured hiding game with 1-3 little ducks, together with another child and the second author, who guided the children in the game. The ducks flew onto their houses, walked into their houses, dived into the pond, etc. providing 20 minutes game with plenty of variation in small numbers. The adult directed the children's attention to numbers of ducks if the children did not spontaneously do so.

2.6 SFON observations at day-care settings of the experimental group

The personnel of the experimental group gathered observational data on the children's SFON manifestation in day-care settings with five tally charts in different areas of the group. The adults were instructed to record every incident, in which they noticed that a child focused his or her attention on numerosity. The personnel had also note books, on which they described informative situations concerning SFON manifestation in children's action. The children's results in the pre- or posttests were not given to the personnel. This made it possible for us to compare the individual child's SFON scores measured by the SFON tasks in the pre- and posttests to the corresponding observational data gathered by the tally charts on the child's SFON manifestation in the day-care settings.

2.7 Statistical analyses

First, Spearman's correlations were calculated for the SFON percentages in SFON assessments and the numbers of children's observed SFON in day-care settings. The three children who were absent from day care for more than 5 days during the two-week period, as well as one child who was especially active in focusing on numerosity were not included in the analyses of covariance. This child focused 59 and 65 times on numerosity during the first and second two-week period, respectively, when the range for the numbers of tallies for all the other children was from 0 to 15 tallies per a child during a two-week period.

Second, in order to examine whether the experimental treatment had an effect on children's SFON tendency and their cardinality-related skills, we first analysed the experimental effect for the children in the experimental and control groups. Secondly, to study whether the experimental effect differed on the basis of a child's initial SFON tendency, we split the group of all participating children into two sub-groups: into those with initially either some (SFON percentage > 33.3) or low SFON tendency (SFON percentage smaller than or equal to 33.3). We then studied the experimental effect among the children with some initial SFON tendency, as well as among the children with low initial SFON tendency. The analyses we conducted were separate ANOVA's with repeated measures (2 Groups x 3 Times) together with planned contrasts for SFON, cardinal skills and counting attempts at pre-, post- and delayed post tests and corresponding analyses (2 Groups x 2 Time) for the results at pre- and delayed posttests. Mann-Whitney's U-test was used to analyse differences in number sequence production of the experimental and control groups at the delayed posttest. All the statistical testing was one-tailed due to our hypothesis of the favourable performance of the experimental group in the skills followed.

3 Results

3.1 Association of SFON percentage and observed SFON incidents

According to the tally charts of SFON incidents in day care, during the first two weeks of SFON enhancement, the personnel noticed that a child focused on numerosity on average of 3.92 times (SD = 4.59). In the following two weeks, the children focused spontaneously, on average, 5.13 times (SD = 5.14) on number. The Spearman's correlations between the number of tallies from the first two-week period and the SFON percentage measured by the SFON tasks at pretest was $r = .36$, $p = > 0.05$, (n = 13). The corresponding correlation between the tallies of the second two-week period and the SFON percentage on the posttest was $r = .55$, $p < .05$, (n = 16).

3.2 Comparison of experimental and control groups

3.2.1 SFON

All children's SFON tendency increased during the entire follow-up period, resulting in a significant main effect of time (see Tables 1 and 2). The interaction of time and experimental treatment from the pretest to the delayed posttest was statistically significant, showing that the experimental group developed more SFON tendency than the control group during the follow-up. The main effect of group and the interaction between time and the experimental treatment were not significant when the posttest was included in the analyses.

Table 1. Descriptives of the variables broken down by experimental and control groups (N = 34)

	Experimental		Control	
	M	SD	M	SD
SFON percentage				
Pretest	42.48	19.73	42.48	21.60
Posttest	64.05	21.70	62.74	26.40
Delayed posttest	79.41	17.46	67.16	21.74
Cardinal number words				
Pretest	2.53	0.62	2.53	0.72
Posttest	2.53	0.87	2.76	0.97
Delayed posttest	3.82	2.22	3.06	0.97
Counting attempts				
Pretest	0.65	1.17	0.82	1.59
Posttest	0.82	1.51	0.76	2.17
Delayed posttest	4.41	8.68	1.00	1.50
Number sequence production at the delayed posttest	10.18	3.76	6.47	2.96

3.2.2 Cardinality recognition skills and counting attempts in the cardinality task

The children's skill to recognise and produce numbers of objects as well as the number of their counting attempts increased during the follow-up period, resulting in a significant main effect of time (Table 2). Neither the main effects of experimental condition nor interaction between the main effects across the measurement points reached statistically significant level.

Table 2. The results of group comparisons made by separate ANOVA's with repeated measures together with planned contrasts for SFON, cardinal skills and the number of counting attempts at pre-, post- and delayed posttests among either all children, children with some, or low initial SFON tendency

Repeated Measures ANOVA	Experimental vs. Control F (degrees of freedom)					
	All (n = 17 exp +17 c)		Some initial SFON (n = 11 exp + 9 c)		Low initial SFON (n = 6 exp + 8 c)	
	Pre-P-DP[1]	Pre-DP[2]	Pre-P-DP[1]	Pre-DP[2]	Pre-P-DP[1]	Pre-DP[2]
SFON						
Interaction	1.96 (2, 64)	3.09 (1,32)*	2.41 (2,36)*	4.61 (1,18)*	0.81 (2,24)	1.90 (1,12)
Time	42.73(2,64)***	78.08(1,32)***	13.81(2,36)***	26.90(1,18)***	41.00(2,24)***	113.3(1,12)***
Group	0.52 (1,32)	1.05 (1,32)	0.16 (1,18)	0.56 (1,18)	0.02 (2,12)	0.10 (1,12)
Cardinality skill						
Interaction	1.84 (2,64)	1.66 (1,32)	4.33 (2,36)*	3.60 (1,18)*	1.17 (2,24)	1.76 (1,12)
Time	6.64(2,64)**	9.45(1,32)**	4.46(2,36)**	5.74 (1,18)*	1.70 (2,24)	3.81 (1,12)*
Group	0.47 (1,32)	1.33 (1,32)	1.11 (1,18)	3.34 (1,18)*	0.37 (1,12)	0.90 (1,12)
Counting attempts						
Interaction	2.58 (2,64)*	2.66 (1,32)	2.78 (2,36)*	3.05 (1,18)*	0.51 (2,24)	1.22 (1,12)
Time	3.22 (2,64)*	3.22 (1,32)*	2.43 (2,36)	2.44 (1,18)	0.46 (2.24)	0.49 (1,12)
Group	1.73 (1,32)	2.20 (1,32)	2.79 (1,18)	2.61 (1,18)	0.24 (1,12)	0.12 (1,12)

[1] Pre-P-DP = Pretest – Posttest – Delayed Posttest. [2] Pre-DP = Pretest – Delayed Posttest.
* p < .05, ** p < .01, *** p < .001.

3.2.3 Number sequence production at the delayed posttest

The experimental group was able to count higher than the control group at the delayed posttest according to Mann-Whitney's test, $p < .01$.

3.3 Comparisons of experimental and control groups among children with some initial SFON tendency and among children with very low initial SFON tendency

As can be seen in Table 2 and Figures 1-3, the interaction between experimental condition and time was significant in all the skills measured among children who had some initial SFON tendency at the beginning of the study. Furthermore, the main effect of time was significant for SFON and cardinality recognition skills. The main effect of experimental condition was significant only in cardinality recognition skills, not in SFON or counting attempts. According to the planned contrasts and confirming Mann-Whitney's tests, comparisons among children with some initial SFON tendency in experimental and control groups at the delayed posttests, showed that the experimental group outperformed the control group in cardinality recognition skills ($p < .05$), in counting attempts ($p < .01$), and in number sequence production ($p < .01$). The experimental group counted accurately from one on up to 11.27 ($SD = 4.17$), and the control group up to 6.22 ($SD = 2.91$).

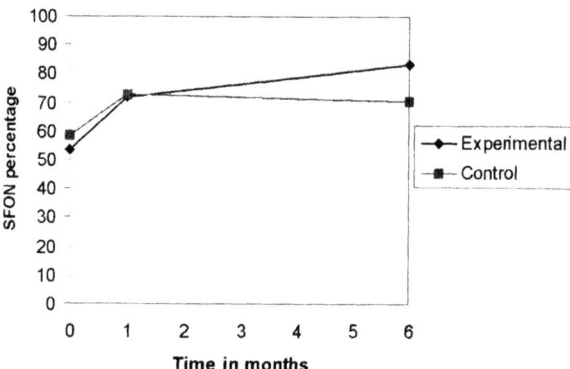

Fig. 1. The means of the SFON percentages of children with some initial SFON tendency at the beginning of the study. The results are presented for the children belonging to the experimental (n = 11) or the control (n = 9) groups in pre-, post-, and delayed posttests.

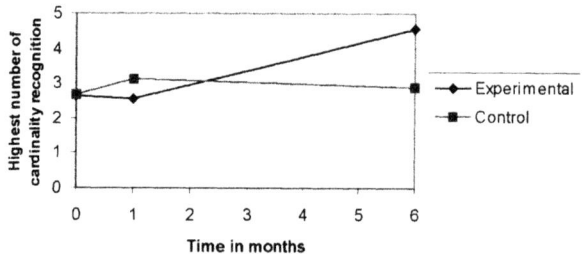

Fig. 2. Cardinality recognition and production skills of children with some initial SFON tendency. The results are presented for the experimental and control groups in pre-, post, and delayed posttest.

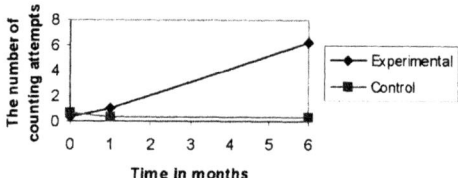

Fig. 3. The number of counting attempts of children with some initial SFON tendency. The results are presented for the experimental and control groups in pre-, post-, and delayed posttests.

Although children with very low initial SFON tendency developed in all the measured skills, no experimental effects were visible in any of the measured skills (see Table 2). This showed that the SFON enhancement had an effect only on those children who had some initial SFON tendency at the beginning of the study.

4 Discussion

In this study, we explored whether it is possible to affect children's spontaneous tendency to focus on numerosity by providing practice in kindergarten aimed to direct children's attention towards small numbers of items. The results show that we were able to have an effect on children's SFON tendency, but the effect varied according to the amount of a child's initial SFON tendency at the beginning of the study. The children who had some initial SFON tendency developed more in SFON tendency during the follow-up than children with a corresponding tendency to focus on numerosity in the control group. Furthermore, children with some initial SFON tendency in the experimental group developed more in cardinality-related skills during the follow-up. This indicates that the SFON enhancement was able to trigger these children's deliberate practice in cardinality related skills. On the contrary, the children, with low SFON tendency at the beginning of the study did not show any effects of SFON enhancement, when their development was compared to the control group with a corresponding amount of initial SFON tendency. The results also showed that the observational data of the children's amount of spontaneous focusing on numerosity in day-care settings was related to the children's SFON percentage in the SFON assessments. At the time of the delayed posttest, the children of the experimental group were able to produce a longer number sequence than the control group.

Conclusions about the order of counting skills and SFON tendency - which comes first - in the development of early mathematical skills can not yet be drawn on the basis of this study. During the SFON enhancement the adults used cardinal number words and counting as an additional way of directing the children's attention towards number of objects, although the child's incorrect counting or enumerating attempts were not actively corrected by the adults. As supposed from earlier studies showing the slow development of the cardinality-related skills in the early phases (Wynn 1992b), there was no improvement in these skills during the period between the pre- and posttests, unlike in SFON tendency.

The small differences between the experimental and control groups must be considered when interpreting the results. The participants in the study were normally developing children, whose SFON tendency may be supported by parents and siblings, in addition to the experimental treatment offered. Furthermore, the experimental treatment was seemingly too short both for the day-care personnel and for the children whose initial SFON tendency was very low. The personnel had to espouse new knowledge on SFON appearance and enhancement, and put this into practice during a very short period of time. It is plausible that during the last two weeks of the enhancement period the personnel was able to really observe and enhance SFON as it was supposed to. It appeared that it was especially difficult for the adults to take the perspective of non-numerically focusing children, and create a zone of proximal development (Vygotsky, 1978) for these children's numerical focusing activities (Mattinen, 2005). This could illustrate what can easily happen in day-care settings with more and less mathematically interested children as well as explain why SFON enhancement had effect only on those children who had some initial SFON tendency. Adults may have noticed and promoted these children's SFON behaviour more efficiently. Further studies are needed to find effective ways of producing SFON enhancement in children with a very low SFON tendency.

Children's cardinality-related development is known to occur slowly in the phase when they learn to execute counting routines (Wynn 1992b). However, after children have achieved the basic skills in counting procedures, cardinality understanding can be efficiently promoted (Bermejo et al., 2004). This could partly explain why the deliberate practice enhanced by the increased SFON tendency produced observable development more clearly in the children who had better initial skills.

This study increased our understanding of the phenomenon of SFON, and how it develops in the community of adults and children. The children seemingly enjoyed the practices, and became very interested especially in the numbers of animals on the board with changeable numbers of animals. Providing variation in small numbers seems to awaken children's interest in the aspect of number. This is the first study indicating that children's focusing on numerosity in SFON tasks is related to their amount of focusing on numerosity in their everyday surroundings in day care. This confirms, firstly, our earlier reasoning that SFON provides practice in number recognition skills in everyday surroundings, and secondly, the validity of our SFON tasks in their ability to measure children's general tendency to focus on number. Moreover, this study indicates that social interaction is a significant factor in children's focusing on numerical aspects of their surroundings. Our studies on SFON like the studies of Lobato et al. (2003) emphasize the need to pay greater attention to the specific ways in which kindergarten teachers and learning materials can direct the child's attention when learning new skills. When designing mathematical learning environments for young children it is important to consider how mathematically children interpret the tasks, and especially to confirm that the mathematically less skilled children actually focus on the numerical aspects.

To conclude, the present study, together with the earlier studies of Hannula and Lehtinen (2001; 2004; in press) and Hannula et al. (2005) indicate that the explanation of why all children do not acquire competent counting and cardinality-related skills during the childhood years, may partly lie in children's own spontaneous activities based on their focusing targets. Children's frequent focusing on numerosity leads to a great amount of deliberate practice in the recognition of numbers of objects and incidents within the meaningful contexts of their surroundings. How to optimally promote these kinds of explorative, active processes of children should be carefully regarded while designing learning environments for young children. Our studies emphasise the significance of these child-initiated activities beginning already at a very early age, long before school. Small numbers of items are constantly recognised and utilized in everyday activities by adults. Uncovering and modelling this kind of mathematical thinking embedded in everyday life could be an efficient tool for promoting young children's mathematical development. Children's learning to utilise even the earliest mathematical skills in a wide variety of meaningful everyday activities, in addition to specific mathematical kindergarten or pre-school tasks, should be a serious goal for the designers of young children's learning environments. Targeting the joint attention of the group of children towards the aspect of number can be an effective way of promoting SFON tendency of individual children. Learning to focus on numerosity may be one of the significant steps on young children's way to learning to take mathematically meaningful perspectives on perceiving the world around them.

References

Anderson, A. (1997). Families and mathematics: A study of parent-child interactions. *Journal for Research in Mathematics Education, 28*, 484-511.

Bermejo, V., Morales, S., & deOsuna, J. G. (2004). Supporting children's development of cardinality understanding. *Learning and Instruction, 14*, 381-398.

Blevins-Knabe, B., & Musun-Miller, L. (1996). Number use at home by children and their parents and its relationship to early mathematical performance. *Early Development and Parenting, 5*, 35-45.

Ericsson, K. A., & Lehmann, A. C. (1996). Expert and exceptional performance: Evidence of maximal adaptation to task constraints. *Annual Review of Psychology, 47*, 273-305.

Fuson, K. C. 1988. *Children's counting and concepts of number.* New York: Springer.

Gauvain, M. (2001). *The social context of cognitive development.* New York: Guilford Press.

Gleissner, B., Meltzoff, A. N., & Bekkering, H. (2000). Children's coding of human action: Cognitive factors influencing imitation in 3-year-olds. *Developmental Science, 3*, 405-414.

Goldin-Meadow, S., Alibali, M. W., & Church, R. B. (1993). Transitions in concept acquisition: Using the hand to read the mind. *Psychological Review, 100*, 279-297.

Hannula, M.M., & Lehtinen, E. (2001). Spontaneous tendency to focus on numerosities in the development of cardinality. In M. Panhuizen-Van Heuvel (Ed.), *Proceedings of 25th Conference of the International Group for the Psychology of Mathematics Education,* (Vol. 3, pp. 113-120). Amersfoort, The Netherlands: Drukkerij Wilco.

Hannula, M. M., & Lehtinen, E. (2004). *Relationships between spontaneous focusing on* numerosity and early mathematical skills. Paper presented at the Annual Meeting of the American Educational Research Association, April 16-20, San Diego, CA.

Hannula, M. M., & Lehtinen, E. (in press). Spontaneous focusing on numerosity and mathematical skills in young children. *Learning and Instruction.*

Hannula, M. M., Räsänen, P., & Lehtinen, E. (2005). Development of counting skills: Role of spontaneous focusing on numerosity and subitizing-based enumeration. Manuscript submitted for publication.

Huntsinger, C. S., Jose, P. E., Larson, S. L., Krieg, D. B., & Shaligram, C. (2000). Mathematics, vocabulary, and reading development in Chinese American and European American children over the primary school years. *Journal of Educational Psychology, 92,* 745-760.

Karmiloff-Smith, A. (1995). *Beyond modularity. A developmental perspective on cognitive science* (2nd ed.). London: The MIT Press.

Lindström, B., Marton, F., Lindahl, M., & Packendorff, M. (2002). *Enhancing arithmetic skills by boosting the sensous experience of numbers through perceptual – bodily interaction with a computer game.* Unpublished manuscript.

Linnell, M., & Fluck, M. (2001). The effect of maternal support for counting and cardinal understanding in pre-school children. *Social Development, 10,* 202-220.

Lobato, J. (2003). How design experiments can inform a rethinking of transfer and vice versa. *Educational Researcher, 32,* 17-20.

Lobato, J., Ellis, A. B., & Munoz, R. (2003). How "Focusing Phenomena" in the instructional environment support individual students' generalizations. *Mathematical Thinking and Learning, 5,* 1-36.

Marton, F., & Booth, S. (1997). *Learning and awareness.* Mahwah, NJ: Erlbaum.

Mattinen, A. (2005). Vaikuttaminen lukumäärien havaitsemiseen päiväkodissa. [Influencing children's focusing on numerosity in day care]. Unpublished manuscript.

Mix, K. S. (2002). The construction of number concepts. *Cognitive Development, 17,* 1345-1363.

Mix, K. S., Huttenlocher, J., & Levine, S. C. (2002). *Math without words: Quantitative development in infancy and early childhood.* New York: Oxford University Press.

Ruff, H. A., & Rothbart, M. K. (1996). *Attention in early development: Themes and variations.* New York: Oxford University Press.

Saxe, G. B., Guberman, S. R., & Gearhart, M. (1987). Social processes in early number development. *Monographs of the Society for Research in Child Development, 52,* Serial No. 216.

Sophian, C. (1998). A developmental perspective on children's counting. In C. Donlan (Ed.), *The development of mathematical skills* (pp. 27-41). Hove, UK: Taylor & Francis.

Spelke, E. (2003). What makes us smart? Core knowledge and natural language. In D. Genter & S. Goldin-Meadow (Eds.), *Language in mind* (pp. 277-311). Cambridge, MA: MIT Press.

Tomasello, M., Carpenter, M., Call, J., Behne, T., & Moll, H. (in press). Understanding and sharing intentions: The origins of cultural cognition. *Behavioral and Brain Sciences.*

Vygotsky, L. S. (1978). *Mind in society: The development of higher psychological thought processes.* M. Cole, V. John-Steiner, S. Scriber, & E. Souberman (Eds.), Cambridge, MA: Harvard University Press.

Wynn, K. (1990). Children's understanding of counting. *Cognition, 36,* 144-193.

Wynn, K. (1992a). Evidence against empiristic accounts of the origins of numerical knowledge. *Mind & Language, 7,* 315-332.

Wynn, K. (1992b). Children's acquisition of the number words and the counting system. *Cognitive Psychology, 24,* 220-251.

Chapter 5

Using mathematical symbols at the beginning of arithmetical and algebraic learning

Annick Fagnant, Joëlle Vlassis, and Marcel Crahay

1 Introduction

In mathematics, objects cannot be grasped by perceptual means. Access to them is only possible with the help of symbolic representations. Mathematics is bound in what Sfard (2000, p. 39) calls "Virtual Reality" which she opposes to "Actual Reality": "*actual reality communication may be perceptually mediated by the objects that are being discussed, whereas in the virtual reality discourse perceptual mediation is scare and is only possible with the help of what is understood as symbolic substitutes of objects under consideration*". Today, several authors (see the books edited by Cobb, Yackle, & McClain, 2000 and by Gravemeijer, Lehrer, van Oers, & Verschaffel, 2002) consider symbolizing activities as an integral part of mathematical reasoning rather than as an external aid to it. For many of them, "the ways that symbols are used and the meanings they come to have are mutually constitutive and emerge together" (Cobb, 2000, p. 18).

Consequently, symbolizing activities become central and are considered in a bottom-up perspective in which "the starting point is students' ways of symbolizing" (Gravemeijer, Cobb, Bowers, Whitenack, 2000, p. 234) or, more generally, pupils' informal and spontaneous approaches.

Far from this "modern view", traditional teaching approaches often adopt a top-down perspective: teachers give ready-made symbols to students, explain what they mean and how they are to be used. In traditional approaches, "manipulative materials and visual models are used to make the abstract mathematics to be taught more concrete and accessible for the students" (Gravemeijer, 2002, p. 8). More precisely, in the top-down perspective, "mathematical symbols are treated as referring unambiguously to fixed, given referents. The teacher's role in this traditional scheme is typically cast as that of explaining what symbols mean and how they are able to be used by linking them to referents" (Gravemeijer et al., 2000, p. 226).

In arithmetic, the above ideas can be applied to the use of more or less concrete materials (such as blocs) to illustrate the formal operations of addition and subtraction. Addition is presented as "putting together" two sets of objects (sometimes as adding one set on the other); it can be symbolized by 3+4=7 (for example). In the same way, the action of "taking away" is considered as a good illustration of subtraction which can be symbolized by 7-4=3. Once symbols are introduced in such a way, traditional approach emphasizes on computation techniques (which are too often proposed outside a real context of problem solving). A significant number of teachers continue to think (despite the lot of researches which has been realized in this domain) that mastery in computation techniques is a pre-requisite to problem solving. Word problems are then proposed only later (mainly in grade 2) to illustrate the applicability of the formal operations. Such a traditional approach is still encountered too often in the French Community of Belgium.

A similar teaching perspective is developed in the domain of algebra in early secondary school. In grade 7 (first year of secondary school), learning is mainly centred on rules and techniques which are considered as a pre-requisite to problem solving and equations. These topics are only proposed in grade 8.

In grade 7, algebraic symbols are introduced in some "pretext situations" with a ready-made meaning (supplied by the teacher). For example, symbols are introduced in geometric situations where the students have to calculate the perimeter or the area of a rectangle for which the dimensions are "a" and "2+b". The letters must be understood as signifying any dimension. The letter is then considered as "introduced" and will be used in a variety of situations (without discussing anymore its meaning in those different contexts). In the same way, the extension of the plus and minus signs from arithmetic to algebra is not explicitly negotiated in an algebraic context.

One of the objectives of this chapter is to present how pupils (in the beginning of primary school) and students (in the beginning of secondary school) can use mathematical symbols in the traditional teaching-learning context we briefly describe here above. The second aim of this chapter is to handle the question of powerful teaching-learning environments by investigating the model of "chain of significations" developed by Gravemeijer (2002).

First of all, this chapter presents this bottom-up model for which meaning and symbols are mutually constitutive. Some results coming from a traditional approach are then proposed. More specifically, in the domain of arithmetic, we will present some results indicating how children can use conventional symbols in problem solving situations. In algebra, the issue of the use of the negative sign in polynomial reductions will be investigated. Finally, on the basis of these results, we finish this chapter by developing didactical issues based on the model of "chain of significations" in both domains investigated here. These realizations will offer a basis to engage a reflection linked with powerful learning environments.

2 The chain of significations

Gravemeijer et al. (2000) focus on the critical part played by the symbolization activities in the evolution process of the various mathematic class practices. According to these authors, the various steps of symbolization form a chain of significations where the basic component is the "sign". On the basis of Saussure's reflections, Gravemeijer (2002) as well as Sfard (2000) define the sign as being made up of a *signifier* and a *signified* that are closely related. In this perspective, the words *signifier* and *signified* refer to two inseparable aspects of the relationship to the signs: "the former (*the signifier*) implies that a sign must have a perceptually accessible form, and the latter (*the signified*) makes it clear that from the user's point of view, there is more to the sign than what meets the eye (or ear)" (Sfard, 2000, p. 48).

The chain of significations developed by Gravemeijer et al. (2000) and Gravemeijer (2002) presents a dynamic view of the *sign*, according to which a previous combination becomes the *signified* of the following combination. This process is illustrated in the Figure 1.

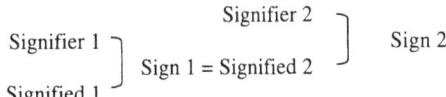

Fig. 1. *Chain of significations (Gravemeijer, 2002, p. 17)*

This process infers that the new *signified* includes the initial sign, whereas the meaning of the initial sign changes. The initial meaning of the previous sign is related to specific concerns and, as a matter of fact, is replaced by a different meaning when the following sign is used in practices motivated by different concerns. We will come back to this model in the section "Conclusions and discussion", where some possible implementation in the arithmetical and algebraic domains will be proposed.

3 Some results from the traditional approach

3.1 First arithmetical learning: Which use of mathematical symbols in word problem solving?

3.1.1 Presentation of the issue

In the past, a lot of researches showed that children can develop a great variety of informal strategies (even before formal instruction in arithmetic or problem solving). Beside these great competencies, some difficulties to use number sentences were also put in light (see Barrouillet & Camos, 2002;

Fagnant, 2002a, 2005; Fayol, 1990; Fuson, 1992; Verschaffel & De Corte, 1997 for some reviews of this topic). On the basis of these studies, a lot of researchers proposed to develop more intensively problem solving at the beginning of schooling.

Teacher practices are sometimes resistant to change and some traditional approaches still exist. For Resnick (mentioned by De Corte, Greer, & Verschaffel, 1996), a persistent idea in education is that knowledge has to be acquired first and that applications for developing reasoning and problem solving have to be postponed. In this top-down teaching condition, conventional symbols are early introduced. But, can children use them? Here, we choose to consider if they are able to use them in problem solving; that means to create connexions between these symbols and the word problems (which are proposed to them) or the strategies (they develop to solve them) (see Fagnant, 2002a, 2005, for a more extensive presentation of this study).

3.1.2 Methodology

The empirical study presented here focuses on 25 grade-1 pupils who were randomly selected from 6 classrooms coming from 4 different schools situated in the French Community of Belgium. In their classical curriculum, they received a traditional teaching such as the approach described in the introduction of this chapter. The methodology consisted in individual interviews around the 14 word problems of Riley's classification (Riley, Greeno, & Heller, 1983): 2 combine problems, 6 change problems and 6 compare problems. The interview consisted of the following steps: the word problem was read aloud by the interviewer; the pupil had to solve the problem (manipulative materials could be used); after solving the problem (correctly or not), the pupil had to write down a number sentence (closed to the problem or to the strategy). He/she had then to circle the answer inside the number sentence. Finally, the child was asked to produce other number sentences with the aim of exploring his/her flexibility in the use of symbols (Carey, 1991).

For the problem solving task, the strategy was considered as correct if it resulted in the expected answer (and this is true for all the different solution processes encountered). Technical errors were avoided by asking the child to count again when needed. For the number sentence writing task, the computation had to fulfil three criteria. First of all: the number sentence had to present a correct structure (3–8=5 was not accepted). Second: the number sentence had to contain the three expected numbers (that means the two data given in the problem text and the expected answer). Third: the answer had to be correctly identified inside the number sentence (by circling the answer after writing the formal operation).

3.1.3 Main results

Informal strategies and number sentences: is one possible without the other? It's important to note the competencies demonstrated by the children in developing informal solution strategies and to remind that they were not submitted to an explicit and intensive teaching of problem solving. Most of the strategies are made up of material or verbal strategies which modelled the actions or relationships described in the problem text. This result confirms young children's inventiveness largely described in the 80'.

Concerning the relationships between the strategies and the use of conventional symbols, the first result is that the number of correct number sentences is always less high than the number of correct answers (which they found by developing informal strategies). This result is true for every child and for every problem. No child is able to produce a correct number sentence if he/she is not able to solve the problem correctly before (by developing an informal strategy). The difference between the number of correct answers and the number of correct number sentences reveals difficulties with the use of symbols which consist here in the inability to create connexions between informal strategies and conventional symbols (used inside the classroom to train computation techniques).

Links between problems, informal strategies and number sentences. The links between the problem solving task and the sentence writing task were analysed carefully. Children mainly develop strategies which closely model the actions or relationships described in the problem text; consequently, many number sentences are linked to the problem as well as to the strategy. That is *relational calculus* and we can see two contrasted examples of these number sentences (one standard and the other not) in the first two following examples (direct or indirect addition).

In problems corresponding to a direct addition (i.e., Change 1 – *Peter has 4 apples. Ann gives 9 apples to Peter. How many apples does Peter have now?*), children generally develop additive strategies: *counting all* or *counting on*. The correct number sentences produced, in link with the strategies, are 4+9=(13) or 9+4=(13). In problems corresponding to an indirect addition (i.e., Change 3 – *Peter has 5 apples. Ann gives him some more apples. Now, Peter has 9 apples. How many apples did Ann give to Peter?*), children develop nearly exclusively *counting up from given* strategies. The correct number sentences produced, in link with the strategies, are 5+(6)=11 or sometimes (6)+5=11 (commutability). No subtractive strategy (consisting in taking away 5 from 11) is observed; correlatively, no child produces a correct subtractive standard number sentence: 11-5=(6).

Unlike these closed links "story/strategy/number sentence", we note an interesting result which permits to pass over the traditional opposition between *relational or numerical calculus* (Vergnaud, 1982): faced with some problems (subtractive situations), many children develop a sort of invention by creating an additive reconstruction (which helps them to avoid the minus sign that seems difficult for them). The following example (direct subtraction) illustrates this case: the additive number sentence which is produced in this situation has no direct link with the story-problem, or with the solution strategy. On the contrary, the subtractive number sentence indicates both links (both with the story-problem and with the strategy); it is a *relational calculus* (like in the first two examples).

In problems corresponding to a direct subtraction (i.e., Change 2 – *Peter has 12 apples. Peter gives 7 apples to Ann. How many apples does Peter have now?*), children develop nearly exclusively subtractive strategies consisting in taking away 7 from 12 and in counting the rest. Two types of number sentences appear in this situation: 12-7=(5) (relational calculus linked to the problem and the strategy) and 7+(5)=12 or (5)+7=12 (additive reconstructions which do not present any link, neither with the strategy, nor with the problem). The same type of analysis can be made for problems involving indirect subtraction.

Children's profiles. An analysis per child profile helps to discover six hierarchical levels in the use of conventional symbols (for a closer description of these profiles, see Fagnant, in press).
– Level 0: no correct number sentence is proposed by the children.
– Level 1: only direct additive situations (like combine 1 or change 1) are correctly symbolized (these problems express the closest link with the way by which addition is introduced: "putting together" or "adding").
– Level 2: the plus sign is correctly used in a variety of additive situations (linked to the strategies, open or closed number sentences – see the first two examples in point b). No subtractive situation is correctly symbolized.
– Level 3, we find the same type of use for the plus sign, but this sign is also used faced with subtractive situations (additive reconstruction mentioned before).
– Levels 4 and 5, the minus sign is used in some subtractive situations. At level 4, some connexions "strategies / symbols" fail to succeed; at level 5, everything is ok (except for some compare problems but we accepted some errors faced with such complex problems, see Fagnant, 2002b; Stern, 1993).

Four children do not fit any profile: the simplest additive situations (change 1 and combine 1) are not symbolized correctly and some more complex situations are correctly symbolized (all by using the plus sign).

The observed results can be summarized as follows: 9 children are situated at levels 4 and 5; they demonstrate a rather pertinent use of conventional symbols (and principally the 5 children situated at level 5); for the other 16 children, the creation of connexions between symbols and problems or strategies is more difficult. For 9 children (the 5 children situated at levels 0 and 1, but also the 4 children who can't be placed in any profile), even the use of the plus sign seems to pose problems; for the other 7 children (situated at levels 2 and 3), additive symbols are used adequately but the subtraction is never proposed.

These results reveal some abilities but also many difficulties with the use of conventional symbols in problem solving situations. The analysis per pupil profile is not meant to build a "model", but rather to supply an original analysis of the abilities and difficulties met by the children. It helps to bring a rather obvious hierarchical organization to light, that raises the following question: does it reflect a developmental sequence or is it strongly influenced by teaching? We need additional researches to bring some clearing up to this question.

3.2 The early steps of algebraic learning: which use of the minus sign in the polynomial reductions?

3.2.1 Introduction of the issue

During earlier researches (Vlassis, 2001, 2002; Vlassis & Demonty, 2002), we focused on significant difficulties facing 8th-grade students when these are required to solve equations involving the minus sign. Those difficulties emerge as well in the solution procedures as in the reduction of equation members. Furthermore, several authors (Gallardo, 1994; Herscovics & Linchevski, 1991; Linchevski & Herscovics, 1996) showed that 7th-grade students make a lot of errors when they are operating on negative numbers. This part of this chapter is dedicated to the review of data collected by Vlassis, in order to discuss more specifically about the use of the minus sign in the polynomial reductions by students of the secondary school (grade 8).

3.2.2 Methodology

Two small-scale studies were conducted in order to identify some of the difficulties met by the students in coping with the minus sign in the polynomial reductions.

The first study was conducted on twelve 8th-grade students from three different schools. All the 8th graders passed an algebra test. Twelve of them were selected for being interviewed on the basis of their score at the test: four low-level students (score: 5/10 or less), four middle-level students (score: 6/10 or 7/10) and four high-level students (score: 8/10 or more). These twelve students were faced with four polynomial reductions. They were interviewed about the way they proceeded and about the reasons for which they proceeded like that. They were also questioned on the meaning they give to the minus sign.

The second in-depth study concerned the meaning of the symbols involved in the polynomial $-18a -2y +5a-y$. Seventeen students from two schools were required to circle the negative numbers and to underline the positive ones, and to explain their suggestion. They were then asked on the kind of numbers that the letters (a and y) can or could replace.

3.2.3 Main results

Use of the "minus" sign in polynomial reductions. The first study (Vlassis, 2004, 2005) shows that most errors made in polynomial reductions are linked to irrelevant extension of arithmetical habits or to inadequate use of algebraic rules.

The most frequent incorrect procedure consists in putting imaginary brackets around two like terms when preceded by the minus sign. For instance, to reduce $20 + 8 - 7n - 5n$, some students change the expression into $20 + 8 - (7n - 5n) = 28 - 2n$. This procedure is very frequent in polynomials where like terms are presented by pairs. This behaviour results from an inability to consider the unary function of the minus sign. In this case, students cannot consider the "minus" as attached to the terms in an expression. In our example, they detach the minus sign placed before $7n$ from this term. These brackets are fictive insofar as they only appear in the oral discourse of the students.

It seems that the irrelevant mobilisation of this procedure can have two origins. First, the most evident origin comes from the arithmetical context, where the minus sign is not attached to numbers and is always used as an operation sign. The "minus" sign before these fictive brackets is considered as a "boundary" (following the terminology used by the students), which divides the polynomial in two operations made on natural numbers. But, an algebraic origin can also be found. In this case, some students confuse with the rule of the priority of operations. One interviewed student suggests this possibility. He says that this error reminds him of the case of an operation such as $7 . 4 + 8 (a - 3) - 2 . 8$, where the multiplications have to be made before the additions or the subtractions. He says the teacher encourages the students to underline the terms $\underline{7 . 4} + \underline{8 (a - 3)} - \underline{2 . 8}$, in order to remind them of the rule. The interviews show that students also present the bracket reasoning with the "plus" sign. But, in this case, it does not lead to mistakes in the written productions. This erroneous procedure only appears in the oral discourse of the students. We also observe a second important kind of errors in the polynomial reductions. Several students mobilise wrongly the signs rule to explain how they reduce the expressions. The use of this rule is more common for the items in which several minus signs are present, such as in the expression $6 - 5a - 3 - 4a$.

When explicitly questioned about the meaning of the "minus" sign in the polynomials, students present a rigid use of the minus. Their discourse can be summarized as follows: *The minus sign cannot have a double status:*

it has only one function in relation with its place in the polynomial. Placed at the beginning of the expression, the minus is considered as attached to the number. Placed between two like terms, students explain that the minus is used for subtracting, and between two unlike terms, that it is used for splitting, operating, or making the following term negative. For most students, a minus sign placed in an expression can only play the part of an operation sign, just like in arithmetic. In this context, the minus sign is rarely considered as an attached sign.

Meaning given by the students to the symbols in the polynomials. In the second study (Vlassis, 2005), students were questioned about the symbols involved in the polynomial $-18a - 2y + 5a - y$. More especially, they had to circle the negative numbers and to underline the positive ones. We are aware that from a mathematical point of view, this question is not very orthodox because it implies we can determine *a priori* that a literal term is positive or negative. But this question led to interesting data which justify this stretching of mathematics. Table 1 presents the answers of the 17 students to that question.

Table 1. Terms considered by the students as negative numbers (circled) and positive numbers (underlined) in the expression -18a - 2y + 5a - y

# category	Circled or underlined terms	Student numbers
1	(-18a) (-2y) + 5a (- y)	9
2	(-18a) (- 2y) + 5a - y	1
	(-18)a (- 2)y + 5a - y	1
	(-18a) - (2y) + 5a - y	1
	(-18a) (- 2y) + 5a - y	1
3	(-18a) - (2y) + 5a - (y)	1
	(-18a) - (2y) + 5a - y	1
	(-18)a - (2)y + 5a - y	1
4	-(18a) - (2y) + 5a - y	1

Nine students give an answer similar to the one expected. Among the other students who give a different answer, six of them do not either circle or underline y. One student in category 2 seems also puzzled by the status of y, since he/she underlines it as if it was a positive number.
Furthermore, we can make the following observations:
– Four students (category 2) answer as if they consider the first term with the sign attached, while the terms inside the polynomial are considered either with their sign or without, according to a logic which varied from one student to another.

- Three students (category 3) stay coherent, whatever the nature of the term: the first one has to be circled together with its sign, while inside the polynomial, the operation signs are independent from the terms. It seems clear for these students that the signs inside the expression are only operation signs.
- One student (category 4) seems to consider systematically independently the terms and the operation signs.

Globally, it can be observed that seven students, who belong to the categories 2 and 3, give a special status to the first term of the polynomial, *-18a*. Indeed, these seven students circle the term with its minus sign while the other terms, which are also preceded by a minus, are circled on a more random pattern.

Only three students perceive the ambiguity of our question. They say they are quite perplexed faced with the guideline requiring to circle the negative numbers and to underline the positive ones. Even while they produced first the expected answer, they explain then they did not really know what they had to circle or underline, because it depends on the number replaced by the letter. For instance, if *a* replaces a negative number, it should be underlined because the expression becomes positive, and if *a* replaces a positive number, it should be circled because the expression becomes negative. In fact, only these students do really consider that the letter replaces a number, whatever this one is positive or negative, and draw the obvious conclusions, which means they examine the different solutions and feel unease faced with the ambiguity of our question.

4 Conclusions and discussion

4.1 Brief conclusion of both studies

Some authors (Radford, 2003; Sfard, 2000) stand up for the opinion that the early uses of symbols are closely linked to the context; the meaning given to them then depends on the situations where they first appeared.

In traditional approach, early learning in arithmetic are focused on computation techniques. The results we present here show that students have some skills but over all significant difficulties in going beyond this restricted context and in using these conventional symbols in a wide range of problem situations. The students show a high-level inventiveness aimed at developing solution strategies which model actions and relationships described in the problems. On the other hand, they have significant difficulties in making connections between these informal and spontaneous approaches and the conventional symbols taught in class. Nevertheless, there is still some form of inventiveness at the level of the symbol production (see the "additive reconstruction") and this could be developed in order to help the students to go beyond the closed context of calculations.

In algebra, the context is quite different. It is a matter of more complex phenomena, where arithmetic and algebraic rules interact: negative signs in the polynomials have been discovered in arithmetic. Furthermore, the negative integers are part of the early algebraic learning as well as the appearance of new rules, such as the sign rule. It seems that a succession of several minus signs in the expression entails this erroneous procedure. Consequently, stemmed from arithmetical and algebraic contexts, the minus sign is used by students either as an operation sign, such as in arithmetic, or in reference to irrelevant algebraic rules. These two reflect a same fundamental inability, that of considering the minus sign as attached to the term that follows it. The results of the second study confirm those of the first one. Indeed, they show that students also attest the tendency of considering the minus inside a polynomial as an operation sign. In this context, when they have to circle the negative numbers, only 9 students out of 17 circle systematically the minus with the term that follows it: all the other ones circle the term and its sign more randomly, and four of them never attach the minus to its term.

4.2 Didactical issue: Realization of Gravemeijer's model "chain of significations"

These observations made in the context of arithmetic and algebra lead to some critical reflection about the instruction received by these students. This instruction, based on techniques, trains the students to consider mathematical symbols as a range of codes on which they need to apply some procedural rules. It appears that students use symbols in a very restricted way, as they appear for the first time. These results show how difficult it is for students to give a relevant meaning to the symbols they use. It seems thus very important to adopt teaching approaches that help to reveal both meaning and symbol together.

In arithmetic, students have important skills that help them to develop a range of informal solution strategies, mainly based on the counting of materials that can be handled. If we refer to Cobb (2000, p. 17), we can already perceive here a kind of symbolization: the term *symbol* is used "to denote any situation in which a concrete entity such as a mark on paper, an icon on a computer screen, or an arrangement of physical materials is interpreted as standing for or signifying something else". Furthermore, students have important difficulties in using conventional symbols in a variety of situations that enable to meet various meanings; for example: *change-take-from meaning, combine-unknown-part meaning* and *compare meaning* for the minus sign (Fuson, 1992). The main question in this issue is to consider how we can help students to evolve from a less conventional symbolization (use of concrete materials) to a more conventional symbolization (production of number sentences using the signs "+", "-" and " =").

According to Gravemeijer's model (2002), we can consider that the use of manipulative materials to solve various problems represents the first level of the "chain of significations". To reach the second level, the students are invited to produce a drawn representation of their solution strategy: they can draw the blocs they counted, circle them to show they counted everything, draw an arrow representing an addition, cross out the blocs they took away, ... Students have to symbolise in order to communicate their solution strategy and thus facilitate the collation of the various approaches met in class (which should induce a progress in their mathematical reasoning). The teacher has a pro-active part to play to help the students to make their representations more precise, more clear for a third party (for instance: "you say you counted everything, can you show it in your drawing?"). Once the students feel comfortable enough with drawn representations, they can gradually leave the use of concrete materials and solve the problem developing directly the drawing of their solution strategy. Going beyond up to the third level of the chain of significations needs then the introduction of the conventional mathematical symbolism. In direct link with the drawings representing the counting strategies, conventional symbols help to communicate the approach in a more economical way and thus, to observe the common aspects between some solution strategies (i.e., the three approaches "to make two piles and count everything, to make two piles, put them together and count everything, or to make a first pile, directly add the second pile on the first one and count everything", are all symbolised by the same number sentence: a+b=(c)). As for the drawings, the conventional symbols are used to communicate mathematical reasoning and to discuss about the similarities and differences between the various procedures. The teacher has a pro-active part to play to encourage the students to produce conventional symbolizations which stick to the strategies. For instance, the "additive reconstructions" produced by the students faced with some subtractive situations will be questioned because they do not stick to the subtractive strategies. The links between "missing-term additions" and "subtractions" can be tackled through the comparison of the various symbolizations associated with the same number sentence (see Fagnant, 2002, for a more detailed presentation of this approach).

In this perspective, symbolizing activities are developed by students to communicate their mathematical reasoning, in order to support shifts in mathematical development. Symbols are used by students "as a resource (...) to express, communicate and reflect on their mathematical activity" (Mac Clain, 2000, p. 189 – see also Bednarz, Dufour-Janvier, Poirier, & Bacon, 1993).

The "Chain of significations" model can also be concretised in algebra in the context of polynomial reductions. Given the results presented here above in this chapter, we need to focus on the purpose of developing the students' ability to "consider" the minus sign as attached to the number. More precisely, the chain of significations should lead them to consider the numerical and literal terms as "signed entities", that is to say entities to which a sign "+" or "-" is attached.

The use of cards representing numbers such as +5, -4,..., might help the students to use the terms as signed entities. Moreover, the fact of moving easily the cards representing the terms might help them to consider the terms on an equal footing, wherever the signed entities could be at the beginning or in the middle of the polynomial (see the results of the second study which showed that several students do not consider the first term of the polynomial on the same level as the other terms present in the expression). Finally, cards enable to make use of the commutative property which, on its turn, can help to reveal the unary notion of the operation signs. The numerical cards constitute the first signified of the chain of significations. This one has then to evolve towards algebraic cards presenting literal terms, passing through "unknown" cards (represented by question marks) presented in the context of missing-term operations (arithmetical equation). Finally, the last level of the chain of significations fits the mathematic notation of the terms (example: $+3x$ or $-6a$) in a context of polynomial reductions and without the support of the model supplied by the cards.

The transition from operations represented by cards to operations mathematically expressed needs the students' work of symbolization at each level of the chain. At that very step, non-conventional models may appear; the teacher has then to play a pro-active part to gradually lead the students to more conventional expressions. The various levels of the chain have to arouse discussions and negotiations which will come to new signification production. In other words, the various steps of the process have to enable a gradual change from an arithmetical model of the operations to an algebraic model of polynomials composed of signed entities (see Vlassis, 2005, for a detailed description of this approach).

These reflections on the arithmetical and algebraic domains have the purpose of illustrating an approach aiming at the co-emergence of meaning and symbols. Gravemeijer's model of the chain of significations presents a significant interest in this sense. Complementary studies are necessary to evaluate the "potential power" of the teaching-learning environments briefly described above.

References

Barrouillet, P., & Camos, V. (2002). *Savoirs, savoir-faire arithmétiques et leurs déficiences*. Paris: Rapport pour le Ministère de la Recherche. Programme cognitique, école et sciences cognitives, document non publié.
Bednarz, N., Dufour-Janvier, B., Poirier, L., & Bacon, L. (1993). Socioconstructivist viewpoint on the use of symbolism in mathematics education. *Alberta Journal of Educational Research, 39*, 41-58.

Carey, D.A. (1991). Number sentences: Linking addition and subtraction word problems and symbols. *Journal for Research in Mathematics Education, 22,* 266-280.
Cobb, P. (2000). From representation to symbolizing: Introductory comments on semiotics and mathematical learning. In P. Cobb, E. Yackel, & K. McClain (Eds.), *Symbolising and communicating in mathematics classrooms. Perspectives on discourse, tools and instructional design* (pp. 17-36). Mahwah, NJ: Lawrence Erlbaum Associates.
Cobb, P., Yackel, E., & McClain, K. (Eds.). (2000). *Symbolizing and communicating in mathematics classrooms. Perspectives on discourse, tools and instructional design.* Mahwah, NJ: Lawrence Erlbaum Associates.
De Corte, E., Greer, B., & Verschaffel, L. (1996). Mathematics teaching and learning. In D.C. Berliner & R.C. Calfee (Eds.), *Handbook of educational psychology* (pp. 491-549). New York: MacMillan.
Fagnant, A. (2002a). *Quelle compréhension du symbolisme mathématique au travers de la résolution de problèmes arithmétiques?* Thèse de doctorat non publiée, Université de Liège, Belgique.
Fagnant, A. (2002b). Mathematical symbolism: A feature responsible for superficial approaches? In A.D. Cockburn & E. Nardi (Eds.), *Proceedings of the 26th Annual Conference of the International Group for the Psychology of Mathematics Education* (Vol. 2, pp. 345-352). Norwich, UK: University of East Anglia.
Fagnant, A. (2005). Résoudre et symboliser des problèmes additifs et soustractifs en début d'enseignement primaire. In M. Crahay, L. Verschaffel, E. De Corte, & J. Grégoire (Eds.), *Enseignement et apprentissage des mathématiques. Que disent les recherches psychopédagogiques* (pp. 131-150)? Bruxelles: De Boeck.
Fagnant, A. (in press). The use of mathematical symbolism in problem solving. An empirical study carried out in grade one in the French Community of Belgium. *European Journal of Psychology of Education, 20.*
Fayol, M. (1990). *L'enfant et le nombre.* Paris: Delachaux et Niestlé.
Fuson, K.C. (1992). Research on whole number addition and subtraction. In D.A. Grouws (Ed.), *Handbook of research on mathematics teaching and learning* (pp. 243-275). New York: MacMillan.
Gallardo, A. (1994). Negative numbers in algebra, the use of a teaching model. In J. Pedro da Ponte & J. Filipe Matos (Eds.), *Proceedings of the Eighteenth International Conference for the Psychology of Mathematics Education* (pp. 376-383). Lisboa, Portugal.
Gravemeijer, K. (2002). Preamble: From models to modeling. In K. Gravemeijer, R. Lehrer, B. van Oers, & L. Verschaffel (Eds.), Symbolizing, modeling and tool use in mathematics education (pp. 7-22), Dordrecht, The Netherlands: Kluwer Academic Publishers.
Gravemeijer, K., Cobb, P., Bowers, J., & Whitenack, J. (2000). *Symbolizing, modeling, and instructional design.* In P. Cobb, E. Yackel, & K. McClain (Eds.), *Symbolising and communicating in mathematics classrooms. Perspectives on discourse, tools and instructional design* (pp. 225-273). Mahwah, NJ: Lawrence Erlbaum Associates.
Gravemeijer, K., Lehrer, R., van Oers, B., & Verschaffel, L. (Eds.). (2002). *Symbolizing, modeling and tool use in mathematics education.* Dordrecht, The Netherlands: Kluwer Academic Publisher.
Herscovics, N., & Linchevski, L. (1991), Pre-algebraic thinking: Range of equations and informal solution processes used by seventh graders prior to any instruction. In F. Furinghetti (Ed.), *Proceedings of the Fifteenth International Conference for the Psychology of Mathematics Education* (Vol. 2, pp. 173-180). Assissi, Italy.

Linchevski, L., & Herscovics, N. (1996). Crossing the cognitive gap between arithmetic and algebra: Operating on the unknown in the context of equations. *Educational Studies in Mathematics, 30*, 39-65.

Radford, L. (2003). Gestures, speech, and the sprouting of signs: A semiotic-Cultural approach to students' types of generalization. *Mathematical Thinking and Learning, 5*(1), 37-70.

Riley, M.S., Greeno, J.G., & Heller, J.I. (1983). Development of children's problem-solving ability in arithmetic. In H.P. Ginsburg (Ed.), *The development of mathematical thinking* (pp. 153-196). New York: Academic Press.

Sfard, A. (2000). Symbolizing mathematical reality into being. Or how mathematical discourse and mathematical objects create each other. In P. Cobb, E. Yackel, & K. McClain (Eds.), *Symbolising and communicating in mathematics classrooms. Perspectives on discourse, tools and instructional design* (pp. 37-98). Mahwah, NJ: Lawrence Erlbaum Associates.

Stern, E. (1993). What makes certain arithmetic word problems involving the comparison of sets so difficult for children? *Journal of Educational Psychology, 85,* 7-23.

Vergnaud, G. (1982). A classification of cognitive tasks and operation of thought involved in addition and subtraction problems. In T.P. Carpenter, J.M. Moser, & T.A. Romberg (Eds), *Addition and subtraction. A cognitive perspective* (pp. 39-59). Hillsdale, NJ: Lawrence Erlbaum Associates.

Verschaffel, L., & De Corte, E. (1997). Word problems: A vehicle for promoting authentic mathematical understanding and problem solving in the primary school? In T. Nunes & P. Bryant (Eds.), *Learning and teaching mathematics: An international perspective* (pp. 69-97). Hove, East Sussex: Psychology Press.

Vlassis, J. (2001). Solving equations with negatives or crossing the formalizing gap. In M. van den Heuvel-Panhuizen (Ed.), *Proceedings of the Twenty-fifth International Conference for the Psychology of Mathematics Education* (Vol. 4, pp. 375-382). Utrecht, The Netherlands.

Vlassis, J., (2002). The balance model: Hindrance or support for the solving of linear equations with one unknown. *Educational Studies in Mathematics, 49,* 341-359.

Vlassis, J. (2004). Making sense of the minus sign or becoming flexible in 'negativity'. *Learning and Instruction, 14,* 469-484.

Vlassis, J. (2005). *Sens et Symboles en mathématiques: Étude de l'utilisation du signe "moins" dans les réductions polynomiales et la résolution des équations du premier degré à une inconnue.* Thèse de doctorat non publiée, Université de Liège. Belgique.

Vlassis, J. (2005). Etude de l'utilisation du signe négatif dans les opérations algébriques élémentaires. In M. Crahay, L. Verschaffel, E. De Corte, & J. Grégoire (Eds.), *Enseignement et apprentissage des mathématiques. Que disent les recherches psychopédagogiques* (pp. 247-269)? Bruxelles: De Boeck.

Vlassis, J., & Demonty, I. (2002). *L'algèbre par des situations-problèmes.* Bruxelles: De Boek.

Chapter 6

Collaboration in small group mathematics problem solving: A case study

Gerard Seegers and Dirk Hoek

1 Introduction

1.1 Approaches to mathematics learning

Starting point is that mathematical knowledge is not transmitted but the outcome of an active and social construction process. This idea, grounded in socio-constructivist perspectives on learning, implies that both the learning context and the didactics for teaching mathematics are changing. Students construct knowledge when confronted with conflicting views, when different solutions are proposed (and defended), and when participants are involved in exploring complex phenomena.

This approach of mathematics learning deviates from a traditional approach where instruction is predominantly based on the information transmission model. Within this instruction model the teachers conceptualize knowledge as a commodity that can be transferred from the teacher to the students (Greeno, 1991; Romberg & Carpenter, 1986). The teacher explains the curriculum content by showing how specific procedures should be applied to solve characteristic mathematics problems. Following these instructions, students practice by solving a number of problems. However, the information transmission model has come under pressure as research showed that students often developed ineffective and incomplete representations ("misconceptions"), and were inefficient in applying knowledge to new types of problems ("lack of transfer") (De Corte, Verschaffel, & Greer, 1996). A result that emphasized the importance of the student in learning and that paved the way for acceptance of alternative constructivist approaches.

Freudenthal (1971, 1973, 1991) expressed a similar point of view. In his work he laid the framework of what later has become known as "Realistic Mathematics Education (RME)". He rejected the idea that in learning mathematics the domain should be presented as a logically coherent system. As this approach starts with the results of the learning process, he referred to this view as an "anti-didactic inversion" He emphasized that students should be given opportunities to discover mathematics by acting as mathematics researchers. Basically, mathematics from a mathematician's point of view starts with the development of methods to analyze and describe real life problems. Students should be confronted with realistic and meaningful problems that can be solved by using adequate mathematical tools. Students develop mathematical knowledge as the outcome of working on these organizing problems with the help of mathematical tools and methods. In working on these problems, they develop mathematical knowledge by refining solution steps and by broadening mathematical concepts. The teacher acts as an expert in the background. Freudenthal refers to this as "guiding reinvention".

1.2 Collaborative learning

According to a socio-constructivist view, knowledge is the result of the individual's active participation in joint learning activities. Opportunities for learning occur during social interaction through collaborative dialogue, explanation, justification and negotiating of meaning (Wenger, 1998). Working in a dialogue situation, students are in a position to determine misconceptions and missing knowledge links. Collaborative learning can be effective but only if collaboration meets high conceptual standards. If standards are met, interactive discourse between students can be assumed to support understanding, to unveil misconceptions and gaps of knowledge, and to contribute to the construction of meaningful concepts (Mercer, 1996; Van Boxtel, Van der Linden, Roelofs, & Erkens, 2002).

Collaborative learning does not make the teacher obsolete, although the teacher's role is subject to change. First, the teacher has to support a learning environment where students can learn collaboratively. Second, the teacher has a role in guiding students to improve collaborative activities e.g., by helping students to verbalize mathematical concepts, by asking challenging questions, by giving suggestions and hints when necessary, by responding to student ideas, and by giving feedback on both solutions and solution process. In this way, teachers make mathematical knowledge accessible to students in the classroom. Mortimer and Scott (2000) refer to this role as controlling "the flow of discourse".

1.3 Goal of the study

Aim of the study is the design of useful learning environments directed at helping teachers to adapt their instruction to support student collaborative problem solving. To achieve this aim, it is important to pay attention to the mathematical and social practices which will contribute to knowledge construction. According to Cobb, Stephan, McClain and Gravemeijer (2001), students' mathematical learning is situated with respect to the culture in which it takes place. Their point is that mathematical learning activities depend on the culture of the classroom. This classroom culture encompasses general norms of participation (classroom social norms e.g., what are accepted rules for interaction) as well as specific mathematical issues (sociomath norms, e.g., what can be accepted as a mathematical argument). Although these elements cannot be considered separately, the study will be focused on classroom social norms. These social norms include how to make sense of explanations given by others, how to indicate agreement or disagreement, and how to question alternatives when conflicts in interpretations become apparent. It is important to emphasize that the teacher shapes the classroom culture and has a crucial position in the enculturation of students into what is allowed as mathematical and what is not.

Even when teachers accept that their role in materializing effective (powerful) learning environments is important, they struggle to implement well fitting instructional activities. They often lack a clear notion of what to expect from their students, or what to do to improve student collaboration. This study aims at supporting teachers to gradually develop and implement instructional activities that support collaborative problem solving. Development of instructional activities took place in cooperation with the teachers that took part in the study. This is similar to what Roth refers to as "co-teaching" (Roth, 1998; Roth & Boyd, 1999; Roth, Tobin, & Zimmerman, 2002). This cooperation has clear advantages. First, teachers will have a clear understanding of goal and purpose of the planned activities. Second, the teachers will agree that the planned activities are meaningful. Third, activities imply changes that comply with teachers' current instructional practice.

As an additional element in the study, the graphic calculator (GC) as a tool that can support exploratory activities is implemented. To enable students to use the GC effectively a number of conditions have to be fulfilled. Students have to learn how to use the interface of the tool (e.g., which keys are needed to draw graphs), they have to learn how to interpret the calculator output (Doorman, Drijvers, & Kindt, 1994), and students have to understand the accuracy of the output (Smith, 1999).

Collaborative learning is not a goal in itself, but must be seen as a means for students to achieve improved problem solving (Schoenfeld, 1992). At this point, teachers have to be aware that they have a modelling and guiding role in both the development of strategies and the implementation of an exploratory use of the GC. Although implementation of the GC can be considered supportive for collaborative learning from a theoretical point of view, former studies found that without teacher guidance the GC might even have a blocking effect on collaboration (Doerr & Zangor, 2000). Most importantly, students have to develop insight in strategies and procedures in which the GC can be applied as an effective supportive tool for problem solving.

Design of the tasks that students work on is a crucial element in the learning environment. Cohen (1994) reported that working on "closed" tasks, where one specific procedure will lead to a unique answer, did not support collaborative activities. On the other hand, open-ended tasks, where both problem space ("what is the problem?") and solution space ("what are effective steps to find a solution?") leave room for discussion, triggered higher levels of collaboration. In this study, a number of problems from the textbook were adapted and extended to make them more open-ended. Collaboration was further stimulated by having students work on a joint product, e.g., a report, a collage or a presentation.

Main research question in this study is twofold: can teachers adapt instructional activities to support collaborative learning when students work on open-ended mathematical problems and do these activities support effective collaboration? Effectiveness in this context depends on raising both social (process) and the cognitive (content) levels. The assumption is that these activities at the social (interpersonal) plane will be internalized by students to develop a problem solving process at the intrapersonal level that is guided by self-addressed meta-cognitive questions (cf., Sfard, 2001). Assuming that collaborative discourse reflects conceptual standards and level of collaborative activities, student verbal interactions are analyzed to determine effectiveness of the learning environment.

1.4 Development of instructional activities

Teachers not only shape the culture in the classroom but also play an active role in *changing* this culture through organizing tasks and activities. In this study, no pre-set intervention was developed that teachers had to implement, but it was decided to gradually develop new instructional activities in cooperation with the participating teachers. These activities concerned whole-class discussions and collaborative activities in small groups. In terms of the distinction that has been proposed by Sfard (2001), instructional activities are aimed at changing both object-level aspects of discourse (by modelling problem solving) and meta-discursive rules (by giving feedback on collaborative process activities).

In the study, instructional activities were developed, implemented and evaluated in a cyclical process. This approach reflects the ideas of a design experiment (Cobb, Confrey, diSessa, Lehrer, & Schauble, 2003; Cobb et al., 2001). Design experiments ideally result in greater understanding of a *learning ecology*. Elements of a learning ecology typically include teachers' instruction, the tasks or problems, the types of discourse that are encouraged, the norms of participation that are established, the tools that are provided, and the practical means by which classroom teachers can orchestrate relations among these elements.

The decision to combine small group and classroom activities was based on the outcome of a preliminary study. In this study, (observational) data confirmed that during classroom activities teachers mostly confined themselves to directed instruction. When a classroom discussion developed, teachers often interrupted the discussion to make sure that students all reached the same conclusion. This had a blocking effect on student contributions because it was the teacher's view that students were expected to accept. Data that were collected while students worked in small groups showed that teachers often neglected the group by responding to individual questions. This behaviour had a negative effect as it allowed students to avoid collaboration. Finally, teachers mostly gave content-related feedback to students, but failed to support collaboration by giving process-related feedback.

To change this behaviour, instructional activities were developed in cooperation with the teachers. At the whole-class level, the main change in teacher behaviour that was aimed for was a shift from *instruction* to discussion. In these whole-class discussions, emphasis had to be put on steps in solving mathematical problems and exploring mathematical phenomena, on discussing the mathematical meaning of solutions, and on modelling a solution process. Teachers were to emphasize questions instead of instructions and explanations, i.e. to stimulate discussions about different mathematical phenomena and concepts, to challenge students by asking to explain their problem solving strategies, and to urge them to clarify how they think and work. As part of these discussions, teachers were to implement the GC as an exploratory tool that could support reasoning and explanation. These discussions were aimed at modelling an effective approach towards problem solving.

As for collaborative *small group* activities, goal of instructional activities was to bring teachers to gradually transfer responsibility to the students. Teachers had to support collaboration actively by redirecting individual questions to the group and by stimulating students to develop their own solutions instead of being dependent on the teacher. Furthermore, bringing teachers to interfere actively in student work by asking questions about how and why students progressed as they did in working on the problem was considered a means to give feedback on the collaborative process. It can be expected that this will force students to clarify their solution steps to the teacher, and to help them to reflect on steps to be taken.

2 Method

2.1 Setting

A case study was set up largely in line with a design experiment (Cobb et al., 2003; Cobb et al., 2001). Design experiments ideally result in a greater understanding of a learning ecology. Elements of a learning ecology typically include teachers' instruction, the tasks or problems, the types of discourse that are encouraged, the norms of participation that are established, the tools that are provided, and the practical means by which classroom teachers can orchestrate relations among these elements.

The research took place in two schools for senior secondary technical education. Two teachers with two different classrooms participated in the study. A number of 45 students were included, 32 male and 13 female. Their age varied from 16 to 18.

In the participating classrooms a newly designed mathematics/science textbook (TWIN; Goris & Van der Kooij, 1997-2000) was implemented. The textbook is based on three basic elements: (1) students work on meaningful problems, (2) where reflection on solution and solution steps is crucial, and (3) use of the graphical calculator is integrated. The research took place while students worked on chapters concerning relations between variables: linear functions ($y = a \times x + b$), power functions ($y = a \times x^n$) and exponential functions ($y = a \times n^x$).

In the study, a number of problems were included that were based on revised and extended versions of the problems in the textbook. These modified problems were more "open-ended" to elicit higher levels of collaboration.

2.2 Procedure

The participating classes were at least visited once a week to observe and to videotape whole-class (instruction and discussion) and small group collaborative activities. Field notes and videotapes made during whole class discussions were used to register teachers' instructional activities. Based on these data, instructional activities were discussed with the teachers. Core of these activities was that teachers modelled an effective approach towards collaborative problem solving and integrated in this approach an exploratory use of the GC.

In addition to observational data that were collected during classroom activities, data were collected for one group of four students in each classroom while working collaboratively. For each group sixteen observations of one lesson (50 minutes) were collected during the school year. These videotapes were used to verbatim transcribe and analyze verbal interactions. In addition, field notes were made to register activities that were not included in the video. These notes also included summaries of discussions with the teachers about adaptations in instructional activities, and were used to support interpretations of the relationships between classroom activities, teacher-student interactions during small group work, and changes in student-student and teacher-student verbal interactions.

2.3 The intervention: Changes in teachers' instructional behaviour

The observations of classroom activities and videotapes were used as a basis for weekly discussions with the teacher as a preparation on forthcoming lesson(s). Main objective of these discussions was to stimulate teachers to reflect on the course of actions and to check consensus on how to achieve specific goals in a stepwise approach.

At the start of the teaching experiment, whole-class instruction was used to instruct students how to use the interface of the graphic calculator. During these instruction-lessons, the teachers had a steering and directing role. Given that they were used to this type of instruction, teachers felt confident and reported no specific problems. Whole-class instruction took about 15 minutes. Next students started to work in small groups.

Observational data showed that students used the GC mainly as a computing tool whereas teachers had difficulties in supporting a more investigative use of the tool. They often gave content related feedback and explanations about the interface to individual students. To alter this behaviour and to force students to discuss specific problems in the group, the strategy of redirecting questions to the group was discussed with the teachers. They agreed to avoid direct answers. However, maintaining this strategy turned out to be difficult. Teachers adhered to the more familiar approach because they considered responding to individual questions and correcting mistakes as a way to control student work progress. Furthermore, students expected their teachers to answer their questions and responded by being frustrated when this did not happen.

Apparently, simply suggesting teachers to redirect questions to the group does not work. Furthermore, teachers felt this approach to be less effective. As they did not succeed in redirecting questions to the group, they were forced to repeat explanations of similar problems that surfaced in diverse collaborative groups. To change this, teachers were asked to observe collaborative activities and to infer conclusions about student errors and misconceptions. As a next step, they were asked to make these errors and misconceptions subject of whole class discussions. In this way, repetitions could be avoided, and support of discussion could be transferred to the level of the classroom where the teacher was in a better position to elicit student activities.

To start whole-class discussions, teachers agreed to invite one of the students to explain how his or her group solved the problem, and how the GC was used. This "student-initiated" model was introduced because it might help students understand how investigating and discussing specific issues can help to solve problems effectively. However, it turned out that this "discussion model" for whole-class discussions was not effective. Students had difficulties in rephrasing solutions in their own words, and often the class interrupted the student in front. Furthermore, teachers frequently broke off the discussion to take control. As a result, it was decided to abandon this approach and leave it to the teachers to take the initiative to start a whole-class discussion, e.g., by challenging solutions that students gave to a problem or by asking them questions on the meaning of the output of the graphic calculator. In this "teacher-initiated" discussion model, the teachers kept control over the whole-class discussion and were in a better position to model specific collaborative activities and an exploratory use of the graphic calculator.

Analyses of whole-class discussions showed that the teachers succeeded in stimulating students to discuss solutions by posing questions and by challenging proposals. However, their behaviour was not consistent in that they were inclined to interrupt discussions to revert to direct explanations and instruction. Discussing this behaviour with the teachers it became clear that in this way they wanted to "to secure results", i.e. to make sure that all students reached certain conclusions.

Gradually teachers succeeded in orchestrating whole-class discussions that left room for students to infer themselves whether a conclusion was right or wrong. However, observational data showed that it was difficult for them to transfer this whole-class discussion approach to the coaching of small group collaboration. We conjectured that this lack of transfer was caused by the teachers' stubborn willingness to give content related feedback to individual students. Teachers felt that this was the most effective way to keep students on a working track. Responding to individual questions also matched student expectations, and prevented feelings of frustration to surface. However, discussing this coaching style helped the teachers to understand that their instructional behaviour inhibited collaborative work and an exploratory use of the graphic calculator during small group work. Consequently, teachers succeeded in gradually avoiding direct answers and stimulated students to help each other and to discuss problems with their peers.

2.4 A framework for discourse analysis

Video registrations of students working in small groups were used to investigate whether changes in teachers' instructional behaviour went together with changes in student collaborative problem solving. Observational data were used to transcribe student verbal interactions. To determine patterns in collaborative discourse, a classification system has been developed to account for verbal interaction patterns. In this system, not individual utterances are taken as the unit of analysis, but units of coherent utterances ("episodes"). An episode starts when a specific problem or question is brought in, and ends either when students reach agreement on this point, or when the process is interrupted.

The system assigns values to the episodes, reflecting types of interactive processing and their definition includes both cognitive (types of questions, levels of arguments) and social (valuing each other's contributions, taking contributions seriously) elements. A somewhat revised version of the model that has been proposed by Mercer and colleagues (Mercer, 1996, Wegerif, Mercer, & Dawes, 1999) best fitted with the learning situation in this study. Mercer distinguishes three different types of verbal interaction patterns (or "modes of talk"): disputational talk, cumulative talk, and exploratory talk. However, applying this distinction to the data, not all interaction patterns could be categorized. Students sometimes worked independent of each other, or students followed critically one student that took a leading role. These situations could not be accounted for by the modes of talk that were distinguished by Mercer. Following a proposal by Cobo and Fortuny (2000), it was decided to include two additional dimensions: parallel work and guided work. This resulted in an extended framework where five interaction patterns are distinguished: parallel work, disputational talk, guided work, cumulative talk and exploratory talk (see also Cobo & Fortuny, 2000; Mercer, 1996). The various patterns are summarized in Table 1.

Table 1. Summary of interaction patterns

Type of pattern	Types of exchanges	Participant roles	Level of collaboration	Cognitive outcome of collaboration
Parallel	Argumentational, reasoning, responsive minimal	Participants work independently	No collaboration	
Disputational	Argumentational, reasoning, responsive minimal	Competitive attitude, with minimal interaction	No collaboration	
Guided	Validation, explanation	Unequal roles, with one student taking a leading role	Low to moderate level of collaboration, unequal distribution of effort	Positive impact on problem solving capacity
Cumulative	Repetition, confirmation, responsive with evaluative minimal	Participants have equal roles (introduction of contributions), with minimal variation	Moderate level of collaboration	Minimal impact on improved problem solving capacity.
Exploratory	Frequent reasoning, interrogative and evaluative exchanges	Equal distribution of roles	High level of collaboration, equal distribution of effort	High impact on problem solving capacity

It is assumed that these modes describe the relevant types of verbal interactions in collaborative learning situations. In *parallel work,* participants work independently and no collaborative activities unfold. This situation often occurs when students are simply told to work together without further adaptations in the learning environment or teacher guidance. *Disputational talk* reflects the situation where one or two dominating participants are focused on a single solution, do not respond to contributions of others, or reject these without arguments. Variation in role taking is minimal and participants will hardly benefit cognitively from other participants. *Guided work* is similar to disputational talk in that there is an uneven distribution of roles among participants, but now the other participants follow critically by asking questions, by formulating doubts, and by demanding argumentations. The interactive pattern is characterized by frequent occurrences of validation and explanation exchanges[1]. *Cumulative talk* is the situation where emphasis is on agreement and participants are willing to accept each other's contributions without critical reflection. Repetitions and confirmations characterize this interaction pattern. Variation in role taking (observing, guiding, correcting, and performing procedures) is minimal. Finally, *exploratory talk* is at stake when participants collaborate actively; evaluate contributions critically, while role taking is complementary (Mercer, 1996). Exploratory talk gives students the best opportunities to (re)construct their knowledge. The various patterns are summarized in Table 1.

During a storm, 6 mm of rain, on average, fell on the city of Eindhoven. In the map below, the boundary is clearly marked with the scale: 2,5 cm is 2 km. Calculate how much water (volume in litres) has fallen in the city during that downpour.

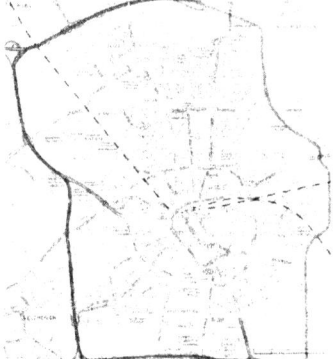

Fig. 1. How many litres poured down on the city?

---

[1] The analysis that Sfard (2001) presents of a dialogue between two students, A and G, suggests another (uncritical) type of guided talk, that is characterized by a dominating participant whereas other participants have "given up their own thinking" and simply try to understand the leading participant's dialogue.

Examples of modes of talk

To clarify the classification scheme, two discourse fragments will be given to illustrate the two most frequently occurring modes of talk, i.e. cumulative and exploratory talk. The first fragment is taken from a situation where students work on the problem that is given in Figure 1.

Cumulative talk is characterized by repetitions, confirmations and lack of critical remarks. An example of an episode that illustrates this mode of talk is given in Table 2.

Table 2. Example of cumulative talk

J	(Reads aloud the problem).
J	So we have to know the surface area of this city. That is clearly marked.
T	We also have to know what the scale of this map is.
P	The scale is written at the bottom of the map.
R	Yes, two and a half centimetres is two kilometres.
R	The length of the city is about 12 centimetres.
R	The width is about 9 centimetres.
T	So, to calculate the circumference we first have to divide the length by two and a half.

The above protocol shows that students build positively but uncritically on what other group members have said, constructing a common knowledge by "accumulation". One of the students starts to read the text of the problem aloud. Then the students jump in to solve the problem. Contributions are simply accepted without further discussion.

To illustrate exploratory talk a fragment is taken from the situation where students work on the problem that is represented in Figure 2.

> In chapter 4, you worked on tasks about power relations. All these relations can be written in the form of the function: $y = a x^n$, a is the proportional quantity. In this case, the n is a negative power. During a whole-class discussion the graphs of the following functions are drawn: $y=x^{-1}$, $y=x^{-2}$, $y=x^{-3}$, $y=x^{-4}$. Below you see the input of the window screen on the left, on the right the graphs of the functions above are drawn.
>
>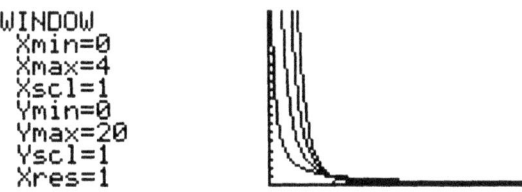
>
> Just below you see a very short fragment of the whole-class discussion.
> Teacher J what do you see and think when you look at those graphs?
> J The higher the power the steeper the graphs. Therefore, the most left graph has the highest power. Further to the right, this graph lies below the other ones.
> You have to investigate whether J is right. To do this it you can use your graphic calculator. Your group has to make a clear, systematic report. I (the teacher) have to understand what you have been doing to find out whether J was right or wrong. I want to get an explanation why you think she is right or wrong.

Fig. 2. Which graph is steeper?

Students are asked to check the correctness of J's statement that raising the variable "X" to a higher power goes together with a steeper graph. To find a solution for the problem, students use the graphic calculator. They enter the functions to investigate the corresponding graphic representations. Exploratory talk is characterized by students being engaged in explaining ideas, and in offering justifications and alternative points of view. The protocol that is given in Table 3 shows the discussion about how they can find out which graph is steeper.

Table 3. Example of exploratory talk

B	These are the graphs in the figure? (Shows his display to the other group members).
C	Yes, but I do not know which graph belongs to which function.
E	How can we find out which one belongs to which function?
B	The first graph that is drawn belongs to the first function on your input display.
M	When you activate the trace function, you see on which graph you are.
E	Oh yeah, I see.
M	I think that as the value of the power is lower, the graph of the function will be steeper.
E	What do they mean by "steeper"?
M	Look, here it declines faster and here it becomes flat.
E	So, you think the higher the power the steeper the graph?
M	Here this graph is steeper than that one (she points first to $y = x^{-4}$ and then to $y = x^{-2}$). So when the power is higher, the graph will be steeper.
C	This is the first one ($y = x^{-1}$).
M	Yes, that is right. As the power is higher, the graph will be steeper.
C	No, it is more negative. This one is $y = x^{-1}$ and that one is $y = x^{-4}$.
M	Yes, when the power is minus four the graph is steeper than when the power is minus one.
C	Yes, that is correct. Minus four, however, is lower than minus one. So as the power is lower, the graph will be steeper.
M	Oh, yes you are right.

The protocol shows how a discussion develops beginning with the question about the gradient of the graphs, and ends when student M agrees with the given explanation. During the discussion, several proposals are made. M hypothesizes that a lower power implies a steeper graph. This hypothesis is critically received by E, who asks for an explanation. To explain this, M indicates at the display of the graphic calculator two graphs ($y = x^{-4}$ and $y = x^{-1}$). Student C reacts by bringing in the problem of negative exponents. He argues that minus four is smaller than minus one and that the conclusion should be that as the value of the power is lower the graph will be steeper. At this point, student M realizes her mistake and she agrees with student C.

This interaction shows that students follow each other's contributions critically. They challenge and counter-challenge suggestions made by others, showing willingness to convince each other. Contributions are justified or rejected, and sometimes alternative hypotheses are offered.

3 Results

As for whole-class discussions, videotapes and field notes confirmed that the teachers gradually succeeded in orchestrating these discussions. Students participated actively in these discussions, and used their graphic calculators to follow the discussion critically. Furthermore, teachers were increasingly aware of their supporting role in small group collaboration. They avoided direct answers and invited students to come up with their own solutions, re-directed questions to the group, gave feedback on the process of collaboration and stimulated discussions about how the graphic calculator could be used during collaborative problem solving. They did so even when this left students "struggling" and they expressed feelings of frustration.

To analyze student collaborative activities, video registrations were used to transcribe discourse protocols verbatim. These written protocols were used to determine the frequency of various types of episodes. In a first step, relevant discourse utterances were marked to leave off-task discourse out of the analysis. In a next step, beginning and end of episodes were determined. Episodes started when a question was posed. The end of an episode was marked either when the question was answered, when attention of the students was diverted, or when the teacher interfered. In a next step, the episodes were assigned values using the scheme for modes of talk. Both researchers analyzed two randomly selected protocol fragments independently. Agreement on classifications was 74 percent (implying a Cohen's kappa higher than .60) whereas differences mainly concerned related modes of talk (guided work vs. disputational talk).

Quantified results of the analysis of the two classrooms will be given separately in Table 4 and Table 5. Table 4 shows the frequency of the modes of talk of the observed group in classroom A.

The data show that the percentage of exploratory talk increases during the school year. In the beginning of the school year, the percentage of exploratory talk is 16 percent while this percentage increases to 66 percent toward the end of the school year. At the same time, discourse patterns that can be classified as cumulative talk decline from 72 to 33 percent, whereas disputational talk was no longer found at the end of the school year.

Table 5 shows comparable results for classroom B. The percentage of exploratory talk increases during the school year from 21 percent at the beginning of the school year, to 74 percent. At the same time, the percentages of patterns that can be classified as cumulative talk declines from 68 percent to 12 percent, whereas this figure for disputational talk declines to 0 percent. At the end of the school year, the percentage of guided talk is 14 percent.

Table 4. Frequencies of the interaction patterns (in %) during a school year for classroom A

Code	Classroom A			
	Chapter 1*	Chapter 2	Chapter 3	Chapter 4
Parallel work	0.8	1.2	4.9	0
Disputational talk	10.8	1.7	4.5	0
Guided talk	0.5	0	0.3	0.4
Cumulative talk	71.9	58.9	57.0	33.5
Exploratory talk	16.0	38.2	33.0	66.1

* Given are the rounded off valid percentages; this means that all off task interaction is taken out of the analysis.

Table 5. Frequencies of the interaction patterns (in %) during a school year for classroom B

Code	Classroom B		
	Chapter 1*	Chapter 3	Chapter 5
Parallel work	8.6	0	0
Disputational talk	2.9	0	0
Guided talk	0	0	14.0
Cumulative talk	67.9	45.6	11.8
Exploratory talk	20.7	54.4	74.2

* Given are the rounded off valid percentages); this means that all off task interaction is taken out of the analysis.

4 Conclusions and discussion

Goal of this study was to design instructional activities to improve student collaboration while solving open-ended mathematical problems. As an additional element, an exploratory use of the GC was integrated. Whole-class discussions were designed as an important element in this approach to model effective problem solving and exploratory applications of the GC. In addition to whole-class discussions, instructional activities were developed for teachers to coach their students during small group collaborative work.

The results showed that the teachers gradually changed their coaching style. Teachers stimulated collaborative activities by avoiding direct responses to individual students. Also, type of given feedback changed from-content related to process-oriented. Teachers stimulated students to reflect on activities by asking questions, by challenging their solutions, and by inviting them to explain solution steps.

These changes in instructional activities went together with changes in student collaborative activities. Analysis of students' interaction patterns during joint learning activity shows an increased effectiveness of collaborative learning. Comparing the beginning and the end of the school year, students were increasingly involved in collaborative activities and the level of these activities became higher. While working together, students discussed more often the mathematical content, made more conjectures, asked more frequently for explanations, and were more critical towards each other's contributions. Interaction patterns showed a development towards what Wegerif et al. (1999) refer to as a "productive pattern". This pattern is characterized by elements such as generation of new ideas, discussion about solutions, explanation of strategies, discussion about the content of the task and giving help to each other to understand the task. In terms of the discourse analysis scheme, discourse patterns showed a shift from cumulative talk to exploratory talk, indicating an increasing quality of collaboration. Co-regulation and willingness to consider contributions from other group members improved. As for the role of the graphic calculator, students gradually used this tool in a more investigative mode to discuss and explore different mathematical phenomena.

To achieve effective collaborative learning participants have to establish common frames of reference, resolve discrepancies in understanding, and negotiate steps in the solution process. This makes collaborative learning a potentially powerful but complex process, and a number of conditions have to be fulfilled to make it an effective learning model (Cohen, 1994). A basic condition is that students must have a clear understanding of the common purpose of the task. However, observational data at the beginning of the study showed that a common responsibility was lacking, and students were persistent in relying on the teacher for feedback and support. This attitude was encouraged by the teacher who felt obliged to respond to individual questions to avoid frustration and to "secure results".

The results confirm that it is possible to design education in which student work collaboratively during problem solving, and where the graphic calculator is used to investigate and to explore mathematical concepts. However, teachers often lack a clear notion of what to do to encourage and to improve student collaboration. To enhance student consciousness of relevant aspects of the problem solving process, instructional activities at whole-class (discussion) and small group (redirecting questions and giving feedback on collaborative activities) level were designed.

Although the results are in line with the interpretation that changes in instructional activities stimulated students' collaborative learning, one has to keep in mind that no control group was included in the study. Furthermore, the two groups that were selected for observations represented students of average capacities. We cannot be sure that the same patterns will be found in all students. However, the participating teachers reported that collaboration was more intense and more effective.

In addition to the restrictions that follow from the design, further caveats have to be formulated. First, the study included only two teachers. This makes it difficult to generalize conclusions. Second, changes in student collaboration were found when students worked on open-ended problems. These problems were revised and extended versions of problems that were selected from the textbook. Former studies have shown that working on open-ended problems had a positive effect on collaboration (Cohen, 1994). Although both field notes and teacher perceptions indicated the relevance of the implemented instructional activities, it is not clear to what degree the results can be attributed to these activities in addition to the effect of open-ended problems.

The results of this study suggest at least three lines for further research in addition to an extension of studies to investigate instructional activities. A first line concerns the relation between social and cognitive aspects of collaboration. (Improvement of) collaboration and (level raising of) the content of mathematical thinking are entangled. The question that has to be answered is how improved collaboration is related with deeper mathematical knowledge. To answer this question one has to realize that there is a constant tension between the social and individual level in that a person at each point is involved in a number of activities at both inter- and intrapersonal level: trying to understand the content, producing new content, presenting oneself, face saving activities, elaborating contributions in an intrapersonal dialogue, etc. Stated differently, learning is an individual process but takes place in a situation where individuals act socially. Eventually, learning depends on how students are able to guide communication processes at the intrapersonal level (Sfard, 2001). At this level, learning, i.e. understanding and developing knowledge and skills that can be applied in new problem situations, takes place. However, this level seems to surpass the level of observation. What can be observed are the *conditions* for learning, not the learning itself. This tension between social and individual level makes it difficult to extend the analysis of observed mathematical discourse to include elements that are typical for a mathematically productive discourse. When *observed* discourse reflects the social level but does not reflect learning, the researcher has to "look through" social elements to interpret how individuals use the "discourse environment", i.e. an *inter*personal dialogue, in learning, i.e. in an *intra*personal dialogue. The question that has to be answered is how data on observed discourse may be interpreted to reflect internal learning processes.

A second line of research concerns what can be done to make sure that each participant will gain from being involved in joint learning activities.

Even when collaboration develops smoothly, in each collaborative learning situation roles are unevenly distributed over participants. For example, the interaction may be dependent on only some of the participants whereas others may avoid active contributions. This avoidance may have several causes, e.g., a face saving strategy or because individuals simply try to understand the ongoing discussion without bringing their own contributions to the fore. However, this does not explain to what level individuals may gain from the collaborative discourse. This point can be restated in the question that, if improved communication on the social level is a likely facilitator to improve individual learning, what can be done to support this facilitating effect? Should responsibilities be more evenly distributed over participants (cf., Palincsar & Brown, 1984), should instructional activities/modelling by the teacher be more explicitly aimed at the content level, and what differences in skills and knowledge between participants are acceptable?

A third line of research concerns the interaction between participating students and classroom variables (e.g., classroom climate). Former studies have found evidence that collaboration may foster socialization and motivation. However, relations between instructional activities, collaborative problem solving, personal characteristics and classroom climate have not been a topic of investigation in this study. This leaves relevant questions unanswered, for example whether the approach in this study affects student motivation in a positive way, and whether level of collaboration is related with the role that individual students play.

To answer these questions, additional research is needed to investigate the relations between what actually happens in groups and changes in student perceptions and classroom climate. The approach in this study allows one to combine the development of gradual adaptations in instructional activities, a detailed analysis of actual learning activities and monitoring changes in characteristics of participants in the learning environment.

References

Cobb, P., Confrey, J., diSessa, A., Lehrer, R., & Schauble, L. (2003). Design experiments in educational research. *Educational Researcher, 32,* 9-13.

Cobb, P., Stephan, M., McClain, K., & Gravemeijer, K. (2001). Participating in classroom mathematical practice. *Journal of the Learning Sciences, 10,* 113-163.

Cobo, P., & Fortuny, J. (2000). Social interactions and cognitive effects in contexts of area-comparison problem solving. *Educational Studies in Mathematics, 42,* 115-140.

Cohen, E.G. (1994). Restructuring the classroom: Conditions for productive small groups. *Review of Educational Research, 64,* 1-35.

De Corte, E., Verschaffel, L., & Greer, B. (1996). Mathematics, learning and instruction of. In E. De Corte & F.E. Wienert. (Eds.), *International encyclopedia of developmental and instructional psychology* (pp. 535-538). New York: Pergamon Press.

Doerr, H.M., & Zangor, R. (2000). Creating meaning for and with the graphing calculator. *Educational Studies in Mathematics, 41*, 143-163.
Doorman, L.M., Drijvers, P., & Kindt, M. (1994). *De grafische rekenmachine in het wiskundeonderwijs* [The graphic calculator in mathematics education]. Utrecht, The Netherlands: CD b-Press.
Freudenthal, H. (1971). Geometry between the devil and the deep sea. *Educational Studies in Mathematics, 3*, 413-435.
Freudenthal, H. (1973). *Mathematics as an educational task.* Dordrecht, The Netherlands: Reidel
Freudenthal, H. (1991). *Revisiting mathematics education.* Dordrecht, The Netherlands: Kluwer Academic Publishers.
Goris, T., & Van der Kooij, H. (1997-2000). *Twin wiskunde (Volumes 1, 2, 3 and 4).* Leiden, The Netherlands: SMD.
Greeno, J.G. (1991). Number sense as situated knowing in a conceptual domain. *Journal for Research in Mathematics Education, 22*, 170-218.
Mercer, N. (1996). The quality of talk in children's collaborative activity in the classroom. *Learning and Instruction, 6*, 359-377.
Mortimer, E.F., & Scott, P. (2000). Analysing discourse in the science classroom. In R. Millar, J. Leach, & J. Osborne (Eds.), *Improving science education: the contribution of research* (pp. 126-142). Buckingham: Open University Press.
Palincsar, A.S., & Brown, A.L. (1984). Reciprocal teaching of comprehension-fostering and comprehension-monitoring activities. *Cognition and Instruction, 1*, 117-175.
Romberg, T.A., & Carpenter, T.P. (1986). Research on teaching and learning mathematics: Two disciplines of scientific inquiry. In M. Witrock (Ed.), *Handbook of research and teaching* (3rd ed., pp. 850-873). New York: McMillan.
Roth, W.M. (1998). Science teaching as knowledgeability: A case study of knowing and learning during coteaching. *Science Education, 82*, 357-377.
Roth, W.M., & Boyd, N. (1999). Coteaching, as colearning, in practice. *Research in Science Education, 29*, 51-67.
Roth, W.M., Tobin, K., & Zimmermann, A. (2002). Coteaching/cogenerative dialoguing: Learning environments research as classroom praxis. *Learning Environments Research, 5*, 1-28.
Schoenfeld, A. H. (1992). Learning to think mathematically: Problem solving, metacognition, and sense making in mathematics. In G. A. Grouws (Ed.), *Handbook of research on mathematics teaching and learning* (pp. 165-197). New York: MacMillan.
Sfard, A. (2001). There is more to discourse than meets the ears: Looking at thinking as communicating to learn more about mathematical learning. *Educational Studies in Mathematics, 46*, 13-57.
Smith, E. (1999). Social constructivism, individual constructivism and the role of computers in mathematics education. *Journal of Mathematical Behaviour, 17*, 411-425.
Van Boxtel, C., Van der Linden, J., Roelofs, E., & Erkens, G. (2002). Collaborative concept mapping: provoking and supporting meaningful discourse. *Theory into Practice, 41*, 40-46.
Wegerif, R., Mercer, N., & Dawes, N. (1999). From social interaction to individual reasoning: An empirical investigation of a possible socio-cultural model of cognitive development. *Learning and Instruction, 9*, 493-516.
Wenger, E. (1998). *Communities of practice. Learning, meaning, and identity.* Cambridge: Cambridge University Press.

Chapter 7

Remedying secondary school students' illusion of linearity: Developing and evaluating a powerful learning environment

Wim Van Dooren, Dirk De Bock, An Hessels, Dirk Janssens, and Lieven Verschaffel

1 Introduction

Linear (or proportional) relations have a wide applicability and are useful for understanding not only numerous everyday life situations, but also many problems in mathematics and sciences. Already very early, children experience the validity of these relations (van den Brink & Streefland, 1979): four handfuls of sand to fill one bucket, so twelve handfuls to fill three buckets; one toy car has four wheels so two toy cars have eight wheels; etcetera. Moreover, during primary and secondary education, much attention is paid to proportional relations and their applicability in mathematical and scientific contexts. Students learn, for example, that there exists a proportional relation between the diameter of a circle and its perimeter, between the weight of an amount of fluid and its volume, between the time and the distance travelled at a constant speed. Throughout education, the linearity concept really appears as a "leitmotiv", from the old-fashioned "rule of three" in primary school to the idea of linear models and approximations in calculus and statistics at the secondary level, and to the abstraction in a vector space sense in university courses (for an overview, see e.g., CREM, 2002). Besides their wide applicability, proportional relationships also seem self-evident and intrinsically simple. Because of their simplicity, linear functions appear immediately in human's mind. Rouche argues that "C'est l'idée de proportionnalité qui vient d'abord à l'esprit, parce qu'il n'y a sans doute pas de fonctions plus simples que les linéaires"[1] (Rouche, 1989, p. 17).

These characteristics of proportional models, along with the attention that they receive during education, may have a serious drawback. Many researchers and math educators warn that it may lead to a tendency in stu-

---

[1] "It is the idea of proportionality that comes immediately in the mind, because undoubtedly there are no functions that are more simple than the linear ones".

dents – and even in adults – to see and apply the linear model "anywhere". As formulated by Freudenthal (1983, p. 267): "Linearity is such a suggestive property of relations that one readily yields to the seduction to deal with each numerical relation as though it were linear".

Examples of this misuse of linearity – often referred to as the "illusion of linearity" – are manifold. They are found at different age levels and in various mathematical and scientific domains. One of the oldest and most often quoted examples is probably the slave in Plato's dialogue *Meno*. When asked by Socrates to draw a square having the double area of a given square, he proposed to double the sides of that square. Another historical example is mentioned by Galilei (1638) describing Aristotle's naïve physics theory: Aristotle thought that an object which is ten times as heavy as another object will fall ten times as rapidly as that other object.

Striking examples of the unwarranted application of linearity originate from recent empirical research too. For example, in the domain of elementary arithmetic, Cramer, Post and Currier (1993) confronted pre-service elementary school teachers with the following problem: "Sue and Julie were running equally fast around a track. Sue started first. When she had run 9 laps, Julie had run 3 laps. When Julie completed 15 laps, how many laps had Sue run?" Thirty-two out of 33 pre-service teachers answered by means of a proportion: $9/3 = x/15$ so that $x = 45$. In the domain of probabilistic reasoning, we observed that many secondary school and university students believe that when rolling a die, the probability of getting a six is tripled if the number of trials is tripled (Van Dooren, De Bock, Depaepe, Janssens, & Verschaffel, 2003).

2 The linearity illusion in geometry

The current chapter focuses on the probably best-known case of the "illusion of linearity", i.e., the misconception about the effect of an enlargement or reduction of a geometrical figure on its area and volume (remember the above-mentioned example in Plato's dialogue *Meno*). The correct mathematical principle is well-known: independently from the type of figure or object (square, circle, pyramid, irregular figure, etcetera), an enlargement or reduction with factor k enlarges/reduces the lengths (and perimeter) of the figure with factor k, (surface) areas with factor k^2 and volumes with factor k^3. Many authors (e.g., Freudenthal, 1983; NCTM, 1989; Rouche, 1989; Tierney, Boyd, & Davis, 1990) mention that students (and even pre-service teachers) pass by this principle and are misled by the illusion of linearity. The *Curriculum and Evaluation Standards for School Mathematics* state that "most students incorrectly believe that if the sides of a figure are doubled to produce a similar figure, the area and volume will also be doubled" (NCTM, 1989, p. 114-115).

Recently, the geometrical misconception that the area and volume of a figure enlarge with factor k when a figure is enlarged k times, has been extensively studied by De Bock et al. (De Bock, Verschaffel, & Janssens, 1998, 2002a; De Bock, Van Dooren, Janssens, & Verschaffel, 2002b; De Bock, Verschaffel, Janssens, Van Dooren, & Claes, 2003). In a series of experimental studies, large groups of 12-16-year old students were administered paper-and-pencil tests with proportional and non-proportional word problems about lengths, perimeters, areas and volumes of different types of figures. For example, they used the following non-proportional item about the area of a square: "Farmer Carl needs approximately 8 hours to manure a square piece of land with a side of 200m. How many hours would he need to manure a square piece of land with a side of 600m?" These experimental studies showed the following results:
- The large majority of students failed on this type of problems because of their alarmingly strong tendency to apply linear strategies.
- Even with considerable support (such as drawings, metacognitive stimuli, or making problems authentic), only very few students made the shift to the correct non-linear reasoning (De Bock et al., 1998, 2002a, 2003).
- When, as a consequence of the provided help, students discovered that some of the problems in the test can not be solved by applying linear strategies, they sometimes started to apply non-linear solution schemes to linear problems too.

In an additional study with in-depth interviews (De Bock et al., 2002b), information was obtained on the underlying problem-solving processes and explanatory factors. This study indicated that
- the majority of students used the proportional model in a spontaneous, almost intuitive way being unaware of their choice for a proportional model, while others really were convinced that linear functions are applicable "everywhere", therefore deliberately choosing a linear solution strategy
- students showed particular shortcomings in their geometrical knowledge (e.g., the misconception that the concept of area only applies to regular figures, or that a similarly enlarged figure is not necessarily enlarged to the same extent in all dimensions).
- many students had inadequate habits, beliefs and attitudes towards solving problems in (school) mathematics (e.g., the belief that drawings are not helpful in solving a problem), leading to stereotyped and superficial mathematical modelling.

The next stage of our research program – which is the focus of this present chapter – involves the design, implementation and evaluation of a learning environment aimed at overcoming the illusion of linearity in the context of the enlargement/reduction of geometrical figures, and at developing in students a deep conceptual understanding of proportional and non-proportional relations and situations in this domain. The next paragraph explains how the conceptual change theory is a valuable framework for interpreting the phenomenon of the illusion of linearity. Later, we will clarify how this theory also guided the development of the intervention study and helped in interpreting its outcomes.

3 Theoretical background: The conceptual change theory

Currently, the widely accepted view in the research community on learning and instruction is that students cannot be considered as "empty vessels" when encountering learning tasks or considering scientific or mathematical knowledge. Rather, they have already constructed a common-sense understanding of the world on the basis of their experiences from every day life and prior schooling (Mason, 2001). This highly individual prior-knowledge base interacts with the new information students are confronted with. Especially when that knowledge base is not compatible with certain new learning contents, classroom learning requires a reorganisation of students' existing knowledge base, which is called conceptual change (Mason, 2001; Vosniadou, Ioannides, Dimitrakopoulou, & Papademetriou, 2001). The conceptual change theory (further called CCT) focuses on knowledge acquisition in specific domains where prior conceptions interact with the new, intended knowledge and describes learning as a process that requires the significant reorganisation of existing knowledge structures (Vosniadou & Brewer, 1987). The conceptual change theory originates from a combination of two theories: one from the philosophy of science (Kuhn, 1962) and one from developmental psychology (Piaget, 1977). Kuhn's work describes how scientific revolutions are caused in scientific communities by the discoveries of various members of these communities coupled with historical crises, finally leading to new methodologies and globally accepted worldviews. Piaget describes how learners learn through the "assimilation" and "accommodation" of knowledge. Posner, Strike, Hewson, and Gertzog (1982) suggest that the conditions for the accommodation of new concepts within individuals are similar to the conditions for acceptance of new scientific paradigms. Kuhn's paradigms shift caused by the scientific revolution can be compared to the accommodation of new knowledge in an individual that leads to a change of that individual's conceptual framework, i.e., conceptual change (Zirbel, 2004).

To what extent can we interpret the origin of students' tendency to apply linearity "anywhere" (as described in the introduction of this chapter) in terms of this theory? Clearly, the early acquisition and repeated confirmation of some important knowledge elements from pre-school and out-of-school experiences – a key assumption in CCT – also holds for linearity. In their most simplistic form, linear relations are acquired from early infancy (van den Brink & Streefland, 1979), and are continuously confirmed by everyday experiences. In elementary school, children experience many times the validity of the proportional model, both implicitly and explicitly. CCT assumes that children's initial and intuitive conceptual knowledge of the world is organized in a so-called framework theory – consisting of a few deeply entrenched presuppositions – that makes it possible for them to function in that world (Vosniadou, 1999). Such framework theory is most often unavailable to conscious awareness and deliberate hypothesis testing. Students are often not aware of the hypothetical nature of their beliefs and presuppositions, but treat them as facts about the world. We would argue that "linearity" can be considered as one such presupposition in children's framework theory: our studies have shown that students are indeed often unaware of the fact that they are using this early-acquired concept (De Bock et al., 2002b).

Such early-acquired naïve framework theory may facilitate the knowledge acquisition processes (Vosniadou, 1999). Particularly for the concept of linearity – being a major topic in the entire mathematics curriculum – the formal and systematic study of this concept will then certainly be facilitated by students' prior knowledge. But such deeply entrenched presuppositions may also hinder later learning. The repeated confirmation of the validity of linearity may cause a deeply entrenched misconception that every relationship between two quantities is linear, and that proportions are a panacea for nearly all problems. When students, then, meet pieces of information that are fundamentally inconsistent with this presupposition, they may try to reconcile the new information with this entrenched presupposition without giving it up, or by changing the presupposition only very partially (Vosniadou, 1999). For example, when students are confronted with cases wherein the area of a figure increases quadratically (and the volume cubically) with the sides of the figure, they might not pick up this information since their preconceptions about the issue are not explicitly addressed. Consequently, they do not fundamentally change their presupposition of linearity and continue to believe that if a figure is enlarged k times, its area and volume become k times larger too. Partial changes in the presuppositions could also occur (for example, accepting the principle for squares but not for any other type of figure, or for the increase of area but not for volume). These newly originated misconceptions are then a result of students' active and creative efforts to establish or maintain mental coherence (Vosniadou & Brewer, 1992) when their presupposition of linearity was confronted with inconsistent information. It is precisely this type of misconceptions that has been observed and studied by De Bock et al. (1998, 2002a, 2002b, 2003). The number of students (even 16-year olds) applying proportional strategies to non-proportional geometry problems was surprisingly large, since the regular mathematics curriculum provided these students with ample opportunities to gain the correct insight in this type of situations: their curriculum already dealt with methods of calculating areas and volumes of a diversity of figures, with quadratic and cubic functions and their applications, andin some cases the students were even explicitly taught about the effects of an enlargement or reduction on the perimeter, area and volume of a figure. But apparently no real conceptual change was achieved, probably because the teaching did not sufficiently take into account students' entrenched presuppositions that were inconsistent with the new learning contents. In retrospect, this is not surprising, considering what Mason (2001, p. 260) stated: "over more than two decades of studies (...) have revealed that conceptual change is rather difficult to achieve, therefore students very often fail to understand disciplinar concepts despite the valuable efforts of teachers".

4 Design of the learning environment

The goal of the current teaching experiment is to break students' deep-rooted tendency to apply linear strategies in non-linear situations, more specifically in the context of the relationship between the linear measures of a figure and its perimeter, area and volume. For this goal, a series of 10 one-hour experimental lessons – including all teacher and learner materials – was developed for use with 8th graders. An overview of the contents that were treated in these lessons, as well as illustrative learning tasks and exercises can be found in the Appendix.

There are a number of instructional design principles for the development of a learning environment with the above-mentioned goal, which derive from the conceptual change approach (see e.g., Vosniadou et al., 2001). These principles are moreover generally in line with other sources of inspiration, such as the literature on realistic mathematics education (Gravemeijer, 1994; NCTM, 1989) and on powerful learning environments and the enhancement of higher order thinking skills in general (Collins, Brown, & Newman, 1989). We will now comment on the way in which these design principles (adopted from Vosniadou et al., 2001) were taken into account in the development of the learning environment (referring to several illustrative elements from the Appendix), in order to maximize the chance of obtaining conceptual change in the students.

The first, most essential principle derived from CCT is the necessity of *being well informed about the prior knowledge* students bring with them in the classroom. We tried to take these into account in developing the learning environment. In our target domain, previous research by De Bock et al. (1998, 2002a, 2002b, 2003) provided this necessary knowledge base about students' misconceptions in our target domain, and revealed the underlying origins. Moreover, a pretest at the beginning of the teaching experiment confirmed the presence of the expected misconceptions in the students participating in the teaching experiment. Our learning environment addressed the major lacks that were observed in students' geometrical knowledge base, such as the principles governing an enlargement or reduction of a figure in lesson 1-2, and strategies to determine perimeters, areas and volumes in several tasks throughout the lesson series. We also aimed at addressing students' conceptions, habits and attitudes during mathematical word problem solving, such as the idea that mathematical problems have nothing to do with reality, or that every problem can be solved through the application of one or two simple operations (see for example, the "doghouse" problem in lesson 6-7).

A second principle is the need to *explicitly address students' preconceptions* in the instruction. Knowing that many students have a tendency to over-rely on linear relations and that linearity is often self-evident to them, we specifically incorporated an exploration of the capacity of linear functions to grasp many relations in similarly enlarged or reduced figures (see e.g., the task in lesson 3), but also demonstrated their limitation in understanding certain other situations. For example, the "pancakes" problem in lesson 4-5 was designed to elicit a cognitive conflict in students and meaningful discussions during small group work and classroom discussions.

Third, Vosniadou et al. (2001) stress the importance of *facilitating students' metaconceptual awareness* (awareness of their beliefs and presuppositions and possible inconsistencies in them) *and metacognition* (monitoring their learning and problem-solving processes) in order to bring conceptual change in the conscious control of the learner (for a thorough discussion on the importance of intentional learning, metaconceptual awareness and metacognition for conceptual change, see Vosiniadou, 2003). Our earlier studies showed that students often implicitly and tacitly assume linearity, and this general unawareness prevents them often from questioning the applicability of the proportional model, from detecting inconsistencies in their reasoning and from discovering alternatives. As can be seen in the Appendix, we applied a combination of instructional techniques that have proven to be successful in enhancing students' metacognitive thinking skills, in inducing cognitive conflict and in obtaining conceptual change (e.g., small-group work, changing roles for the group members, exchanges between groups, whole-class discussions, etcetera) (Collins et al., 1989). Indeed, while conceptual change as such is an individual process, social factors may help to promote awareness of one's own beliefs, and therefore awareness of possible conflicts, which in turn may lead to conceptual change (Limon, 2001).

A fourth principle raised in the CCT literature is the *motivation source* for obtaining conceptual change. If we want students to invest substantial effort to change their original conceptual structures and presuppositions, they need to have meaningful learning experiences. In line with one of the major principles of realistic mathematics education (Gravemeijer, 1994), our lesson series was interspersed with a rich variety of meaningful, realistic and attractive problem situations, challenging particular mathematical (mis)conceptions, beliefs and habits observed in the students. As an illustration, we refer to the integrative project that the students worked on during lessons 8, 9 and 10. These lessons were devoted to a project (to be realized in small groups) about the book "Gnomes" (Poortvliet & Huygen, 1977), describing in a very detailed and touchingly realistic way all aspects of the life of the gnomes. During the project, the students had the opportunity to apply all newly acquired mathematical insights in complex, attractive and challenging problems situated in the world of gnomes, where all lengths are 12 times smaller. The most challenging task was the examination of the claim (made in that book) that a gnome of 15 cm weighs about 300 grams. Applying the taught principles about the change of volume in a reduced object and their real-life knowledge about the size and weight of a human, the students discovered that a more appropriate estimation would be 70 000 grams / 12^3 = 40.6 grams (see Appendix).

A final important principle mentioned by Vosniadou et al. (2001), is the need for *providing appropriate mathematical models and related external representations*. Students' knowledge base does not consist of isolated pieces of knowledge. Rather, it tends to be organised in more or less internally consistent models (whether correct or not). Instruction aiming for conceptual change should then be based as much as possible on the provision of such organised models captured in adequate external representations. These representations often have the ability to clarify aspects of an explanation that are not apparent when the explanation is given in a purely linguistic or purely symbolic way. We aimed at enhancing deep-level learning by the use of multiple external representations of all central learning contents, and at accentuating their reciprocal relationships (see e.g., Ainsworth, Bibby, & Wood, 2002; NCTM, 1989). For example, the Appendix shows how the quadratic relationship between the side and the area of a square was analysed in the following representations:
– the formula "A = side × side = $side^2$" for the area of a square (in which a quadratic factor can be observed, and in which side can be algebraically substituted by 1.5 side, 2 side, 3 side etcetera, or by different numerical values)
– a table in which the area is calculated for several values of the side (and in which the areas for different sizes of sides can be compared)
– a graph representing the relation between the side and area (and which illustrates the non-linear character of the relationship)
– a drawing (in which a large square can be "covered" with small squares to get a visual comparison of their areas).

5 Research method

In this study, 35 eighth graders (aged 13-14) were involved. They belonged to two intact classes from two secondary schools in Flanders

(Belgium), attracting comparable regular student populations. Both groups consisted of about equal numbers of boys and girls. One class (of 18 students) was assigned to the experimental condition and followed the experimental lesson series. All lessons in this group were videotaped and all student notes were collected. The other group (of 17 students) acted as a control group. These students followed the regular lessons (in which none of the contents under consideration was treated) and prior to the teaching experiment, the mathematics teacher in this group was not informed about the topic of the study.

Learning gains in both groups were assessed by means of a word-problem test consisting of 2 proportional items (about the perimeter of an enlarged square and of a circle), 4 non-proportional items (about the area and the volume of an enlarged square/cube and an irregular figure) and 2 unrelated buffer items. Table 1 gives an example of a proportional and a non-proportional item. Three parallel versions of this test were constructed (ensuring comparability for each item with respect to the type of figure and complexity of formulation and calculations). Each student of the experimental group solved one version of the test before the intervention (pretest), another version after the intervention (posttest), and a third version three months afterwards (retention test). Students in the control group received only a pretest and a retention test.

Table 1. Examples of word problems used in the test

Proportional item (perimeter)	Non-proportional item (volume)
Steve needs 10 minutes to dig a ditch around a square sandcastle with a side of 50 cm. How much time will he approximately need to dig a ditch around a square sandcastle with a side of 150 cm?	In his toy box, John has dice in several sizes. The smallest one has a side of 10 mm and weighs 800 mg. What would be the weight of the largest die (with a side of 30 mm)?

All problems were open-ended questions, and students had to write down their answer and their calculations. Answers were scored either as correct or as incorrect, and incorrect answers were further categorized as follows (based on an analysis of the students' solution steps): application of proportional methods to non-proportional items (P), application of non-proportional methods to proportional items (NP), other errors (O).

6 Results

A 2×2×3 repeated measures ANOVA was conducted with "group" (experimental vs. control), "item" (proportional vs. non-proportional) and "test" (pretest vs. posttest vs. retention test) as independent variables and students' performance on the word problems as the dependent variable. We expected a significant "item"×"group"×"test" interaction effect, which was confirmed by the ANOVA, $F(1,488) = 4.80$, $MSE = 0.784$, $p = 0.0290$. An overview of the percentages of correct answers is given in Table 2. Because of the significant three-way interaction effect, all pairwise differences in this table were statistically tested by means of post-hoc Tukey tests (correcting for multiple comparisons) and Cohen's d effect sizes were calculated.

Table 2. Percentage correct answers (and standard deviations) of the experimental and control group on the proportional and non-proportional items at the three test moments

	Proportional items						Non-proportional items					
	Pre		Post		Retent		Pre		Post		Retent	
	%	SD	%	SD	%	SD	%	SD	%	SD	%	SD
Experimental	83.3	7.8	58.3	7.8	52.8	7.8	29.2	6.2	61.1	6.2	50.0	6.2
Control	85.3	8.1			73.5	8.1	13.2	6.4			16.1	6.4

As expected, on the pretest there was a significant difference between the performance on the proportional items (which were solved very well) and the non-proportional items (which were mostly solved incorrectly due to linear reasoning), both in the experimental group, $t(488) = 6.56$, $p = 0.0001$, $d = 7.68$, and in the control group, $t(488) = 8.48$, $p = 0.0001$, $d = 9.90$. Again, this is evidence for students' tendency to produce linear answers in non-linear situations. Furthermore, at the pretest there was no significant difference between the experimental and control group, indicating that both groups were indeed comparable. Both groups performed almost the same on the proportional items, and the difference for the non-proportional items was also not significant[2].

We will first discuss the results of the control group. Afterwards, we will contrast these results with those of the experimental group.

We did not expect a significant evolution from pretest to retention test in the control group. In line with this expectation, we observed only a very small, non-significant increase in the performance on the non-proportional items (from 13.2% to 16.1% correct answers) and a non-significant decrease

---

[2] Despite the non-significant outcome of the Tukey test, both groups' performances on the non-proportional items seemed to differ considerable. An additional analysis of covariance (ANCOVA) was performed, predicting the performances on the non-proportional items on the retention test on the basis of the group (experimental/control) *correcting for the performances on these items on the pretest* (thus cancelling out any differences between the groups at the pretest). The corrected means of both groups at the posttest (44.3% and 22.3% for the experimental and control group respectively) were still statistically different, $F(1,32) = 6.42$, $MSE = 0.977$, $p = 0.0164$.

in the number of correctly answered proportional items (from 85.3% to 73.5%) from pretest to retention test. A qualitative analysis of the protocols in this group showed that in about 80% of the cases, students applied linear strategies to the non-linear items on the pretest and the retention test (P-errors). A small increase in the number of overgeneralisations of non-linear strategies to linear items (NP-errors) could be observed (from about 11% to 18%) between pretest and retention test. Apparently, a small effect of retesting was that a few students started to apply non-linear solution methods to the linear problems they solved correctly before. This is similar to observations made in earlier studies (De Bock et al., 1998, 2002a, 2003).

The experimental group significantly improved on the non-proportional items from pretest (29.2%) to posttest (61.1%), $t(488) = 3.09$, $p = 0.0001$, $d = 5.14$, followed by a non-significant decrease in the performances on the retention test (to 50.0% correct answers). This means that the experimental group significantly progressed in its performance on the non-proportional items, and that this progress persisted over several months. However, this improvement in performance was not as high as we had anticipated. Contrary to the results for the non-proportional items, the score of the experimental group on the proportional items decreased from 83.3% correct answers on the pretest to 58.3% on the posttest, $t(488) = -2.62$, $p = 0.0090$, $d = 3.21$, and went further down from posttest to retention test (although not significantly) to 52.8%. Apparently, in line with our earlier studies, when these students discovered that some problems can not be solved by applying proportions, they started applying non-proportional solution schemes to proportional problems too (De Bock et al., 1998, 2002a, 2003). A qualitative analysis of the answers of the experimental group revealed first of all that on the pretest about 70% of all the solutions on the non-proportional items could be characterized as proportional. This number of erroneous linear answers strongly decreased in the posttest to about 18%, while in the retention test, the percentage raised again to about 30%. But students who no longer applied linear solutions to solve non-linear problems during the posttest or the retention test, did not always perform better than at the pretest: in the posttest and retention test, many of them made errors in applying non-linear solutions on these non-linear problems (e.g., confusing area and volume, taking the square of a given number, ...). The qualitative analysis also confirmed the overgeneralisation of non-linear strategies (NP-errors) after the lessons: while on the pretest only 13% of all the solutions to linear items could be characterised as applications of non-linear strategies (NP-errors), this number raised to 36% on the posttest and on the retention test!

The evolution of the performance of the experimental group on the tests revealed that in most students the intended conceptual change was not accomplished. An analysis of the videotaped experimental lessons supports this conclusion. Due to space restrictions, we cannot elaborate on these lessons fragments as such, but we restrict ourselves to the most important conclusions of the analysis of these fragments in an attempt to explain the somewhat disappointing test results of the experimental class students.

First of all, certain lesson fragments revealed that non-linear relations and the effect of enlargements on area and volume remained intrinsically difficult and counterintuitive for many students. A striking example comes from a student raising the following question in the final lesson: "I really do understand now why the area of a square increases 9 times if the sides are tripled in length, since the enlargement of the area goes in two dimensions. But suddenly I start to wonder why this does *not* hold for the perimeter. The perimeter also increases in two directions, doesn't it?"

A second, related issue coming forward from the video analysis is that for the students in our intervention study, proportional reasoning was already well established and practiced, so that they initially overgeneralised proportionality to nearly all problems. But as soon as its applicability was questioned for some situations, the students again started to make hasty overgeneralizations. Some students went on switching back and forth between applying proportionality "anywhere" and applying it "nowhere" during the course of the experimental program, thereby relying only on superficial cues just as they did before. Whereas the instructional goal was that students would make fundamental changes in their conceptual framework to reflect and deliberately discriminate between the concepts and strategies that are adequate in a certain situation, some students seemed to perceive the goal of our intervention as if the old linear thinking should entirely disappear.

Third, the analysis of the videotaped lessons showed that while working in groups on the learning tasks, students very often did not engage in thoughtful, effortful processing as much as we wanted them to do. Instead, they often stuck to very superficial cues, prompting rapid, global strategy choices and evaluations. Contrary to our expectations, the experimental learning tasks – that were based on realistic and attractive learning tasks and that induced cognitive conflict where possible – often failed to create a real feeling of "personal relevance" (Limon, 2001) in the students. When cognitive conflicts arose during group work, local inconsistencies in students' thinking were often "patched up" (Vosniadou, 1999) in a rather superficial way. And whereas the instructional methods of group work, exchanges of ideas and results between groups, and classroom discussions were expected to enhance metacognitive awareness, most of the time the discourse only shortly focused on the genuine exchange and grounded discussion of ideas. These exchanges were moreover often based on the "authority" of the mathematically more able students. In sum, the realistic character of the learning tasks and the interactive and thought-provoking character of the instructional methods did not always reach their goal.

7 Conclusions and discussion

In general, the results of this study confirmed our expectations. Initially, both the experimental and the control group performed well on the proportional items but often failed on the non-proportional items, due to the application of linear methods. After the experimental lesson series, the experimental group applied linear solution methods less often on the non-linear items on the test. Apparently, the illusion of linearity was to a certain extent de-constructed in these experimental group students. However, a considerable part of the non-linear items on the posttest and retention test were still solved erroneously, either due to linear reasoning or to errors in the application of non-linear strategies. Moreover, at the posttest and retention test, the experimental group students suddenly began to make more errors on the proportional problems, because they overgeneralised the newly learnt non-proportional strategies to the proportional problems they previously solved very well. Apparently, after the lessons, the students still experienced serious difficulties in knowing which model to use in which situation. Therefore we can hardly argue that the lesson series has yielded the intended conceptual change. Many students did not develop a deeper understanding of proportionality and non-proportionality, and a disposition to distinguish between situations that can and cannot be modelled proportionally. The non-proportional reasoning scheme that emerged in some experimental students' still remained very fragile and unsteady.

In order to foster a more radical conceptual change for a more substantial part of the students, a teaching intervention during a longer time period or spread out over a longer time period seems necessary. The 10-hour experimental lesson series could deal with the core mathematical content knowledge that is necessary to appropriately solve problems about the change in perimeter, area and volume of enlarged or reduced geometrical figures. But this 10-hour intervention, which was quite separated from the regular mathematics curriculum and the regular classroom practice and culture – was clearly not sufficient to enhance students' metaconceptual awareness, or to change the students' habits and beliefs with respect to mathematical problem solving. And precisely these factors are important facilitating factors in the occurrence of improper linear reasoning (De Bock et al., 2002b) and in the process of conceptual change in general (Vosniadou, 1999, 2003). Evidence on the possibility of changing students' inappropriate conceptions and beliefs with respect to mathematical modelling by immersing them during an extensive period in a new classroom culture can be found in Verschaffel and De Corte (1997).

Besides the difficulty of changing students' metaconceptual awareness, habits and beliefs in a limited time range and a restricted instructional setting, we wonder whether such intervention should not take place earlier than in grade 8. We actually chose for this age group since its regular mathematics curriculum corresponded most to the contents treated in our experimental lesson series. But since these 8th graders already had so much opportunity to practice the proportional reasoning scheme and experienced usefulness of that scheme, this prior knowledge seems to continue interfering in their learning process. A recent study by Van Dooren, De Bock, Hessels, Janssens and Verschaffel (2005) on students' solutions of arithmetic word problems confirmed that students over-application of proportionality runs parallel with students' growing proportional reasoning skills and the curricular attention this topic receives: the illusion of linearity proved to be already present in the 2nd grade, increased up to grade 5, before only slightly decreasing from grade 6 to 8. Therefore, it might be more appropriate to intervene much earlier in order to prevent (rather than remedy) the illusion of linearity. At the first time when students meet proportional relationships in their mathematics curriculum in a more formal way (i.e., in fourth and fifth grade), they should also be confronted with counterexamples (of situations where linearity does not work), and learn to distinguish between situations that can be modelled proportionally and situations with another underlying mathematical structure. In this way, one can possibly avoid or early remedy the presupposition that any relation between quantities is proportional. And when at a later age, students discover, for example, that an area increases k^2 times if a figure is enlarged k times, they might experience less incongruency with their presuppositions and be more susceptible to generalizing and formalizing this principle, which was the goal of the current teaching experiment.

References

Ainsworth, S., Bibby, P., & Wood, D. (2002). Examining the effects of different multiple representational systems in learning primary mathematics. *The Journal of the Learning Sciences, 11*(1), 25-61.

Collins, A., Brown, J. S., & Newman, S. E. (1989). Cognitive apprenticeship: Teaching the crafts of reading, writing and mathematics. In L. B. Resnick (Ed.), *Knowing, learning and instruction. Essays in honor of Robert Glaser* (pp. 453-494). Hillsdale, NJ: Lawrence Erlbaum Associates.

Cramer, K., Post, T., & Currier, S. (1993). Learning and teaching ratio and proportion: Research implications. In D. T. Owens (Ed.), *Research ideas for the classroom: Middle grades mathematics* (pp. 159-178). New York: Macmillan.

CREM (2002). Des *grandeurs aux espaces vectoriels: La linéarité comme fil conducteur*. Nivelles: Author.

De Bock, D., Van Dooren, W., Janssens, D., & Verschaffel, L. (2002b). Improper use of linear reasoning: An in-depth study of the nature and the irresistibility of secondary school students' errors. *Educational Studies in Mathematics, 50*, 311-334.

De Bock, D., Verschaffel, L., & Janssens, D. (1998). The predominance of the linear model in secondary school students' solutions of word problems involving length and area of similar plane figures. *Educational Studies in Mathematics, 35*, 65-83.

De Bock, D., Verschaffel, L., & Janssens, D. (2002a). The effects of different problem presentations and formulations on the illusion of linearity in secondary school students. *Mathematical Thinking and Learning*, 4(1), 65-89.
De Bock, D., Verschaffel, L., Janssens, D., Van Dooren, W., & Claes K. (2003). Do realistic contexts and graphical representations always have a beneficial impact on students' performance? Negative evidence from a study on modelling non-linear geometry problems. *Learning and Instruction*, 13, 441-463.
Freudenthal, H. (1983). *Didactical phenomenology of mathematical structures.* Dordrecht: Reidel.
Galilei, G. (1638). *Discorsi e dimostrazioni matematiche intorna a due nuove scienze.* New York: Dover.
Gravemeijer, K. (1994). *Developing realistic mathematics education.* Utrecht, The Netherlands: Freudenthal Institute, University of Utrecht.
Kuhn, T. S. (1962). *The structure of scientific revolutions.* Chicago: University of Chicago Press.
Limon, M. (2001). On the cognitive conflict as an instructional strategy for conceptual change. *Learning and Instruction*, 11, 357-380.
Mason, L. (2001). Introduction to special issue "Instructional practices for conceptual change in science domains". *Learning and Instruction*, 11, 259-263.
NCTM. (1989). *Curriculum and evaluation standards for school mathematics.* Reston, VA: Author.
Piaget, J. (1977). *Equilibration of cognitive structures.* New York: Viking Press.
Poortvliet, R., & Huygen, W. (1977). *Gnomes.* New York: Harry N. Abrams Inc.
Posner, G. J., Strike, K. A., Hewson, P. W., & Gertzog, W. A. (1982). Accommodation of scientific conception: Towards a theory of conceptual change. *Science Education*, 66, 211-227.
Rouche, N. (1989). Prouver: amener à l'évidence ou contrôler des implications? In Commission inter-IREM Histoire et Epistémologie des Mathématiques (Ed.), *La démonstration dans l'histoire* (pp. 8-38). Lyon: IREM.
Tierney, C., Boyd, C., & Davis, G. (1990). Prospective primary teachers' conceptions of area. In G. Booker, P. Cobb, & T. N. de Mendicuti (Eds.), *Proceedings of the 14th PME-Conference* (Vol. 2, pp. 307-314). Oaxtepex, Mexico.
van den Brink, J., & Streefland, L. (1979). Young children (6-8) – Ratio and proportion. *Educational Studies in Mathematics*, 10, 403-420.
Van Dooren, W., De Bock, D., Depaepe, F., Janssens, D., & Verschaffel, L. (2003) The illusion of linearity: Expanding the evidence towards probabilistic reasoning. *Educational Studies in Mathematics*, 53, 113-138.
Van Dooren, W., De Bock, D., Hessels, A., Janssens, D., & Verschaffel, L. (2005). Not everything is proportional: Effects of problem type and age on propensities for over-generalization. *Cognition and Instruction*, 23(1), 57-86.
Verschaffel, L., & De Corte, E. (1997). Teaching realistic mathematical modeling and problem solving in the elementary school. A teaching experiment with fifth graders. *Journal for Research in Mathematics Education*, 28, 577-601.
Vosniadou, S. (1999). Conceptual change research: State of the art and future directions. In W. Schnotz, S. Vosniadou, & M. Carretero (Eds.), *New perspectives on conceptual change* (pp. 3-13). Oxford: Pergamon.
Vosniadou, S. (2003). Exploring the relationships between conceptual change and intentional learning. In G. M. Sinatra & P. R. Pintrich (Ed.), *Intentional conceptual change* (pp. 377-406). Lawrence Erlbaum Associates: London.
Vosniadou, S., & Brewer, W. F. (1987). Theories of knowledge restructuring in development. *Review of Educational Research*, 57, 51-67.
Vosniadou, S., & Brewer, W. F. (1992). Mental models of the earth: A study of conceptual change in childhood. *Cognitive Psychology*, 24, 535-585.

Vosniadou, S., Ioannides, C., Dimitrakopoulou, A., & Papademetriou, E. (2001). Designing learning environments to promote conceptual change in science. *Learning and Instruction, 11*, 381-419.

Zirbel, E. L. (2004). Framework for conceptual change. *The Astronomy Education Review, 1*(3), 62-76.

Appendix.
Overview of the lesson contents and exemplary learning tasks and exercises

Lesson 1-2 : Similar figures / objects

Goals: Recognize and construct similarly enlarged and reduced figures/objects and understand their properties.

Example: *Which reproduction of the original painting by Margritte is the best one?*

Original painting

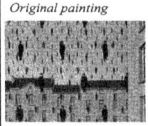 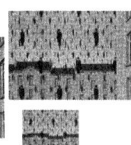 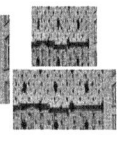

Other activities: Examination of similarity of diverse drawings and three-dimensional objects (cans, envelopes, bottles, ...), constructing similar enlargements and reductions of a given figure, finding "easier" strategies to construct similar figures.

Afterwards: Whole class discussion leading to
- the properties of similar (two-dimensional) figures and (three-dimensional) objects
- methods of constructing similar figures in different sizes
- the meaning of the enlargement/reduction factor k

Lesson 3 : Linear relations in similar figures

Goals: Understand the proportional relations in similar figures, and know how they can be used to predict lengths in other sizes of the figure.

Example: *Complete the tables, and put the data from each table in a graph.*

	A	B
Picture width		
Picture diagonal		
Cupboard height		
(various other lengths)		

	Height	Diagonal
A		
B		
C		
D		

Afterwards: Group discussions leading to conclusions such as:
- each length in figure A is k times that length in figure B
- the ratio of two random lengths is the same in each figure
- predictions about lengths in other sizes of the figure can be made by interpolation or extrapolation of the linear graph

Lesson 4-5 : Linear growth of perimeter and quadratic growth of area

Goals: Understand and apply the principle that if a figure is enlarged or reduced k times, the perimeter of that figure enlarges k times too, but the area enlarges k^2 times.

Example: *Is a big cola bottle of 1.5 litres similar to a small cola bottle of 0.5 litres?*
If you strip the labels of the bottles, the label of the small bottle is 5 cm high by 20 cm wide. The label of the big bottle is 7.3 cm high. When both bottles are similar to each other, what should be the width of the label of the big bottle?

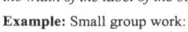

Example: *Small group work:*
It's Anne's birthday and her mother is going to make pancakes, using three pans of different sizes. Anne asks her friend: "You may choose between two big pancakes (30 cm diameter), four regular ones (20 cm diameter) or six small ones (15 cm diameter)."
Her friend reasons as follows: "You better choose six small pancakes because 2 x 30 cm = 60 cm, 4 x 20 cm = 80 cm and 6 x 15 cm = 90 cm"
What do you think about the reasoning of Anne's friend? Compare your solutions.
How many of the smallest pancakes do you need to have the same amount as one large pancake? Why?

+ **Classroom discussion** on different group solutions, exploring possible approaches: calculating areas, using cardboard discs as models (weighing the cardboard discs, cutting and covering a large disc with pieces of a smaller disc, ...)

Afterwards: Class discussion investigating the effect of enlargements and reductions on their perimeter and area
- by means of multiple representations (formula, table, drawing, graph)
- for a diversity of figures (squares, circles, rectangles, irregular figures)
- example:

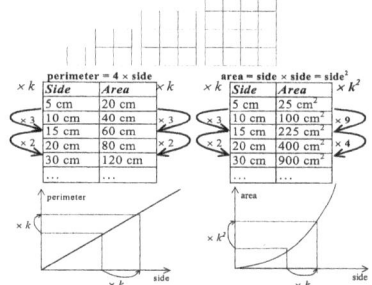

+ **Several application exercises (individual & in dyads):**
e.g. *Tiny's parents bought 25 m^2 of floor tiles. They needed 19 m^2 for the living room. Tiny's bedroom is only half as long and half as wide. Are there enough tiles left to put a new floor in her bedroom?*

132   Remedying the illusion of linearity

Lesson 6-7 : Cubic growth of volume

Goals: Understand and apply the principle that if an object is enlarged or reduced k times, the volume of that object enlarges k^3 times (and the area enlarges k^2 times).

Example: Small group work: *Tommy wants to make a doghouse, following the model below. What's the area of all components? How much wood should he approximately order?*
His uncle has a much larger dog. If he would construct exactly the same doghouse, but twice as large, how much wood would he need?
Calculate the volume of the small doghouse, and then estimate the volume of the large doghouse. How much larger is it? (Try to explain using a simpler model like a cube)

+ **Classroom discussion** on different group solutions, exploring possible approaches and solutions.

Afterwards: Class discussion investigating the effect of enlargements and reductions of an object on their area and volume
- by means of multiple representations (formula, table, drawing, graph)
- for a diversity of objects (cubes, rectangular prisms, cylinders, spheres, …)
- example:

+ **Several application exercises (individual & in dyads)**
e.g., *An apple grower sells two sizes of apples: The first one has an average diameter of 6 cm and costs 10 eurocent and the second one has an average diameter of 9 cm and costs 20 eurocent.*
Compare both sizes of the apples. What is the enlargement factor (k)?
The apples have a similar shape. How much more weighs a big apple compared to a small apple?
Which apple size is the most economical to make apple sauce?
Another apple grower has other prices for the two kinds of apples: "The apples with an average diameter of 6 cm costs €1/kg, those with an average diameter of 9 cm costs €1,20/kg". Which apple is the most economical now?

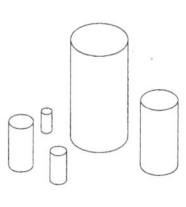

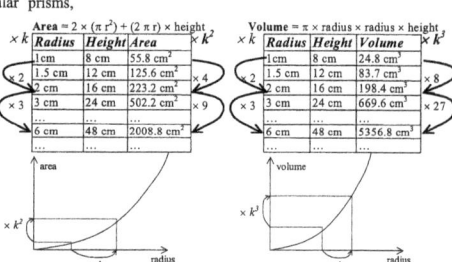

Lesson 8-10 : Integrative project

true height: 15 cm   a gnome weighs 300 grams

Assuming that a gnome is similar to a human being, is it possible than that a gnome with length 15 cm weighs 300 grams?

Gnome	Human
15 cm – (×12)→	180 cm
300 g – (×12³=1728)→	518 400 g (impossible!)
(better!) **40.6 g** ← (:12³=1728) –	70 000 g

Small group work: *Let us assume that a gnome is similar to a human being, but 12 times smaller. Answer the following questions about the world of gnomes, using knowledge about your own world. Collect additional information when necessary.*

- *How long is the belt of a gnome?*
- *What is the area of the sole of a gnome shoe?*
- *How much coffee is there in a cup for gnomes?*
- *How much fabric do you need to make a skirt for a woman gnome?*
- *How much water does a gnome need to take a bath?*

Chapter 8

Improving procedural transfer in mathematics with interactive animations

Peter Gerjets, Katharina Scheiter, and Richard Catrambone

1 Introduction

Understanding mathematical solution procedures is a necessary prerequisite in order to be able not to solve only familiar problems, but also to work on novel problems requiring an adaptation of known solution procedures. However, it has been noted that students often face severe difficulties in understanding solution procedures even when they have received elaborated instructional explanations of the individual solution steps. This may result from the fact that the solution steps are often conveyed in a rather abstract way so that learners experience difficulties in imagining which changes in the problem state are achieved by applying a specific solution step to a problem.

The use of multimedia learning environments may offer ways to overcome these difficulties that can hardly be achieved by traditional instructional means (Mayer, 2001). In multimedia learning environments information presentation can be accomplished by using different representational formats (textual and pictorial) which may be processed in different sensory channels (auditory and visual). Additionally, information presentation is not restricted to static displays (e.g., diagrams, pictures, written text), but the representations used can involve changes over time (e.g., dynamic visualizations, spoken text).

In the current chapter we are interested in the effects of augmenting a purely text-based hypertext environment called HYPERCOMB by different kinds of visualizations. HYPERCOMB teaches how to calculate the probability of complex events. Problems of calculating complex event probabilities are related to situations where the probability of selecting a particular configuration of elements randomly out of a set of elements has to be determined (cf. Figure 1).

The main instructional principle underlying HYPERCOMB is the use of worked-out examples for conveying knowledge on different problem categories. Research over the last 20 years has shown that worked-out examples are of great help for knowledge acquisition in particular in well-structured domains like mathematics, physics, or programming (Atkinson, Derry, Renkl, & Wortham, 2000). However, although we have identified a way of designing worked-out examples that boosts performance compared to conventionally designed examples (Gerjets, Scheiter, & Catrambone, 2004) there is still space left for improvements. We assumed that this space might be claimed by the benefits achieved through the use of visualizations.

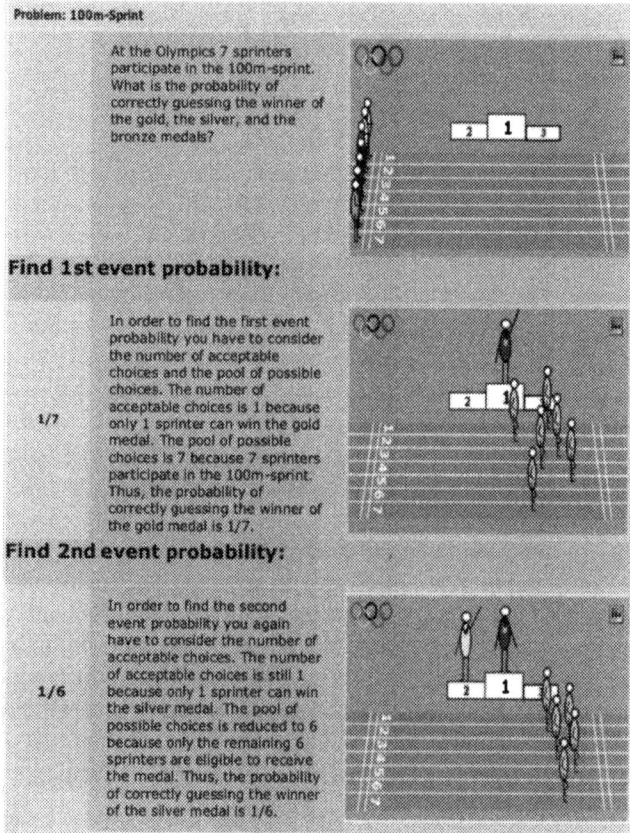

Fig. 1. Screenshot of a worked-out example with external visualization.

According to the multimedia principle (Mayer, 2001) augmenting textual learning materials by static pictures or dynamic visualizations (i.e., animations) helps to promote learners' understanding of instructions. With regard to the acquisition of problem-solving knowledge visualizations of worked-out examples may first help learners to understand the situation described in the problem statement (i.e., the initial problem state) and thus to correctly represent its meaning in a situation model (Nathan, Kintsch, & Young, 1992). Second, visualizations of the solution steps may promote an understanding of changes with regard to the initial problem state that are achieved by applying a solution step to a problem. Visualizing worked-out examples can be done by presenting either static pictures, animations, or an instruction to mentally imagine the examples' contents.

Static pictures. Static pictorial representations are known to foster the immediate and delayed retention of facts contained in the accompanying text (cf. for a review Levin, Anglin, & Carney, 1987). Moreover, with regard to the acquisition of problem-solving knowledge in domains like mathematics and physics the added value of abstract diagrammatic and graphical representations has been acknowledged (e.g., Shah & Hoeffner, 2002). These types of visualizations are said to be computationally effective in that they facilitate specific inferential processes needed for some learning tasks (Larkin & Simon, 1987). However, there is no research to our knowing on whether concrete pictures that depict a problem statement and its associated solution procedure promote the acquisition of problem-solving knowledge. Representing the problem statement in a picture might help to understand which object features and interrelations are relevant to the solution of the problem. For instance, in the sprinter example seven sprinters on the racetrack are depicted out of which three can win the gold, silver, and the bronze medal – represented by the pedestal. Additionally visualizing the solution steps may support learners in inferring which change is achieved by applying a solution procedure when they compare the new problem state to the previous one. For instance, comparing the picture illustrating the second solution step to the one of the first step helps to clarify the fact that only six sprinters are eligible for guessing the winner of the silver medal, because one sprinter has already been assigned to the gold medal in the first solution step and thus already stands on the pedestal.

Animations. An animation is "any application which generates a series of frames, so that each frame appears as an alteration of the previous one, and where the sequence of frames is determined either by the designer or the user" (Bétrancourt & Tversky, 2000, p. 313). Thus, animations do not only depict the current status of objects; rather they additionally deliver information concerning changes of objects and of their position over time (motion) as well as information concerning the direction of these changes (trajectory, Rieber, 1990). Several findings suggest that animations can be used successfully for delivering abstract contents like mathematical rules, Newton's laws, or computer algorithms (Baek & Layne, 1988; Byrne, Catrambone & Stasko, 1999; Catrambone & Seay, 2002; Rieber, 1990). With respect to conveying problem-solving knowledge the visual-spatial properties of the visualization may be used to deliver information on the current problem state and its relevant structural features. Moreover, the changes over time that can be depicted in an animation may be used to reflect the changes in problem states that result from applying a solution step to a specific problem state of the example – without the need to compare multiple representations as it is necessary when learning from static pictures.

However, learning from animations is known to impose certain requirements onto the learners that they may have difficulty to meet (Bétrancourt & Tversky, 2000). Pane, Corbett, and John (1996) have demonstrated that learners often fail to use animations to a sufficient extent and thus miss important information. The results of Lowe (1999) additionally suggest that learners have trouble focusing on the most relevant parts of an animation and are often distracted by salient, but irrelevant details. Furthermore, due to the dynamic changes of the display the information that has to be remembered can only be viewed for a limited amount of time and may therefore have vanished before learners have identified it. Finally, dynamic visualizations may lead to an overly passive information processing and prevent learners from performing effortful cognitive processes required for a deeper understanding (Palmiter & Elkerton, 1993). In line with Salomon's principle of least effort (Salomon, 1984) learners may refrain from deeply processing the contents of an animation and passively watch it as an ongoing movie.

Imagery. To circumvent the problem of passive information processing we implemented a third visualization condition in our experiment in which we instructed learners to imagine the contents of a text-based worked-out example. That is, learners did not receive any pictorial representations at all; rather, they were told to construct their own visualizations. Hodes (1992) compared the effectiveness of imagery instructions and instructional visuals for fact recall and understanding. Both instructional methods were helpful in inducing an imagery strategy and in improving posttest performance; however, for some performance measures achievements due to presenting external visuals were larger than for the imagery instructions. Ginns, Chandler, and Sweller (2003) showed that imagining (vs. studying text-based materials) was helpful only for learners who possessed sufficiently high prior knowledge in the domain. The authors explained this finding by assuming that "to successfully imagine a procedure or a concept, all of the relevant elements must be processed simultaneously in working memory. That may be possible only after a schema had been constructed" (p. 231).
Comparing the three different visualization methods (static pictures, animations, and imagery) to each other yields insights on specific promises as well as on drawbacks associated with these methods. The trade-off between these promises and drawbacks may determine learning outcomes (Table 1). Learning from *static pictures* may engage learners in a more active way, because they have to compare multiple visualizations in order to understand the to-be-learned solution procedures. As this information is permanently visible these comparisons may be conducted without overloading the cognitive system. However, learners may make wrong inferences and they may

miss important information so that their internal representation of the solution procedures may be incorrect as well as incomplete. Moreover, because the external representations cannot be modified by a learner they are not adapted to his or her preferences or prior knowledge level. *Dynamic pictures* may on the other hand reduce learner activity and induce a rather passive style of processing. The cognitive demands imposed by the need to extract the relevant information from a changing display and to memorize this information may be rather high. Unless animations are highly interactive they do not allow for any adaptation to a learner's preferences or prior knowledge. However, an advantage of dynamic visualizations of solution steps is that all the information that is needed to understand problem states and their changes is in principle contained in the representation and thus it is correct as well as complete. Finally, *imagery instructions* should foster learner activity in an optimal way; however, the need to envision all information may at the same time require rather demanding processes (Ginns et al., 2003). There is also the danger that learners may miss important information or that they make incorrect inferences. A possible advantage of mental imagery is that because it is based on self-generated images, these images are adapted to a learner's preferences and prior knowledge level.

Table 1. Promises (+) and drawbacks (-) of visualization methods

	Static pictures	Dynamic pictures	Imagery
Learner activity	+	-	+
Cognitive load	+	-	-
Correctness / completeness	-	+	-
Adaptation to learner preferences / knowledge	-	-	+

These trade-offs between possible promises and drawbacks were investigated in the experiment outlined in the remainder of the chapter.

2 Experiment

2.1 Method

Participants. Participants were 124 students (88 female, 36 male) of the University of Tuebingen, Germany, who participated for either course credit or payment. One subject in the static-pictures condition had to be excluded from the analysis, because the person's learning time was more than four standard deviations above the mean learning time in this condition. Average age was 23.6 years. Most of the subjects were familiar with the domain of probability theory and were experienced computer users.

Materials and procedure. HYPERCOMB consisted of a technical instruction, a short introduction to the domain, an example-based learning phase and a subsequent test phase. Before starting with the experiment participants filled in a multiple-choice questionnaire with eleven questions on important concepts and definitions from the field of probability theory. This questionnaire was used to measure participants' prior knowledge. In the first part of HYPERCOMB learners were given a short technical introduction to the system and to the experiment. Consequently, the basic notion of random experiments and the general rationale behind calculating the probability of outcomes were explained in a short introduction to the domain. In the subsequent example-based learning phase learners had to acquire knowledge on four different problem categories, whereby each category was explained by means of two worked-out examples. Depending on the experimental condition subjects additionally received an imagery instruction or they could retrieve static pictures or dynamic visualizations that augmented the worked-out examples. Subjects were not forced to process these visualizations; rather, they had to select them by clicking on a button in order to view them. The visualizations depicted the contents of the worked-out examples in a concrete way (cf. Figure 1). For every worked-out example there was always one visualization of the problem statement and one of every worked-out solution step. Following the coherence principle (Mayer, 2001) the visualizations were kept as simple as possible and were not cluttered with any irrelevant details. Participants could decide by themselves when to start working on the test problems. The instructional materials were no longer available during problem solving. For the eleven test problems we varied the transfer distance with respect to the worked-out examples by presenting isomorphic as well as novel problems. Isomorphic test problems differed from the instructional examples only with regard to their surface features. Novel test problems were constructed in a way that two complex-event probabilities had to be considered whose outcomes had to be multiplied in order to calculate the required probability.

Design and dependent measures. Subjects learned in one of four instructional conditions. In the text-only condition only the written worked-out examples were available. In the imagery condition learners were additionally told to mentally imagine the contents as vividly and with as many details as possible. Mental imagery was trained at the beginning of the experiment by instructing learners to imagine the contents of a short text passage describing a traffic situation involving multiple cars which approach a crossing from different directions. Moreover, they were constantly reminded to use imagery in the example-based learning phase by a sticker "imagine the situation" attached to the computer screen. In the pictures condition static visualizations could be retrieved for each component of the worked-out examples, whereas in the animation condition clicking the play-button for any of the example components resulted in the presentation of a dynamic visualization. For instance, in the sprinter animation the sprinters were first entering the racetrack (problem statement) and were then running across the racetrack. The visualization of the solution steps always depicted one sprinter passing the finishing line and ascending the pedestal. As static pictures we always used the last frame of the animations (cf. Figure 1) that depicted the problem state resulting from the application of the respective solution step.

As dependent measures we registered problem-solving performance for isomorphic and novel test problems and the time spent on learning (learning time).

2.2 Results

Overall analyses. Prior knowledge was comparable across all four instructional conditions. Moreover, it did not moderate the effects reported in this chapter. In a first step we analyzed problem-solving performance and learning time across all four conditions by means of one-factorial ANOVAs. Performance on isomorphic problems (Figure 2, left) varied slightly as a function of instructional condition ($F(3,119) = 2.32$; $MSE = 769.06$; $p < .10$), while performance on novel problems (Figure 2, right) was left unaffected by the experimental manipulation ($F < 1$). Learning time (Figure 3) increased rather naturally with the more instructional materials being available for processing ($F(3,119) = 6.21$; $MSE = 48052.96$; $p = .001$).

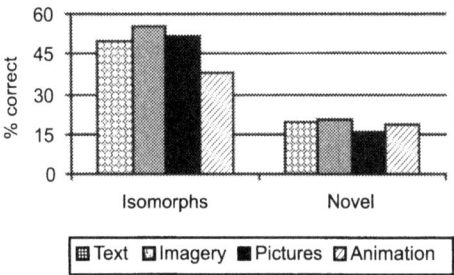

Fig. 2. Problem-solving performance (in % correct) for isomorphic (left) and novel problems (right) as a function of instructional condition.

Thus, at first sight it seems that although presenting external visualizations increased the time learners devoted for learning, these increases in learning time were not accompanied by respective gains in performance. On the contrary, performance for isomorphic problems was worst in the animation condition. However, it is not clear whether the finding that problem-solving performance was only slightly affected by variations of the instructional materials is due to the ineffectiveness of these variations or whether it is due to the fact that learners did not sufficiently use the external visualizations. To address this question we analyzed the frequency by which learners retrieved these visualizations in a next step.

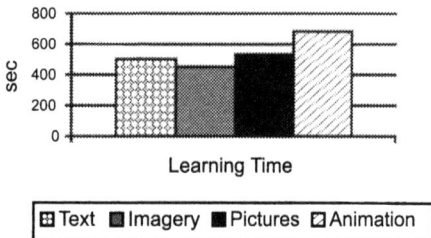

Fig. 3. Learning time (in sec) as a function of instructional condition.

Utilization of external visualizations. For every participant it was possible to determine how often (s)he had retrieved visualizations. Though there were a total of 31 visualizations available in each of the conditions, these visualizations were seldom retrieved (see Figure 4). The figure displays the number of participants using a specific number of visualizations in each of the two conditions. For instance, nine participants in the animation condition and 11 participants in the static pictures condition used only one or two visualizations. On average, static pictures were viewed 7.0 times, animations 10.3 times. Thus, less than one quarter of the available static pictures and only one third of the animations were used for learning. For the further course of the statistical analyses a median split within each of the two conditions was conducted to distinguish between learners who sparsely used external visualizations and those who made frequent use of the representations. In the static pictures condition the median for visualization retrieval was $Mdn = 3$, with 18 participants being classified as sparse users and 12 as frequent users. In the animation condition the median was

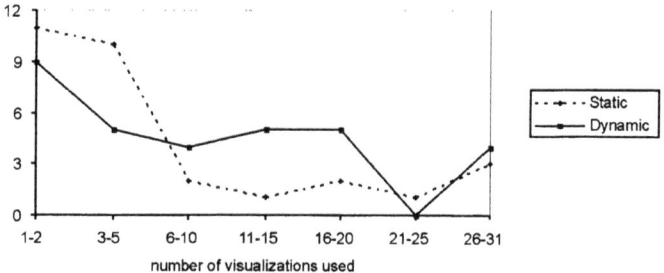

Fig. 4. Number of participants using external visualizations and frequency of use in the static and in the dynamic visualization condition.

$Mdn = 9$ with 17 participants classified as sparse users and 15 as frequent users of visualizations. The resulting variable was used as a second factor in an ANOVA (instructional condition x visualization utilization).

Analyzing performance in the conditions with external visualizations by means of this ANOVA revealed no significant effects for performance on novel problems (instructional condition: $F < 1$; information utilization: $F(1,58) = 1.30$; $MSE = 474.28$; $p > .20$) nor interactions ($F(1,58) = 1.12$; $MSE = 474.28$; $p > .20$). However, for performance on isomorphic test problems (Figure 5) there were significant main effects of external visualization and visualization utilization. Learners showed a superior performance when learning from static pictures ($F(1,58) = 5.56$; $MSE = 743.58$; $p < .05$). Furthermore, learners who made use of the visualizations more frequently tended to outperform those who only used them sparsely ($F(1,58) = 3.08$; $MSE = 743.58$; $p < .10$). Finally, there was a significant interaction ($F(1,58) =7.20$; $MSE = 743.58$; $p < .01$) indicating that – when frequently used – static pictures were superior to animations ($t(25) = 3.44$; $p < .01$), while there were no differences when the visualizations were retrieved only sparsely ($t(33) = -0.24$; $p > .80$).

Figure 5 additionally displays the performance in the text-only condition as a baseline. Contrasting the various conditions with this baseline indicated that the frequent use of static pictures was associated with performance improvements, while frequently using animations correlates with worse performance. Both comparisons yielded differences that were significant at the .05 level.

Furthermore, analyzing the learning times (Figure 6) revealed that this deterioration in performance due to frequently using animations was accompanied by an increase in time learners needed to study the instructional materials. Learning times were longer for students in the animation condition than in the static pictures condition ($F(1,58) = 7.97$; $MSE = 44333.61$; $p < .01$) and increased dramatically with a frequent use of visualizations ($F(1,58) = 18.02$; $MSE = 44333.61$; $p < .001$). Moreover, a significant interaction ($F(1,58) = 8.78$; $MSE = 44333.61$; $p < .01$) revealed that frequently using static pictures compared to retrieving them only sparsely had no impact on learning time ($t(33) = 0.11$; $p > .90$), while the frequent use of animations almost doubled the time spent with the instructional materials ($t(25) = -3.95$; $p = .001$).

To sum up, using static pictures frequently did not increase learning time demands and nevertheless improved performance. On the contrary, frequently using animations was rather harmful in that it required more learning time and did not yield any performance improvements. On the contrary, performance even worsened compared to the text-only condition. Therefore, while concrete visualizations of the contents of the worked-out examples proved beneficial for learning, the dynamics contained in the animations

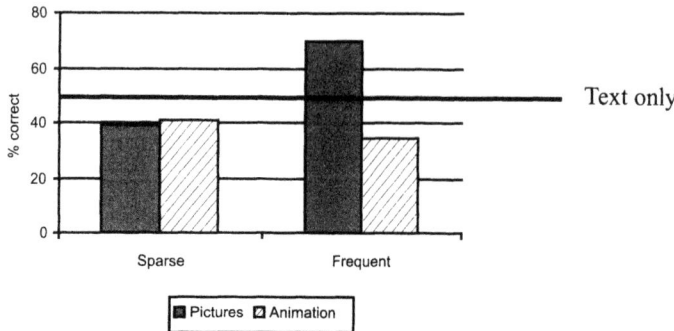

Fig. 5. Performance on isomorphic problems (in % correct) as a function of external visualization and visualization utilization.

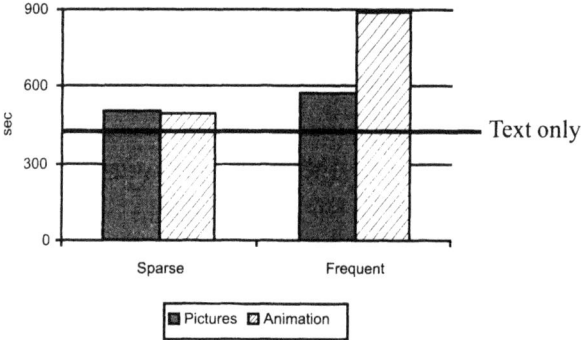

Fig. 6. Learning time (in sec) as a function of external visualization and visualization utilization.

were unnecessary or even harmful. If complex dynamic visualizations cannot be recommended for learning, the question arises whether there is a need for external visualizations at all. That is, if already simple visualizations like static pictures of the content help to achieve an understanding of the principles, then maybe learners are able to generate these images by themselves. The question whether external visualizations are more helpful than the instruction to imagine the contents of the worked-out examples was addressed in the last analysis.

The benefits of imagery compared to external visualizations. In this final section we compared the imagery condition to the two external-visualization conditions whereby in the latter two we further distinguished between sparse and frequent use of visualizations. Because none of the analyses revealed any effects for performance on novel problems we will report the results for isomorphic problems only.

The imagery condition had no impact on performance for isomorphic problems when compared to the group of learners who had frequently used static pictures ($t(42) = 1.42$; $p > .10$); whereas imagery improved performance slightly compared to a sparse use of static pictures ($t(48) = -1.96$; $p < .10$).

Using animations frequently was worse than receiving an imagery instruction only ($t(45) = -2.51$; $p < .05$), while there were smaller differences between the sparsely use of animations and the latter condition ($t(47) = -1.70$; $p < .10$). With regard to learning time, the frequent use of external visualizations increased the time spent studying the instructional materials compared to the imagery instruction (imagery vs. frequent picture use: ($t(42) = 2.30$; $p < .05$; imagery vs. frequent animation use: $t(45) = 7.32$; $p < .001$), whereas the sparse use did not yield any longer learning times (imagery vs. sparse picture use: $t(48) = 0.88$; $p > .30$; imagery vs. sparse animation use: $t(47) = 0.71$; $p > .40$). Thus, imagining the contents of the worked-out examples was as effective as viewing static pictures that depicted these contents and more efficient because it required less time for learning. Moreover, mental imagery was slightly more effective than receiving dynamic visualizations and was again accompanied by less learning time.

3 Conclusions

In this chapter we presented evidence for the differential effectiveness of external and internal visualizations for cognitive skill acquisition. Our results support the assumption that learners might benefit from a concrete visualization of problem states that is tied to the cover stories of worked-out examples. However, while we were able to show that a frequent use of static pictures fostered performance at least on isomorphic problems, including dynamics in the external visualizations worsened performance. The initial idea of using animations had been that the dynamics of an animation might be used to depict information on changes in problem states that occur due to applying a specific solution step. However, it seems that representing these changes explicitly was more harming than helpful in that it may even have distracted learners. These results are in line with prior findings (Lowe, 1999; Pane et al., 1996) showing that learners are often overwhelmed by the number of details they need to identify, select, and to remember in a limited period of time (i.e., while the information is present on the changing display) when learning from animations.

In our current research we thus pursue the idea of further reducing the cognitive demands imposed by animations by using abstract rather than concrete dynamic visualizations of the worked-out examples. These abstract animations are characterized by the fact that the visualizations of all examples share a common representation of objects and of the relevant relations among them. That is, irrespective of an example's cover story objects like the sprinters are represented by marbles which are selected from an urn.

This common representation across examples should help learners to focus on the structural similarities and differences between the examples while being able to ignore their surface features. Thus, there is not only less information that needs to be processed in total; moreover, the ratio between relevant and irrelevant information is improved compared to the concrete animations investigated in the current chapter. Thus, this simplified representation should be less demanding and should leave free cognitive resources in order to cope with the dynamics of the animation.

Additionally, we want to continue our work based on the promising results with regard to cognitive skill acquisition from static pictures and imagery. First, we would like to investigate means of improving learners' use of static pictures. In particular, we aim at testing the effectiveness of *retrieval prompts* which guide learners to use static pictures more often. In prior studies we were able to demonstrate that prompting learners to retrieve profitable information units is an effective means to foster problem-solving performance in particular for students with low prior knowledge (Gerjets, Scheiter, & Schuh, 2005). Second, once static pictures have been retrieved to a sufficient extent, their processing should be supported by additional instructional guidance. In particular, learners may receive *instructions to compare multiple static pictures* to enable them to extract changes in problem states that have occurred due to applying a solution step more easily. Finally, we are also convinced that the use of imagery might be further improved. In the current experiment learners were instructed to use imagery only at the beginning of the experiment and the reminder during the learning phase could be easily overlooked. Thus, we would like to investigate the use of computer-based prompts that frequently remind learners to envision the examples' contents. All three instructional devices (retrieval prompts, comparison instruction, and imagery prompts) aim at increasing the time learners devote for studying the instructional materials as well as at improving the quality of processing the worked-out examples.

References

Atkinson, R. K., Derry, S. A., Renkl, A., & Wortham, D. (2000). Learning from examples: Instructional principles from the worked examples research. *Review of Educational Research, 70*, 181-214.

Baek, Y. K., & Layne, B. H. (1988). Color, graphics, and animation in a computer-assisted learning tutorial lesson. *Journal of Computer-Based Instruction, 15*, 131-135.

Bétrancourt, M., & Tversky, B. (2000). Effect of computer animation on users' performance: A review. *Le Travail Humain, 63*, 311-329.

Byrne, M. D., Catrambone, R., & Stasko, J. T. (1999). Evaluating animations as student aids in learning computer algorithms. *Computers & Education, 33*, 253-278.

Catrambone, R., & Seay, F. A. (2002). Using animations to help students learn computer algorithms. *Human Factors, 44*, 495-511.

Gerjets, P., Scheiter, K., & Catrambone, R. (2004). Designing instructional examples to reduce intrinsic cognitive load: Molar versus modular presentation of solution procedures. *Instructional Science, 32*, 33-58.

Gerjets, P., Scheiter, K., & Schuh, J. (2005). Instruktionale Unterstützung beim Fertigkeitserwerb aus Beispielen in hypertextbasierten Lernumgebungen [Instructional support for skill acquisition from examples in hypermedia-based learning environments]. *Zeitschrift für Pädagogische Psychologie, 19*, 25-38.

Ginns, P., Chandler, P., & Sweller, J. (2003). When imagining information is effective. *Contemporary Educational Psychology, 28*, 229-251.

Hodes, C. L. (1992). The effectiveness of mental imagery and visual illustrations: A comparison of two instructional variables. *Journal of Research and Development in Education, 26*, 46-56.

Larkin, J. H., & Simon, H. A. (1987). Why a diagram is (sometimes) worth ten thousand words. *Cognitive Science, 11*, 65-99.

Levin, J. R., Anglin, G. L., & Carney, R. N (1987). Validating functions of pictures in prose. In D. M. Willows & H. A. Houghton (Eds.), *The psychology of illustration: Vol. 1. Basic research* (pp. 51-86). New York: Springer.

Lowe, R. K. (1999). Extracting information from an animation during complex visual learning. *European Journal of Psychology of Education, 14*, 225-244.

Mayer, R. E. (2001). *Multimedia learning*. Cambridge: Cambridge University Press.

Nathan, M. J., Kintsch, W., & Young, E. (1992). A theory of algebra-word-problem comprehension and its implications for the design of learning environments. *Cognition and Instruction, 9*, 329-389.

Palmiter, S., & Elkerton, J. (1993). Animated demonstrations for learning procedural computer-based tasks. *Human-Computer Interaction, 8*, 193-216.

Pane, J. F., Corbett, A. T., & John, B. E. (1996). Assessing dynamics in computer-based instruction. In M. J. Tauber (Ed.), *Proceedings of the ACM Conference on Human Factors in Computing Systems* (pp. 797-804). Vancouver: ACM.

Rieber, L. P. (1990). Animation in computer-based instruction. *Educational Technology Research & Development, 38*, 77-86.

Salomon, G. (1984). Television is "easy" and print is "tough": The differential investment of mental effort in learning as a function of perceptions and attributions. *Journal of Educational Psychology, 76*, 647-658.

Shah, P., & Hoeffner, J. (2002). Review of graph comprehension research: Implications for instruction. *Educational Psychology Review, 14*, 47-69.

Chapter 9

Teaching percentages in the primary school: A four country comparative study

Fien Depaepe, Erik De Corte, Peter Op 't Eynde, and Lieven Verschaffel

1 Introduction

During the last decade international comparative research on mathematics education has flourished, as is exemplified by a number of large-scale studies. TIMSS (Third International Mathematics and Science Study) and PISA (Programme for International Students Assessment) represent a first series of comparative studies. TIMSS investigated students' mathematical and scientific competence in 41 countries all over the world (Beaton, Mullis, Martin, Gonzales, Kelly, & Smith, 1996). In 1999 there was a replication study in 38 countries (Mullis, Martin, Gonzales, Gregory, Garden, O'Connor, Chrostowski, & Smith, 2000). PISA investigates the degree to which students' can apply their knowledge in everyday situations (OECD, 2003).

These large-scale studies that were based on an extensive dataset have certainly contributed to a better understanding of mathematics education at a worldwide level. However, there are still important gaps in this kind of large-scale investigations. First of all, these studies mainly use quantitative methods resulting in a ranking of students' mathematical performances across the participating countries. However, such an approach does not lead to a deep understanding of the interaction patterns and culture of the classroom. Therefore, these studies insufficiently succeed in explaining the variety in students' performances across different educational cultures (Leung, 2001). Moreover, large-scale quantitative studies are dominated by the view that curriculum effects in a number of countries can be compared by means of administering a relatively simple test. Such an approach implies that the curriculum is perceived as fixed across different countries, without taking account its interpretation by teachers and students (Keitel & Kilpatrick, 1999).

The TIMSS video project belongs to a second series of comparative studies in mathematics education. Different from previous comparative research is that the TIMSS video project made use of an "innovative"

Fien Depaepe is research assistant of the National Fund for Scientific Research – Flanders.

methodology by comparing video recordings of mathematics and science lessons. This study aimed at identifying characteristics of classroom practices that foster students' performances (Stigler & Hiebert, 1998). In 1995, the first video study compared mathematics education in three economically comparable countries: Germany, Japan, and the United States. The videotapes were analysed according to three main categories: the nature of the tasks, the nature of students' work, and the nature of the instructional practices (Stigler, Gonzales, Kawanaka, Knoll, & Serrano, 1999; Stigler & Hiebert, 1997). In the second video study, in 1999, seven countries were involved: Australia, Czech Republic, Hong Kong, Japan, the Netherlands, Switzerland, and the United States (TIMSS Video Mathematics Research Group, 2003).

Notwithstanding the undeniable surplus value of the TIMSS video project, it can be criticized for several reasons. First, although the samples in these studies are very large, and also representative for the participating countries, the observation of the lessons is restricted to only one lesson per teacher/class. Such research makes it impossible to investigate how certain mathematical concepts are elaborated over a sequence of lessons. Furthermore, there is a lack of correspondence between the analysed mathematical domains and themes within the different countries that are involved in the TIMSS video project, which hinders a faithful comparison. Finally, large-scale comparative studies seem to result in a reduction of variation in mathematics education instead of an exchange of "good practices". The focus is competitive rather than descriptive. According to Clarke (2003), "attempts at measurement of student mathematics achievement internationally using a single metric, employing a single instrument, can be interpreted as an attempt at the globalisation of mathematics education: the reduction of mathematics education in all countries to a single common denominator. Globalisation seeks to minimise international differences (whether by consensus or imposition) whereas internationalisation seeks to celebrate both the similarities and the differences and to learn from them" (p. 147-148). It is evident, and good too, that all countries use other methods to teach mathematics. For example, one country will emphasise more the understanding and proficiency in mathematical proof, while another attaches greater priority to an understanding of mathematical procedures and proficiency to use them in everyday practical situations. The aim of comparative research in mathematics education should be one of mutually enriching for each society, where one community can learn from the differences and similarities within other communities, without a globalisation of the "Western" thoughts. In fact, the spirit should be more cooperative, than competitive.

This chapter presents a small-scale videobased, comparative study of the teaching of percentages in four European countries which is part of the METE-project (*M*athematics *E*ducation *T*raditions in *E*urope). This project has made an attempt to partly overcome the above mentioned shortcomings of the previous studies, for instance, by comparing quantitatively as well as qualitatively a sequence of lessons about the same mathematical topic. The project aims at a comparison of mathematics education in the upper primary (grades 5 and 6) and the lower secondary school (grades 7 and 8) in Flanders, England, Hungary and Spain. Major criteria for the selection of these countries were the diverse geographical location in Europe, their different socio-economical status, and their various performances on large-scale studies, such as TIMSS and PISA. In each country sequences of four or five lessons relating to several topics of the mathematics curriculum were videotaped in the same classroom: percentages and polygons in the upper primary school (age 10-12), and polygons and linear equations in the lower secondary school (age 12-14).

In this chapter, we will restrict ourselves to a discussion of the percentage part of this comparative study. The next section describes a perspective on the teaching of percentages that was derived from the literature on mathematics education in general and the teaching of percentage in particular, and that relates to its objectives, conceptual aspects, and didactic tools. In the third section, the aims and methodology of the METE-project – and more specifically the percentage part – is outlined. The fourth section situates the observed lessons within their specific sociocultural context. The main outcomes of the study are presented in the fifth section. We conclude by discussing some principal ideas and the constraints of our approach.

2 A perspective on the teaching of percentages

The available research relating to the teaching of percentages is rather restricted. Nevertheless we have made an attempt to frame the observed lesson series in the four countries within a perspective on the teaching of percentages that is derived from the recent literature, and that draws inspiration from a realistic view on mathematics education. In this section, this perspective will be outlined focusing on the objectives of percentage instruction, conceptual aspects of percentages, and some didactic tools used in teaching percentages.

2.1 Objectives

The instruction of percentages serves different goals, namely computational, conceptual, and applicational goals. First, attention should be paid to computational goals (Van den Heuvel-Panhuizen, 1994). In other words, students should master one (ore more) procedure(s) to compute percentages. The attainment of this objective results in the development of procedural knowledge. Although this is an important goal, it is not the only objective to focus on. Indeed, there is some criticism on the teaching of percentages that "is primarily focused on procedures and recall instead of getting a real understanding of percentage" (Van den Heuvel-Panhuizen, 1994, p. 350).

Therefore, a second important goal is students' development of a deep understanding of the concept "percentage" (Van den Heuvel-Panhuizen, 1994). They need to acquire insight in the key features of percentages so that meaningful learning is realised. To meet this objective the acquisition of a good and consistent conceptual knowledge system is required.

Finally, a third goal is the development of skills to apply percentages in all kind of (meaningful) situations. Students should acquire adaptive expertise allowing them to apply procedures flexibly to new, as well as familiar tasks, and to solve percentage problems in a variety of ways. Important for the development of adaptive expertise is the acquisition of a well-structured knowledge base wherein the concept of percentages is related to prior knowledge and to other mathematical entities. This also requires that students' procedural (objective 1) and conceptual (objective 2) knowledge get interconnected (Baroody, 2003).

In the next section, we will describe some characteristics of percentages that should be addressed in the classroom to enable students to acquire a deep understanding of percentages.

2.2 Conceptual aspects of percentages

Through solving appropriate tasks and problems students should discover that a percentage expresses a relation between two numbers or quantities by means of a ratio. They should become aware that percentages are always related to something and have, therefore, no meaning without taking into account to what they refer (Van den Heuvel-Panhuizen, 1994). This characteristic of percentages is illustrated by the following two problems. "You need 50% correct answers to succeed. Loes solved 14 tasks wrongly. What do you think? Can we congratulate Loes or not?". Through such a problem students can experience that a percentage has no meaning if the number to which it is referring, is missing. Consequently, no judgement can be made about Loes' performance. A similar problem is: "Two shops are having a sale. In the first shop one can get a discount of 25%, and in the other one the discount is 40%. Both shops have put up a big poster in the shop window. The manner in which the two shops advertise their discount could convey the suggestion that the two shops do not sell wares of the same quality. In which of the two shops can you get the best buys? Explain your answer." (Van den Heuvel-Panhuizen, 1994, p. 356-357). This last problem illustrates that two percentages cannot be compared without taken into account to what they refer. They have no absolute meaning, but are only used to express the relation between two numbers. So, not enough information is given to answer the problem.

A second characteristic of percentages is that they describe a fixed situation representing how different kinds of substances are related to each other. This means that the size of the whole has no influence on the percentages of the substances. The following problem illustrates this characteristic: "Black currant jam, which contains 60% of fruit, is sold in large (450g) and small pots (225g). Someone forgot to put the percentage of fruit on the small pot. Fill in this missing information. Explain your strategy for finding this percentage. How many grams of fruit does each pot contain? The large one contains ...? The small one contains ...? Show how you got your answers." (Van den Heuvel-Panhuizen, 1994, p. 357). By means of such examples, students can overcome the (potential) misconception that percentages change linearly with the size of the whole. This problem also illustrates that different learning objectives (see section 2.1) can be realised through one and the same activity; indeed, this problem emphasises computational aspects as well as the conceptual development of percentages.

A third characteristic is that the reduction or adding up of percentages has a non-linear character. For example: a whole plus 20%, plus 30%, is not the same as the same whole plus 50%. In fact, in the first situation, the amount of reference changed after adding up 20%. Parallel with that, the decrease or increase of a part behaves asymmetric if it is expressed by percentages. This characteristic is illustrated by the following problem: "Instead of 25% extra to the small bar [chocolate bar] a discount could have been offered to the extended bar. What percent of discount do you get on the extended bar?" (Van den Heuvel-Panhuizen, 1994, p. 357). This example shows that as a result of the change in the amount of reference, the percentage changes. Applied to the example, the chocolate bar enlarges by 25%; but in the inverse case, the price decreases by 20%. The reason for the asymmetry in adding and removing parts is the fact that the reference amount changes (in the latter case the reference amount is larger). But, the part that was added or removed stayed the same. The next problem deals also with the asymmetric characteristic of percentages: "Two stores compare their prices (10 euro and 20 euro). Dirk van den Broek says: 'You are 100% more expensive than I am'. Albert Hein doesn't agree with that: 'That's not true. Your prices are only 50 percent cheaper'" (Streefland, 1995, p. 61). The students are asked to argue whether the statements of Dirk van den Broek and Albert Hein are true. Another illustration of the asymmetric nature of the increase and decrease of percentages is the following one: "Jochen only receives 50% of the pocket-money of Inge. By how many percent should the mother of Jochen increase his pocket-money in order that he receives as much as Inge?" (Velghe & Vervenne, 2000).

Finally, percentages can be used to describe two different types of situations. First, they can describe the substances of a whole. In that case, they describe the size of a part in relation to the whole (Streefland, 1995). For example, to bake bread you need 73% flour, 25% water, 1% yeast, and

1% butter. Or, those stockings consist of 40% cotton and of 60% synthetic materials. Second, percentages can describe situations about a whole that is increased or decreased with a part (Streefland, 1995). For example, "100 visiting cards including V.A.T. cost €10. What's the price of the visiting cards excluding the V.A.T.?" In real world you also can find a lot of examples in which percentages describe a whole plus or minus a part, for instance, in the case of sales, interest, and so on. From a certain point of view, situations in a "part in relation to a whole"-format are easier to solve than situations in a "whole plus/minus a part"-format. This is due to the fact that a "part in relation to a whole"-situation is static so that it is mostly obvious what equals the whole, thus what equals 100%. To the contrary, increase- and decrease-cases are situations of transformation in which it is not always so clear what equals 100%, since the problem is sometimes formulated from the point of view before transformation, while sometimes it is from the point of view after transformation (Van den Heuvel-Panhuizen & Streefland, 1993).

2.3 Didactic tools

To initiate the teaching of percentages, the teacher can use a lot of everyday situations that are intelligible for students. In fact: "Teaching percentages does not start when the name percentage is mentioned for the first time, but it has its roots in all kinds of 'so-many-out-of-so-many' situations that have been dealt with long before, at least in everyday situations" (Van den Heuvel-Panhuizen, 1994, p. 353-354). Indeed, students already have a lot of informal knowledge, for example concerning "anchor" percentages, such as 25, 50 and 100 percent and their equivalent fractions (Streefland, 1998). Therefore, attention should be paid to the relationship of the formal concept "percentage" to students' informal prior knowledge. For example, a teacher can use newspaper-articles, advertisements, boxes of all kinds of food that involve reference to percentages as a starting point for a whole-class discussion in view of making explicit the meaning that students already have about percentages.

To induce meaningful learning in children, especially to foster adaptive expertise (see section 2.1) strong emphasis should be given to the relationship of the concept percentage to other mathematical entities. Some connections are self-evident, such as with fractions, ratios, decimal numbers, ... (Streefland, 1995). To explain the relation between percentages and those other concepts a variety of materials can be used. For example, a double number line (see Figure 1) is easy to represent the relation between percentages and fractions, and it also makes the calculation of percentages easier (Treffers, Streefland, & de Moor, 1994).

In general, the instruction of percentages can be conceived as progressive mathematisation in which models and concrete materials have an

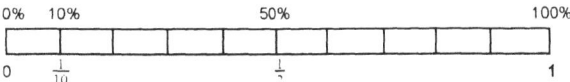

Fig. 1. Example of a double number line.

important role to play. Van den Heuvel-Panhuizen (2003) defines models as "representations of problem situations, which necessarily reflect essential aspects of mathematical concepts and structures that are relevant for the problem situation, but that can have different manifestations" (p. 13). Examples of models are manipulatives, graphs, visual sketches, tables, schemes, metaphors, stories, ... (Middleton & Goepfert, 1996). With respect to percentages, some models are very common to use during the instruction, such as the pizza model or pie chart, the ratio table, and the bar model. The simultaneous use of different models should be encouraged, since it can foster students' conceptual development. Powerful models have at least two important characteristics. First, they are rooted in realistic and imaginable contexts. Second, they are sufficiently flexible to be applied on a more advanced and general level. If models meet those requirements, they can bridge the gap between the informal understanding connected to the "real" and imagined reality, on the one hand, and the understanding of formal systems, on the other hand. While shifting from the informal to a more formal level, models undergo a change from "model of" into "model for": at the beginning of instruction, models are very closely connected to the problem situation, but they gradually evolve to models that are generalised over contexts and can be applied to new and unfamiliar situations. Applied to the bar model, during the instruction of percentages it can shift in function and in form. As a result of the change in function the bar model evolves from a concrete context-connected representation into a more abstract representational model that is applicable to divergent contexts and that also serves as a calculation model. The change in form results into the double number line, which is simpler, easier to use and more flexible. For instance, building up the bar model can start from an exploratory activity in which the students are asked to indicate for different performances how busy the theatre will be. They can do this by colouring the part of the theatre that is occupied and then writing down the percentage of the seats that are occupied. Later on, they can use similar drawings to express what is said in particular statements including percentages. Consequently, this colouring in of theatre halls also becomes a way to express other kinds of situations. In other words, a shift from a "model of" to a "model for" is made (Van den Heuvel-Panhuizen, 2003).

A not so common, but very useful model for the instruction of percentages is the elastic percent meter. This meter is a piece of elastic, which the students divide into ten equal pieces to represent 0% to 100%. The elastic can be enlarged or reduced, just as needed according to the situation that should be solved. Different percent meters with different lengths can be made. The right percent meter should be chosen as a function of the size of the whole that is used in the problem situation (Velghe & Vervenne, 2000). The elastic percent meter is a model that can be used when percentages are introduced for the first time to students. It fosters their understanding of different percentage situations, and they can use that instrument to read off rapidly a certain percentage, without any hard calculations (Abels, 1991). The elastic percent meter is useful for situations in a "part in relation to a whole"-format, but also in decrease- and increase-situations (Bokhove & de Moor, 1993). After some time the connection can be made between the elastic percent meter and the bar model.

Another model that can foster students' conceptual development of percentages is the "slide-slip" (see Figure 2). It consists of a paper slip that is divided into two parts: a white part and a coloured part. Through a vista window cut out of a paper, one can see that slip, which can be moved from one side to the other. The vista window represents a percentage meter and can be combined with a double number line. While sliding the slip from one side to the other, the coloured part is moving from 0 to 100 percent. The slide-slip is a dynamic model since it can be used in many situations, to represent an increase as well as a decrease of percentages, dependent on the context.

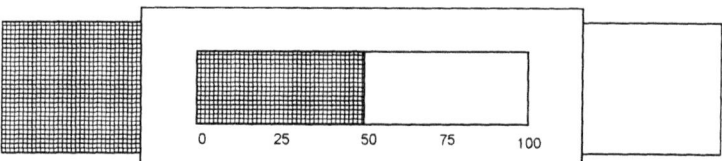

Fig. 2. *Illustration of a slide-slip.*

Using the slide-slip during percentage instruction the teacher can connect new knowledge with the informal prior knowledge students acquired in situations in or out of school. The slide-slip also helps the students to estimate and calculate percentages; for instance, the model fosters the estimation of the percentage that is left or is already used up (e.g., with respect to a battery that begins to empty). Moreover, it evokes the use of different and flexible strategies to solve percentage problems. For example, to calculate 45% of 1200, one can calculate 1%, which is 12, and multiply the result by 45, which equals 540. Another way to solve this task using the slide-slip is to start with the calculation of 50%; when the coloured part is at the half of the vista window. The overestimation can be counterbalanced by a reduction of 5%. Another strategy is to relate 45% to 10%, in a way that 40% is four times 10%, and 5% is half of 10%. Finally, the slide-slip can promote students' insight in the relationship between percentages and other mathematical entities, such as fractions and decimal numbers. Some numbers used in the contexts of percentage problems evoke the use of fractions (e.g., students will often express 50% or 75% as $^1/_2$ or $^3/_4$) (Faes, 1999).

3 Aims and methodology of the comparative study

3.1 Aims

A socioconstructivist view on learning and teaching constitutes the background of the study: learning is conceived as a social construction mediated by teaching, and can only be understood if one takes into account the sociocultural setting in which learning takes place (McCaslin & Hickey, 2001). Educational studies from a socioconstructivist perspective focus on the analysis of learning-in-context. They try to understand the world of signification and meaning in which students act and learn guided by instruction (Cobb & Bowers, 1999).

Similarly, the present study tries to understand some mathematical practices within their specific educational context. It is designed to identify characteristic patterns of classroom activity in general and effective approaches to the teaching of percentages, in the age range of 10-12, in particular. Moreover, the study aims at framing the distinctive features of percentage instruction in the participating countries within current thinking relating to teaching and learning percentages (see section 2). It does, however, not aim at evaluation and generalisation of the different educational practices.

3.2 Methodology

As mentioned before, the focus of the project was on comparing sequences of four or five lessons relating to the teaching of percentages, polygons, and linear equations. However, in view of analysing the videotaped lessons the international research team was confronted with the challenge to develop and try out the necessary instruments. Therefore, during the first phase of the project, which lasted more than one year, live observations by members of the four country teams took place in all countries. Spread over one week a range of lessons was observed, and at the same time videotaped. The teams collaboratively worked on the development of instruments for describing mathematics teaching-learning practices through discussions starting from watching the videoregistration of the lessons observed. This iterative process (see Andrews et al., 2004 for a detailed description) resulted in two instruments: a lesson coding scheme and a lesson synthesis sheet.

We subdivided each observed lesson in different episodes and analysed each episode according to the *lesson coding scheme*. A new episode starts when the didactic intention(s) of the teacher changes. For instance, a lesson starts with a brief review of the content of the previous lesson (episode 1); thereafter students are asked to solve exercises in their workbook (episode 2). Each episode of that lesson is analysed with regard to the lesson coding scheme. That scheme covers four basic categories: mathematical focus, mathematical context, didactics, and materials used by the teacher and students. Each category is subdivided in subcategories that are coded (with a 1 if present and a 0 if absent) for every episode of the lesson.

The mathematical focus of a lesson refers to the underlying objectives of teacher's actions and decision-making. Seven different foci are distinguished:
- conceptual (emphasis on students' conceptual development);
- derivational (emphasis on developing new mathematical entities from existing knowledge);
- structural (emphasis on connections between different mathematical entities);
- procedural (emphasis on the acquisition of skills, procedures, techniques or algorithms);
- efficiency (emphasis on students' understanding or acquisition of techniques that develop flexibility, elegance or critical comparison of working);
- problem solving (emphasis on solving non-trivial or non-routine tasks);
- reasoning (emphasis on students' development of justification and argumentation)

During one episode several of these foci can be addressed.

Mathematical context relates to the conception of mathematics underlying the tasks posed in a lesson, and involves two dimensions. One dimension considers whether or not the task is related explicitly to the real world; the second axis relates to the genuineness of the data on which the task is based. The combination of both dimensions leads to four subcategories of tasks:
- related to the real world and based on data invented by the teacher;
- not related to the real world and based on data invented by the teacher;
- related to the real world and based on genuine data;
- not related to the real world and based on genuine data

Didactics refers to the didactic strategies teachers use in their lesson. Ten subcategories are distinguished:
- activating prior knowledge (revision of prior knowledge as preparation for activities to follow);
- exercising prior knowledge (revision of prior knowledge unrelated to any activities that follow);
- explaining (explaining of an idea or solution with little or no student input);

- sharing (public sharing of ideas, solutions or answers);
- exploring (exploring new mathematical ideas, without explicit teacher direction);
- coaching (offering hints, prompts or feedback to facilitate students' understanding);
- assessing/evaluating (assessing/evaluating students' responses to determine the overall attainment of the class);
- motivating (addressing students' attitudes, beliefs or emotional responses towards mathematics);
- questioning (using a sequence of questions in order to build up new mathematical ideas or clarify existing ones);
- differentiation (different treatment of students in terms of the kind of tasks, the kind of materials provided, and/or the kind of expected outcome)

Materials relates to concrete didactic tools used by the teacher or by the students to support the teaching-learning process. We distinguish between the following materials:
- answer book;
- board (use of black or whiteboard);
- computer;
- calculator;
- coloured writing materials (the purposeful or functional use of coloured pens, pencil, chalk);
- display materials (poster or other prepared materials);
- game (game like activities that use concrete materials);
- pupil whiteboards (small individual whiteboards used by the students, or any equivalent where the teacher can see each students' answer);
- manipulatives;
- overhead projector;
- practical equipment (e.g., protractor, compasses, set squares, scissors...);
- real world materials (e.g., newspaper cutting, cardboard boxes, tins, catalogues...);
- worksheet;
- textbook

The *lesson synthesis sheet* is inspired by the work of Reusser (www.didac.unizh.ch). It summarises the essence of a lesson on one page, and includes the following information: brief details about the lesson and the class involved (grade, topic, and teacher); a photograph of the classroom; a timeline showing a summary of the pedagogic activities; a second parallel timeline showing a summary of the social activities observed; and a narrative summary linking a qualitative description of the lesson to the two timelines as well as to the activities identified in the lesson coding scheme.

The following pedagogic activities are distinguished: theory or conceptual development; working on problems/tasks; reporting solutions to problems/tasks; introducing a problem/activity; homework-related activities; task-related management; and non task-related management. The different forms of social activities are: whole class, group, paired, and individual activities.

As already mentioned, in each of the four countries a sequence of four or five successive lessons on percentages was videorecorded in a fifth or sixth grade classroom. A consecutive series of lessons was videotaped because this allows a better understanding of the different mathematical practices that emerge through interactions between teacher and students in the social context of the classroom. Moreover, studying a sequence of lessons enables a more thorough analysis of important aspects of the teaching process, such as the methods used by the teacher or linking lessons together into units that stretch out over a certain period of time (Stigler & Hiebert, 1997).

The participating teachers were representative of what is commonly accepted as good but not exceptional teaching practice in their community. The following information was collected with regard to each classroom: location and nature of the school; socio-economic background of the pupils and their overall ability level; age and teaching experience of the teacher (see section 4).

The percentage lessons were analysed according to the two instruments described above. The analyses were done by the team of the country in which the lessons were videotaped. A sample of all project lessons was scored by two independent coders, and an interscorer-reliability of .80 was obtained.

4 Context of the videotaped percentage lessons

4.1 Flemish percentage lessons

The five Flemish percentage lessons were videotaped in a fifth-grade class of a primary school in a middle-sized city in Flanders. The school had approximately 350 students. The teacher of the class was in her early thirties and had more than ten years teaching experience. Next to mathematics, she also taught the other subjects in this class. It was a mixed-ability class with 19 students of middle to high SES. The nature of the school was rather comprehensive than selective.

4.2 English percentage lessons

The four English percentage lessons were videotaped in a fifth grade classroom in the urban district of Northampton, a large country town in the

East Midlands of England. The school had 605 pupils on role, from grade five to eight. The teacher of the class was in her thirties and had more than ten years experience. Next to mathematics, she taught most other curriculum subjects excluding, science, physical education and music. The number of students in the class added up to 32. The proportion of immigrants was 1.4 percent, which is a little higher than in other English schools. A little over a third of the pupils were designated as having a special educational need. This is more than average. The social backgrounds of pupils were equally diverse.

4.3 Hungarian percentage lessons

The five successive Hungarian percentage lessons were videotaped in a school that was situated in the heart of Pest, one of the poorest districts of Budapest. The district had a very bad reputation but the school was outstanding. The school was committed to high level education, good results on nation wide competitions, and excellent rates in university entrance exams. Because of its high reputation children from all over the country tried to come here to study, which made it an extraordinary school: all or almost all children were eager to learn and to learn more. The school was rather large and had classes from grade one to twelve. Every grade had approximately two or three classes with 30-35 students. The lessons were videotaped in a sixth grade class with 30 mixed ability students. The teacher had approximately 30 years of experience. She was a mentor teacher, wrote textbooks, and usually gave lectures to in-service teachers.

4.4 Spanish percentage lessons

The four Spanish percentage lessons were videotaped in the fifth grade of a primary school, which was situated in a neighbourhood of Huelva, characterised by its low average socio-economic level, and where the sale and consumption of drugs was commonplace. The school included all six grades of primary education, and each grade had two classes. The school had a very diverse student population involving a number of immigrants as well as students with hearing, visual and mental impairments; attempts were made to pay an adequate amount of attention to their educational needs. The class counted three children with special needs: a very slow learner, a blind child, and a South American immigrant. The teacher had been in the profession for forty years. Besides mathematics he taught also other subjects. From the start in the eighties, he participated in the Pedagogic Renovation Movements, which were groups of teachers who attempted to promote a democratic alternative teaching during the dictatorship.

5 Outcomes

This section reviews both the differences and the similarities in the distinct approaches of the four countries to the teaching of percentages. First, a comparative analysis on the distinct categories of the lesson coding schemes (mathematical focus, mathematical context, didactics, and materials) is outlined. Thereafter, we use the results of that comparative analysis to frame the sequence of lessons in the current thinking on teaching percentages as described in section 2 (the objectives, the conceptual aspects, and the didactic tools). Due to place restrictions, we will not discuss the results of the comparative analysis of the lesson synthesis sheets. We will use the country name to label the sequences of lessons; however, it is obvious that the restricted dataset does not allow to generalise the results of that specific approach to the teaching of percentages in general in each country.

5.1 Analyses of the lesson coding schemes

Mathematical focus. The sequence of percentage lessons in the four participating countries were analysed in terms of the seven different mathematical foci: conceptual, derivational, structural, procedural, efficiency, problem solving, and reasoning. The frequencies of the foci in each lesson sequence were compared and are presented in Figure 3.

In all four countries the two strongest foci were the procedural and the conceptual ones. A wide variation was observed in the codings for the other mathematical foci.

The data were subjected to a Mann-Whitney U-test in order to determine the effect of the specific country approaches on the mathematical

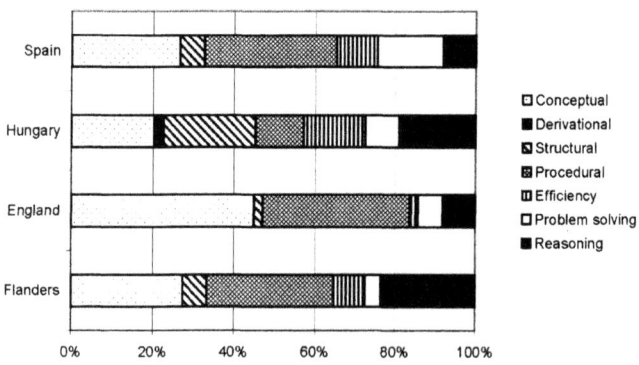

Fig. 3. Comparative analysis of the mathematical focus.

focus. This test contrasts the mean score on each specific focus in one country approach with the average score on that focus in the other three country approaches. The results are shown in Table 1. (We accepted a maximum level of p = .05 for statistical significance. The direction in which the focus of one approach differs statistically from the other approaches can be read off from Figure 3.)

Table 1. Results of the Mann-Whitney U-test for mathematical focus

Mathematical focus		Flanders	England	Hungary	Spain
Conceptual	Z	-1.612	**-1.961**	-0.260	-0.504
	p	0.107	**0.050**	0.795	0.645
Derivational	Z	-0.904	-0.779	**-2.351**	-0.779
	p	0.366	0.436	**0.019**	0.721
Structural	Z	-1.427	-1.423	**-3.329**	-0.626
	p	0.154	0.155	**0.001**	0.574
Procedural	Z	-0.101	-1.414	**-2.221**	-0.870
	p	0.920	0.157	**0.026**	0.442
Efficiency	Z	-0.878	**-2.226**	**-2.996**	-0.056
	p	0.380	**0.026**	**0.003**	0.959
Problem Solving	Z	-1.980	-0.505	-0.625	-1.965
	p	0.048	0.613	0.532	0.061
Reasoning	Z	-0.608	-1.637	**-2.431**	-1.637
	p	0.543	0.102	**0.015**	0.127

These results reveal that the sequence of the Hungarian lessons significantly differed for the major part of the mathematical foci from the other lesson sequences. Compared to other country approaches, the Hungarian lessons had a stronger derivational, structural, efficiency, and reasoning focus, while there is less emphasis on procedural knowledge and skills. Statistically significant differences for the English lessons were found for the conceptual (i.e., a stronger conceptual focus than in the other country approaches) and the efficiency focus (i.e., a weaker efficiency focus than in the other country approaches). The approaches of the Flemish and the Spanish teacher show no significant differences with the other approaches.

Mathematical context. The tasks involved in the four country approaches to teach percentages were analysed with regard to their relatedness to the real world and the genuineness of their data. Figure 4 presents the frequency of the four subcategories: real world fabricated data, not real world fabricated data, real world genuine data, and not real world genuine data.

Figure 4 shows a very homogeneous picture for the use of different contexts over the four approaches. As appears from Figure 4, most of all activities (approximately two thirds) were embedded in a context that was not explicitly related to the real world and that consisted of fabricated data. The second most used context was related to the real world and based on fabricated data. Real world genuine data were absent in the English approach, while the other teachers used them in almost the same frequency. Not real world genuine data were not frequently present in all approaches.

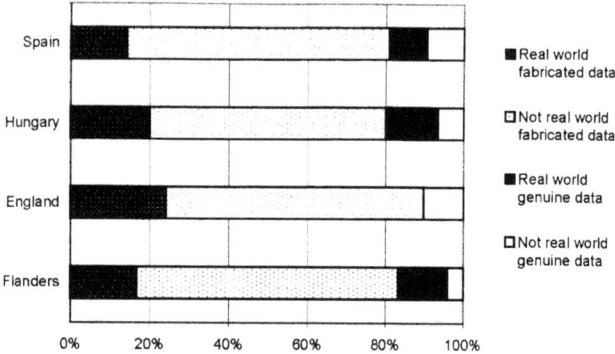

Fig. 4. Comparative analysis of the mathematical context.

The results of the Mann-Whitney U-test on these data are presented in Table 2.

As shown in Table 2, there are no statistically significant differences in the use of mathematical contexts between the analysed approaches to teach percentages.

Table 2. Results of the Mann-Whitney U-test for mathematical context

Mathematical Context		Flanders	England	Hungary	Spain
RWFD	Z	-0.156	-1.007	-0.260	-1.119
	p	0.876	0.314	0.795	0.327
NRWFD	Z	-0.255	-1.209	-0.765	-0.110
	p	0.799	0.227	0.444	0.959
RWGD	Z	-0.118	-1.521	-1.647	-0.380
	p	0.906	0.128	0.099	0.798
NRWGD	Z	-0.339	-0.365	-0.135	-0.146
	p	0.735	0.715	0.892	0.959

Note. RWFD = real world fabricated data, NRWFD = not real world fabricated data, RWGD = real world genuine data, NRWGD = not real world genuine data.

Didactics. Next, we analysed the didactic strategies of the teachers from the four countries. The following didactic strategies were distinguished: activating prior knowledge, exercising prior knowledge, explaining, sharing, exploring, coaching, assessing/evaluating, motivating, questioning, differentiation. Their frequency across the different approaches is compared in Figure 5.

Figure 5 reveals that four didactic strategies were used quite frequently in all country approaches: sharing, questioning, explaining, and coaching. The others were used (much) less frequently. A wide diversity was observed in the codings of these didactics over the different country approaches. Table 3 shows the results of the Mann-Whitney U-test.

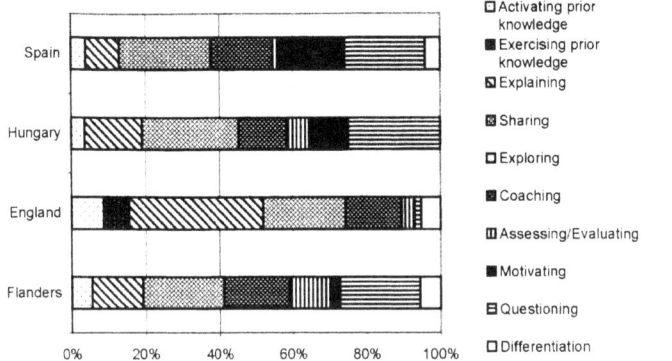

Fig. 5. Comparative analysis of the didactics.

Table 3. Results of the Mann-Whitney U-test for didactics

Didactics		Flanders	England	Hungary	Spain
Activating prior	Z	-0.275	**-2.012**	-1.099	-0.533
knowledge	p	0.784	**0.044**	0.272	0.645
Exercising prior	Z	-1.144	**-3.450**	-1.144	-0.986
knowledge	p	0.253	**0.001**	0.253	0.574
Explaining	Z	-1.480	**-2.529**	-0.408	-1.374
	p	0.139	**0.011**	0.683	0.192
Sharing	Z	-1.560	-0.217	-0.654	-1.192
	p	0.119	0.828	0.513	0.277
Exploring	Z	-1.612	-0.535	-0.620	-0.535
	p	0.107	0.593	0.535	0.878
Coaching	Z	-0.406	-0.383	-0.609	-1.475
	p	0.685	0.702	0.543	0.158
Assessing /	Z	-1.550	-0.954	-1.107	-1.909
Evaluating	p	0.121	0.340	0.268	0.101
Motivating	Z	-1.828	**-2.251**	-0.992	**-3.151**
	p	0.068	**0.024**	0.321	**0.001**
Questioning	Z	-0.203	**-2.951**	-1.522	-1.530
	p	0.839	**0.003**	0.128	0.158
Differentiation	Z	-0.886	-0.477	**-2.214**	-0.954
	p	0.376	0.633	**0.027**	0.442

Table 3 shows that the English approach was responsible for most of the observed differences in didactics between countries. More specifically, the English teacher activated prior knowledge more, exercised prior knowledge more, explained more, motivated less, and questioned less than in the other country approaches. The two other observed deviations were the Hungarian teacher's lesser attention to differentiation and the Spanish teacher's greater attention to motivating pupils.

Materials. The materials used by the teachers and the students to support the teaching-learning process were analysed in the four approaches. Table 4 shows the results of this (comparative) analysis of the fourteen didactic tools.

Table 4. Comparative analysis of the materials used by the teacher and the students

Materials	Teacher				Students			
	F	E	H	S	F	E	H	S
Text book	0%	3%	9%	0%	9%	6%	18%	0%
Worksheet	0%	0%	0%	0%	35%	9%	0%	20%
Game	0%	3%	23%	0%	0%	3%	23%	5%
Manipulatives	4%	0%	0%	5%	43%	9%	9%	25%
Practical equipment	0%	0%	0%	0%	0%	0%	0%	0%
Overhead projector	0%	13%	18%	0%	0%	3%	14%	0%
Computer	0%	3%	0%	0%	0%	0%	0%	0%
Calculator	0%	0%	0%	0%	17%	9%	0%	0%
Real world materials	9%	3%	0%	0%	13%	0%	0%	5%
Pupil whiteboards	0%	0%	0%	0%	0%	53%	0%	0%
Board	43%	59%	73%	75%	9%	3%	82%	5%
Coloured writing materials	0%	22%	23%	0%	4%	3%	0%	0%
Answer book	0%	0%	0%	0%	9%	0%	0%	0%
Display material	13%	6%	14%	10%	0%	0%	14%	10%

Note. F = Flemish approach, E = English approach, H = Hungarian approach, S = Spanish approach. The percentages given in this table were obtained by dividing the number of episodes in which the material was used by the total number of episodes of each lesson. For each material, the obtained percentages were added up for all the lessons of that specific country approach.

In general, the data presented in Table 4 reveal that teachers frequently use the board during their instructional practices. To the contrary, real world materials were only used to a small extent by both the teacher and the students. Some materials were never used by the teacher, such as worksheets, practical equipment, calculators, real world materials, and answer books. Students also did not use computers and practical equipment.

Besides, the results also show a wide diversity in the frequency of the materials that were used to support the teaching-learning process over the four country approaches. Flemish students frequently completed worksheets, while their Hungarian peers did not use them at all. Manipulatives were often used by the Flemish and Spanish, whereas this was clearly less the case in the English and Hungarian lessons. Both the English and Hungarian teacher and students frequently used the overhead; this never occurred in the Flemish and Spanish lessons. Only the Flemish and English students used their calculator. As already mentioned above, real world materials were not frequently used in the different approaches; only in the Flemish lessons a substantial amount of real world materials was used. The English students frequently wrote down their solution(method)s on their whiteboards, whereas the Hungarian students worked frequently on the blackboard.

5.2 Framing the four approaches within the current perspective on teaching percentages

The quantitative results obtained by comparing the different approaches to the teaching of percentages with respect to their mathematical focus, mathematical context, didactics, and materials, enable us to frame these different approaches within the current perspective on teaching percentages, as described in section 2. Therefore, the four sequences of lessons will be qualitatively described according to their objectives, the conceptual aspects of percentages that are addressed, and their didactic tools. This qualitative description will be linked to the categories and subcategories of the lesson coding scheme.

Objectives. According to the perspective on teaching percentages presented in section 2, three major kinds of goals should be aimed at when teaching this topic: computational goals, conceptual goals, and applicational goals. As shown by the analysis of the mathematical focus (see section 5.1.1), all four country approaches served computational goals. Indeed, the procedural focus was clearly present in all four lesson sequences, although significantly less in the Hungarian lessons. But we also observed substantial differences among the kind of procedures that were taught in the four countries. In the Flemish percentage lessons, students' computational process was initially supported by manipulatives (MAB-material). Gradually children learned to calculate percentages without these manipulatives. They applied the following procedure: dividing the given amount by hundred to calculate 1% of that amount; and multiplying that result by the percentage. Another, and more flexible, procedure Flemish students used to solve percentage tasks, was the arrow scheme (see Figure 6).

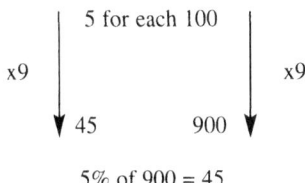

Fig. 6. Example of the use of the arrow scheme.

The English students learned two different procedures to compute successfully percentage tasks. A first procedure was to convert easy percentages (such as 10%, 20%, 25%, and 50%) into fractions simplified to their lowest term (e.g., with numerator one). This translation revealed by which number you should divide to calculate 10%, 20%, 25%, and 50%

(which is respectively 10, 5, 4, and 2, since the equivalent fractions are $^1/_{10}$, $^1/_5$, $^1/_4$, and $^1/_2$). The "percentage-web" was another procedure that was applied to solve percentage tasks. In this procedure all percentages were related to 10%. For instance, 20% is the double of 10%. Consequently, 20% was calculated by dividing the whole by ten, and multiplying it by two. The more gifted children learned, in a similar way, to calculate more difficult percentages, such as 17.5% (e.g., 17.5% = 20% - 2.5% = (10% x 2) – (10%: 4)). Contrary to the Flemish students, the English students did not acquire the procedure to solve percentage tasks by dividing the whole by hundred to calculate 1% of that amount. Like the Flemish and English students, the Hungarian students also learned different procedures to solve all kind of percentage tasks. For instance, they translated percentages into their equivalent fractions (like in the English lessons), and they divided the whole by 100 (like in the Flemish lessons). Some other tasks were solved by means of estimation. For example, during the second lesson the teacher asked the students: "Could you show me – without any calculation – that 101% of the 90% of a number means a decrease of that number?". Students solved that exercise at the blackboard with a bar model. The Spanish teacher put strong emphasis on computational goals too. The students acquired a procedure to solve simple percentage tasks. Like in the English and Hungarian lessons, the Spanish students converted percentages into equivalent fractions in order to calculate the percentage. At the end of the lesson sequence, more difficult percentages were computed (e.g., 83% of 100). Gradually, students learned the skill to calculate percentages of an amount by multiplying the given percentage by 1% of the given amount.

The comparative analysis of the mathematical focus revealed that students' conceptual development was also a major concern of the instructional approaches to percentages in the four countries. The next section gives a more detailed description of the conceptual aspects that were dealt with in the lesson sequences.

Mainly in the Hungarian, and to a less extent in the Flemish approach, the students were frequently and strongly encouraged to apply known procedures flexibly and meaningfully to new and unfamiliar tasks. For instance, Hungarian students were faced with a wide variety of tasks each of which needed an appropriate solution procedure (e.g., the percentage and the solution were given, and the students had to find the original amount; or different parts of two circles were coloured, and the students had to calculate the percentage in degrees; or the students had to solve exercises that contained a combination of increase and decrease of a certain percentage). Some tasks were even solved in many different ways. This helped students to acquire adaptive expertise. For instance, students had to estimate percentages about the human population (e.g., the percentage illiterates); they were asked if a number increases or decreases after a combination of an increase and a decrease of a certain percentage. In the English and Spanish approach, adaptive expertise was not aimed at, since students were always asked to apply the same procedures to familiar tasks.

Conceptual aspects of percentages. Although, students' conceptual development of percentages was a major goal in all four sequences of lessons, the different aspects of percentages that, according to the current literature lead to a deep understanding of this mathematical concept, were hardly addressed in the four approaches. All teachers mainly focused on the "basic ideas" of the concept percentage, such as: a percentage always expresses something out of hundred, 100% equals the whole, etc. Moreover, the different formats of the tasks in the distinct approaches, reflected that percentages describe two kinds of situations: a part plus/minus a whole, and a part of a whole.

The most important and inherent characteristics of the percentage concept were revealed, most clearly, most deeply, and most systematically in the Hungarian approach. For instance, Hungarian students learned that percentages are always related to "something" and that they have no meaning without taking into account to what they refer. Moreover, they acquired the idea that percentages describe a fixed situation while representing how different percentages are related to each other (e.g., students had to represent the total human population by means of hundred pieces of paper; the teacher told them that the ratios in those 100 pieces and in the human population stay the same). Other exercises revealed the asymmetric nature of the increase and decrease of percentages. For instance:

> T: 120% of its 80%. Is that an increase or decrease?
> S: Increase ... it remains the same.
> T: Raise your hand if you think it increased. 120% of its 80%. Prove it! If I take 80% then it decreases. If I take its 120% then it increases. Who can prove it? Come on, Kinga.
> S: [at the blackboard, with a bar model] We had 80%. We took away 20%. That increases by the 20% of this. But this is smaller than this, so its 20% is smaller too. So it does not increase back.
> T: Good. Can you tell exactly, Kinga, what part is it that we got? If I think of a number. I think of 100.
> S: Then it is 96.

Although it did not happen as explicitly and as systematically as in the Hungarian class, the Flemish teacher addressed some of these important conceptual aspects of percentages. For instance, class discussions revealed that percentages describe a fixed situation representing how different kinds of substances are related:

> S: A pot of yoghurt with 9% fruit.
> T: 9% fruit. What does that mean?

S: That there are 9% of 100 fruit in that.
T: 9% of the 100. I do not understand this very well. Who can explain it? Does that mean that there are nine pieces of fruit in that?
S: No.
T: Maybe 9 grams?
S: No.
T: Would it make a difference if it is a large or a small pot?
S: It depends ... Yes, I think it would stay the same.

Moreover, pupils were also given a task to illustrate and explain the fact that percentages are always related to "something" and that they therefore have no meaning without taking into account the referent.

Didactic tools. As explained in section 2.3, teachers can use everyday situations that are intelligible for students when teaching percentages. However, the analysis of the mathematical context revealed that in neither approach a lot of real world genuine data was used (see Figure 4). Similarly, the analysis of the materials showed that real world materials were used only to a small extent in the Flemish, English, and Spanish lessons (see Table 4). Nevertheless, all four teachers, while introducing the concept of percentage, made explicit attempts to connect the newly introduced concept to students' informal everyday knowledge and experience. For instance, the situation of sales was used in every country to let the students explain what they already new about percentages.

To induce meaningful learning, especially to foster adaptive expertise, strong emphasis has to be put on the relationship of the concept percentage to other mathematical entities, like fractions, decimals... In all approaches, percentages were explicitly and strongly related to fractions. Interestingly, only the Hungarian teacher connected percentages with decimals and with the degrees of a circle (e.g., how many degrees equal one percent of a circle).

Furthermore, models and concrete materials have an important role to play in the instruction of percentages. Manipulatives, such as MAB-material and place-value-cards, were used in all four lesson sequences (see Table 4). Popular models to teach percentages were the ten by ten grid (in the Flemish, Hungarian, and Spanish approach), the pie chart model (in the English and Hungarian approach), and the arrow scheme (in the Flemish and Hungarian approach). Dynamic and powerful models such as the slide-slip and the elastic percent meter (see section 2.3), were not observed in any country approach.

6 Discussion

In this chapter we made an attempt to describe differences in approaches to the teaching of percentages across four European countries: Flanders,

England, Hungary, and Spain. This description is based on videotaped sequences of four or five consecutive lessons about (exactly) the same topic in one class that can be considered as typical (but evidently not perfectly representative) for the instructional approach in each of these four countries. Like for the research project as a whole, the goal was not to make a comparative evaluation of the quality of the instruction of percentages in these countries. Rather, we used the videotaped lessons to make an inventory of the variety in the different possibilities and traditions of the teaching of percentages within Europe, and to provide a critical reflection on these possibilities and traditions.

From a methodological perspective, we want to underline the need for using multiple methods to get a good understanding of the educational practice. As McCaslin and Hickey (2001) state: "Multiple methods no longer mean three quantitative instruments and their statistical relation; rather, multiple methods now routinely encompass qualitative work with quantitative" (p. 134). In that perspective, we complemented quantitative data obtained by means of a coding scheme consisting of four categories (mathematical focus, mathematical context, didactics, and materials) with qualitative descriptions of the analysed lessons involving their objectives, conceptual aspects, and didactic tools. This complementary use of quantitative and qualitative data has yielded an added value, in the sense that it enabled us to interpret the (quantitative) codings in light of the broader (qualitative) outlines of the lessons. For instance, the qualitative analyses of the procedures students acquired to solve percentage tasks facilitated a deeper understanding of the strong procedural emphasis in the four country approaches. Indeed, although all approaches focused (relatively) strongly on procedural skills, the qualitative analyses enabled us to grasp the similarities and differences in students' procedures in the distinct country approaches. However, in some cases, the qualitative analyses of the lessons also helped us to refine the outcomes of the quantitative outcomes on the lesson coding scheme. For instance, as the comparative analysis of the mathematical focus revealed (see Figure 3), the Spanish students seemed to be more involved with solving non-routine problems than in the other country approaches. Although this difference was not statistically significant (see Table 1), the qualitative analyses of the country lessons' objectives suggested that in the Spanish lessons the students did not acquire adaptive expertise, since they were always asked to apply the same procedures (routinely) to familiar tasks. Probably this gap between the outcomes of the quantitative and the qualitative analyses can be explained by the fact that the tasks in the Spanish lessons were experienced by the students and by their teacher as problem solving because of their rather low abilities (see section 4.4). But, when compared to other country approaches (like Hungary and Flanders), the tasks of the Spanish lessons were rather easy and would by most mathematics educators not be labelled as illustrations of problem solving.

Another valuable outcome of this project is the development of instruments for lesson analysis containing an internationally shared vocabulary, and possessing an acceptable interscorer-reliability. For sure the elaboration of these instruments was a time-consuming and difficult challenge.

Finally, it is desirable to supplement the outcomes of our analyses with other kinds of data gathering and data analysing techniques, such as interviews, questionnaires, and so on. In this study we necessarily restricted our analyses to observable teacher behaviour. We did not make any inferences about the learning processes and outcomes of the students involved in our investigation, because the methodology did not enable us to make such inferences.

References

Abels, M. (1991). Procenten in W12-16. *Nieuwe Wiskrant. Tijdschrift voor Nederlands Wiskundeonderwijs, 10*(3), 20-25.

Andrews, P., & the METE project team. (2004, July). *International comparisons of mathematics teaching: Searching for consensus in describing opportunities for learning.* Paper presented in a Discussion Group on "International comparisons in mathematics education" at the 10th International Congress on Mathematical Education, Copenhagen, Denmark.

Baroody, A.J. (2003). The development of adaptive expertise and flexibility: The integration of conceptual and procedural knowledge. In A.J. Baroody & A. Dowker (Eds.), *The development of arithmetic concepts and skills. Constructing adapative expertise* (pp. 1-34). Hillsdale, NJ: Lawrence Erlbaum Associates.

Beaton, A.E., Mullis, I.V.S., Martin, M.O., Gonzales, E.J., Kelly, D.L., & Smith, T.A. (1996). *Mathematics achievement in the middle school years: IEA's Third International Mathematics and Science Study (TIMSS).* Chestnut Hill: TIMSS International Study Center.

Bokhove, J., & de Moor, E. (1993). Bakens voor een leerlijn procenten: op de grens van basisschool en basisvorming. In M. Dolk & W. Uittenbogaard (Eds.), *Procenten: op de grens van basisschool en basisvorming* (pp. 11-24). Utrecht: Freudenthal Instituut.

Clarke, D. (2003). International comparative studies in mathematics education. In A.J. Bishop, M.A. Clements, C. Keitel, J. Kilpatrick, & F.K.S. Leung (Eds.), *Second international handbook of mathematics education* (pp. 143-184). Dordrecht: Kluwer Academic Publishers.

Cobb, P., & Bowers, J. (1999). Cognitive and situated learning perspectives in theory and practice. *Educational Researcher, 28*(2), 4-15.

Faes, W. (1999). De schuifstrook: een dynamisch model. *Willem Bartjens, 19*(2), 14-18.

Keitel, C., & Kilpatrick, J. (1999). The rationality and irrationality of international comparative studies. In G. Kaiser, E. Luna, & I. Huntley (Eds.), *International comparisons in mathematics education* (pp. 241-256). London: Falmer Press.

Leung, F.V.S. (2001). In search of East Asian identity in mathematics education. *Educational Studies in Mathematics, 47*(1), 35-51.

McCaslin, M., & Hickey, D.T. (2001). Educational psychology, social constructivism, and educational practice: A case of emergent identity. *Educational Psychologist, 36*, 133-140.

Middleton, J.A., & Goepfert, P. (1996). *Psychology in the classroom. Inventive strategies for teaching mathematics: Implementing standards for reform.* Washington, DC:

American Psychological Association.
Mullis, I.V.S., Martin, M.O., Gonzales, E.J., Greogory, K.D., Garden, R.A., O'Conner, K.M., Chrostowski, S.J., & Smith, T.A. (2000). *Gender differences in achievement: IEA's Third International Mathematics and Science Study (TIMSS)*. Chestnut Hill: TIMSS International Study Center.
OECD. (2003). *The PISA 2003 assessment framework: Mathematics, reading, science and problem solving knowledge and skills*. Paris: OECD.
Reusser, K. (2003). *Schweizerisch-internationale Video-Studie: Mathematiklernen in unterschiedlichen Unterrichtskulturen*. Retrieved June 7, 2004, http://www.didac.unizh.ch/scvs/index.htm
Stigler, J., & Gonzales, P., Kawanaka, T., Knoll, S., & Serrano, A. (1999). *The TIMSS videotape classroom study: Methods and findings from an exploratory research project on eight-grade mathematics instruction in Germany, Japan, and the United States*. Washington, DC: National Center for Educational Statistics.
Stigler, J., & Hiebert, J. (1997). Understanding and improving classroom mathematics instruction: An overview of the TIMSS video study. *Phi Delta Kappan, 79*, 14-21.
Stigler, J., & Hiebert, J. (1998). *The teaching gap*. New York: Simon & Schuster.
Streefland, L. (1995). Procenten en verhoudingen. In L. Verschaffel & E. De Corte (Eds.), *Naar een nieuwe reken/wiskundedidactiek voor de basisschool en de basiseducatie*. Leuven: Acco.
Streefland, L. (1998). Zonnige kortingen. Een leergang voor procenten. *Willem Bartjens, 18*(1), 4-10.
TIMSS Video Mathematics Research Group. (2003). Understanding and improving mathematics teaching: Highlights from the TIMSS 1999 Video Study. *Phi Delta Kappan, 84*, 768-775.
Treffers, A., Streefland, L., & De Moor, E. (1994). *Proeve van een nationaal programma voor het reken- en wiskundeonderwijs op de basisschool. Deel 3A breuken*. Tilburg: Zwijsen.
Van den Heuvel-Panhuizen, M., & Streefland, L. (1993). Per sense: een onderwijsleerpakketje over procenten. In M. Dolk & W. Uittenbogaard (Eds.), *Procenten: op de grens van basisschool en basisvorming* (pp. 25-48). Utrecht: Freudenthal Instituut.
Van den Heuvel-Panhuizen, M. (1994). Improvement of didactical assessment by improvement of the problems: An attempt with respect to percentage. *Educational Studies in Mathematics, 27*, 341-372.
Van den Heuvel-Panhuizen, M. (2003). The didactical use of models in realistic mathematics education: An example from a longitudinal trajectory on percentage. *Educational Studies in Mathematics, 54*(1), 9-35.
Velghe, C., & Vervenne, F. (2000). Percentberekening: lessenreeks voor het zesde leerjaar. *Schokla: school- en klassepraktijk, 41*(165), 27-39.

Part III
Promoting deep conceptual and strategic learning in other major curricular domains

Chapter 10

Teaching-learning environments and student learning in electronic engineering

Noel Entwistle, Jennifer Nisbet, and Adrian Bromage

1 Introduction to the project as a whole

1.1 The ETL Project

The ETL project (Enhancing Teaching-Learning Environments in Undergraduate Courses) is part of the UK-wide Teaching and Learning Research Programme of the British ESRC, and is now one of four projects (out of 31) focusing on teaching and learning in higher education. The programme is trying to strengthen the impact of educational research by requiring that each project is carried out in collaboration with "users" of the research findings. In our project, these users are academic staff, but our findings will also be directed towards staff developers, institutional managers, and policy makers. The ETL project is exploring differences in the teaching-learning environments across four contrasting subject areas – biological sciences, economics, electronic engineering, and history. Within each subject area, staff in six or more course units across distinctively different institutional settings have agreed to participate collaboratively in our study over a two-year period.

In the first year, baseline data are collected. Staff are interviewed to allow the researchers to discover more about teaching and learning within the subject area, as well as details of the particular unit, supplemented by the documentation provided for the students. Two questionnaires were completed by students – one at the beginning and one at the end of the course

---

The ideas being developed in the ETL project are a product not only of the whole project team, but also of our subject advisors, international consultants, and colleagues in our collaborating departments. At the time of writing, researchers on the project team, besides the authors, were Charles Anderson, Kate Day, Dai Hounsell, Jenny Hounsell, Ray Land, Velda McCune, Erik Meyer and Nicola Reimann, while Glynis Cousin, Liz Beaty and Hilary Tait made important contributions earlier in the project. In writing this chapter we also drew, specifically, on the collaboration with Peter Whitaker at Coventry City College, Brian McQuillin in Sheffield Hallam University, Alister Hamiliton and Bob Kelly in the University of Edinburgh, and Bob Chapman, Gordon Hayward and Tony Gachagan at Strathclyde University. More generally, we also drew on discussions held with Les Haworth, Martin Reekie, and David Renshaw at the University of Edinburgh, the late Geoffrey Smith from Strathclyde University, Tim Mulroy and Ian Robinson, at Sheffield Hallam University, and Sherri Johnstone at the University of Durham.

unit. The first looked at students' reasons for taking the degree course and the course unit, and explored students' general approaches to learning and studying in the subject area. The second concentrated on the approaches used in the specific unit and the experiences of teaching and learning. Groups of students were also interviewed to explore those experiences in more depth.

These baseline data were analysed and confidential reports provided for the staff teaching the unit. Discussions were then held to establish whether the feedback from students suggested there would be any value in developing a collaborative initiative designed to enhance certain aspects of the teaching-learning environment. Where such an initiative was agreed, the second year of collaboration involved the same data collection from the following year group to evaluate what changes in teaching and learning had occurred, and the extent to which these can be attributed to the *collaborative initiative*. Further details about the project can be found on the project web site – http:/www.ed.ac.uk/etl/publications.html

1.2 Concepts and measurements

Analyses of the feedback from students provided in the baseline data have been considered in the light of the notion of *constructive alignment*. Biggs (2003) has stressed the importance of designing curricula in higher education so as to ensure that, as far as possible, all the teaching-learning activities are aligned with high level (constructivist) aims. This formulation was developed partly from the student learning research to which Biggs has contributed and summarised, and partly from ideas from the school-based *Teaching for Understanding* framework produced by Project Zero in Harvard (Wiske, 1998). A particularly valuable aspect of that work was the use of *throughlines* representing high-level aims which are outlined to the students at the beginning of the course and repeatedly mentioned in relation to new topics as they arise.

Our project is concerned with helping staff to develop high-level learning outcomes, considered in terms of the *ways of thinking and practising in the discipline* which departmental partners suggested were most important in their course unit. This term was introduced to indicate the broad aims that seemed to underlie course development and assessment procedures in the department.

The ETL team coined the phrase "ways of thinking and practising" in a subject area (WTP) to "describe the richness, depth and breadth of what students might learn through engagement with a given subject area in a specific context. This might include, for example, coming to terms with particular understandings, forms of discourse, values or ways of acting which are regarded as central to graduate-level mastery of a discipline or subject area... WTP can potentially encompass anything that students learn which helps them to develop a sense of what it might mean to be part of a particular disciplinary community, whether or not they intend to join a given community in the future" (McCune & Hounsell, in press).

We were then able to explore how the various teaching-learning activities were expected to fulfil those aims and expectations for student learning and also to consider to what extent the course units we examined were constructively aligned to those broad aims. The evidence that was collected and analysed is now described.

1.3 The conceptual framework

Although a wide range of disciplinary perspectives has been used in considering the nature of teaching and learning across the five contrasting subject areas in our project, Figure 1 indicates in broad outline the main concepts used in considering how various aspects of the teaching-learning environment are likely to influence the quality of learning achieved. Further discussion of this model has been provided elsewhere (Entwistle, 2003).

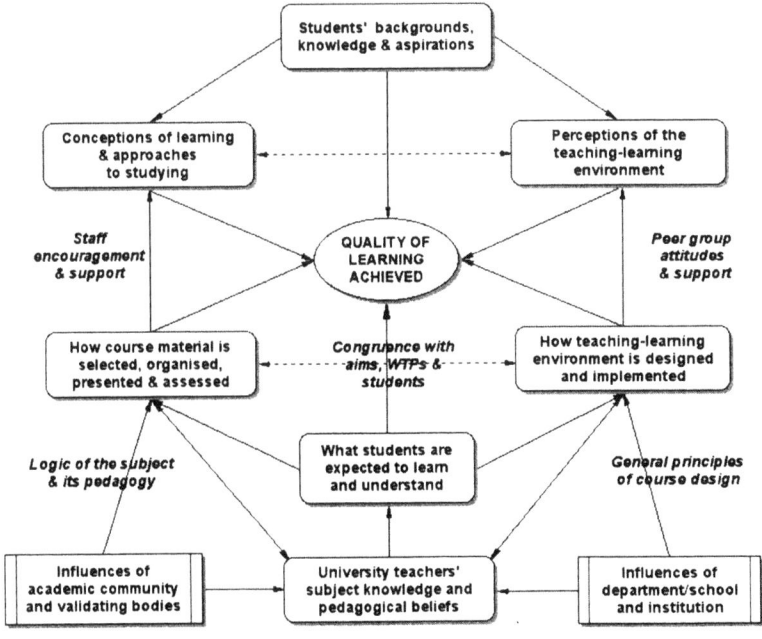

Fig. 1. Concept map indicating influences on student learning.

1.4 Collecting the base-line data

As already indicated, our data involve course documentation, interviews with both staff and students, and two questionnaires. During the first year of our collaboration with departments, we collected the baseline data against which the results of the collaborative initiatives to be evaluated. The *Learning and Studying Questionnaire* (LSQ) was given out in the first few weeks of each course unit, while the *Experiences of Teaching and Learning Questionnaire* (ETLQ) was completed towards the end of the unit. Both questionnaires contain sets of items that have been found to form coherent scales, although the analyses have also looked at individual items as well where these provide additional, more specific information. This set of variables was drawn from the set of concepts shown in Figure 1, but restrictions in the length of the questionnaires, and the time allowed with students, forced us to include only a subset of these. Those included will be described shortly.

Small-group interviews were carried out around the same time that the second questionnaire was completed to explore the students' experiences in more detail. A semi-structured interview schedule was used to guide the focus of the discussions, but we also encouraged students to raise any other aspects that they felt were important; and that frequently happened. Transcripts of the interviews were produced and analysed, leading to an additional form of evidence that could be triangulated with the questionnaire findings.

1.5 Student entry characteristics

"Entry" here refers to the ways students see themselves in relation to the degree course as a whole, before they embark on the target course unit. The first two sections of the first questionnaire (LSQ) invited students to describe "What you expect to get from the experience of higher education" and "Reasons for taking this particular course unit or module". Both these sections drew on the distinction between intrinsic and extrinsic orientations to learning (Beaty, Gibbs, & Morgan, 1997). All four aspects of intrinsic interest (academic, vocational, personal and social) held together under factor analysis to form a scale, but the extrinsic items remained separate. Prior knowledge, and confidence in it, was indicated by an item in the second questionnaire (ETLQ) which asked about the perceived demands of the unit in terms of "What I was expected to know to begin with". Students were also asked to rate themselves on their academic performance before beginning the unit, "based on the grades you have been obtaining".

1.6 Approaches to learning and studying

First-year students in our sample were generally in the second semester of their course when they completed the questionnaires and so had sufficient experience to report on their studying. The third section of the LSQ asked students to describe their *typical* approaches to studying prior to starting the target course unit through a 36-item inventory developed from earlier inventories (ASI: Entwistle & Ramsden, 1983 and ASSIST: Tait, Entwistle, & McCune, 1998). The first section of the ETLQ used half the items to indicate the approaches to studying they had used *in the course unit itself*. Item factor analyses indicated five scales.

1. *Deep approach* involves a combination of intention and process, with items covering "intention to understand" along with the associated thinking processes of "relating ideas" and "use of evidence" that parallel Pask's holist and serialist strategies (Pask, 1976). Additional items cover aspects of constructivist thinking, although these proved indistinguishable from those describing "relating ideas".
2. *Monitoring studying* combines items describing "monitoring understanding", "monitoring generic skills" and "monitoring study effectiveness". The first component is also related to the deep approach while the whole scale is conceptually linked with self-regulation of learning processes and content (Vermunt, 1998).
3. *Organised studying* also includes time-management and overlaps the more general form of study regulation described by Vermunt.
4. *Effort management* indicates the amount of effort generally put into studying and also the ability to maintain concentration while studying, even when work is not particularly interesting.
5. *Surface approach* includes four aspects – "unreflective studying", "unthinking acceptance", "memorising without understanding" (Meyer, 2000) and "fragmented knowledge" (Meyer, 1991).

1.7 Experiences of the teaching-learning environment

The second section of ETLQ asks students about their experiences of teaching and learning in the unit, intended to cover the teaching and the more general teaching-learning environment. Factor analysis identified five main groupings of items.

1. *Course organisation and management* indicates how well the students recognised the main aims of the course unit, and how well organised the unit was perceived to be. Items also include the extent to which teaching and assessment aligned with the aims, as well as the amount of perceived choice of topics to study or the ways of doing that.
2. *Teaching for deep learning* includes items derived from the literature describing the types of teaching and learning activities related to "con-

structivist" aims (Phillips, 2000) and likely to encourage a deep approach to learning. Crucial to this aspect is also the extent to which the assignments and assessments are believed to require using evidence and developing understanding. There are also items about the effectiveness of feedback in improving ways of learning and in clarifying what had not been fully understood.

3. *Interest and relevance* partly reflects the student's own interest in the subject matter ("I found most of what I learned in this course unit really interesting"), but also indicates a recognition of the teachers' efforts to make the content interesting and relevant.

4. *Support from* staff indicates the extent to which teachers were seen to have provided patient explanations, shown both enthusiasm and empathy, and valued students' views.

5. *Support from students* suggests how much mutual support and collaboration came from other students.

The third section of ETLQ asks about the perceived demands of the course unit and indicates how easy the knowledge and skills were perceived to be, as well as the rate at which new material was introduced and "the amount of work I was expected to do". And in two of the subject areas an additional group of ten items was added to cover specific aspects of the collaborative initiative.

The group interviews allowed us to interpret the questionnaire findings with more confidence and provided important additional insights into the course unit from the students' perspective. These were considered in relation to the scale scores and individual responses from the questionnaire and together generally have provided a strong indication of where a collaborative initiative might prove fruitful.

1.8 The collaborative initiatives

The baseline data collection provided a great deal of detailed information about students' attitudes, ways of studying and reactions to the course unit which could be amplified and extended through analyses of the group interviews with students. The scores on approaches to learning indicated the relative balance between deep and surface approaches adopted by students in the course as a whole prior to the unit, and also any changes in that balance in the target unit. Taking that evidence along with the questionnaire responses on students' experiences of teaching in the unit (both as scales and as individual items), and with the comments made in the group interviews, we were able to see if any aspects of the teaching-learning environment seemed to be out of line with the aims specified. Previous findings from student learning research could then be used in conjunction with an understanding of the course aims to suggest possible changes for the following year, which could then be discussed with staff. These discussions established whether a collaborative initiative would be feasible and acceptable and, where agreed, explored how best to implement it. This initiative was then introduced for the following year's intake of students and the same sets of data were again collected.

2 Teaching and learning in electronic engineering

Having established the overall research design of the project, we can now look at the research carried out within electronic engineering. Six course units were identified across four contrasting institutions. One was a first-year course unit on microprocessors in a city college, leading to the award of a Higher National Certificate with a small intake of students from industry on day-release. The next course unit was in a post-1992 university, a former polytechnic, which was preparing some 40 students through an Honours BEng for qualification as an Incorporated Engineer. The remaining five units were attended by larger classes of students in two research-intensive universities; one was a 1960s university with particular strengths in applied technology, while the other was an ancient university covering the whole range of academic subject areas. Both the research-intensive universities were preparing students for the higher status qualification of Chartered Engineer. In all the universities the course units selected were on analogue electronics, the area being chosen because students generally find it difficult and there are concerns in industry about a lack of graduates with this specialism.

The ways in which teaching and learning of electronics were carried out all six course units were sufficiently similar to summarise within a single diagram (Figure 2) which also indicates the presence of other less immediate influences on learning within and outside the institution.

The first analysis reported here is derived from the whole sample of students taking the seven course units. Thereafter, the following two sections introduce the work carried out in the city college and the new university, after which the research in the remaining five settings is described more fully, as the larger samples make quantitative analyses possible.

2.1 Relationships between selected variables from the two questionnaires

Table 1 compares the results of maximum likelihood analyses with rotation to simple structure of the total sample of students for both years of the study with those taking electronic engineering; these were the students who had completed both questionnaires at the time of this analysis. Four factors provided the clearest delimitation of the pattern of variation between the main components. Further subdivisions, although taking out an increased proportion of the variance, reduced the clarity of the pattern.

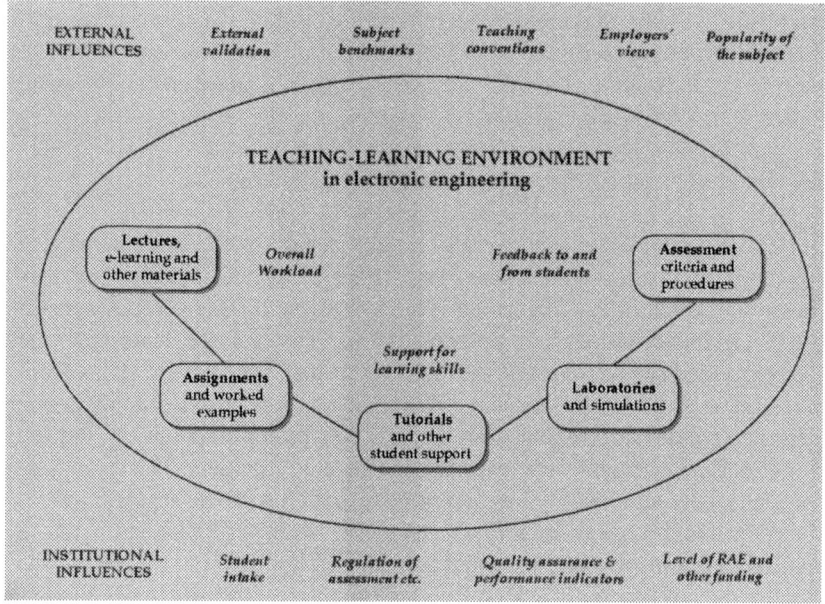

Fig. 2. Teaching–learning environments in electronic engineering.

The main purpose of this analysis was to test one of the main aims of the project, namely that the provision of a teaching-learning environment which was organised to ensure constructive alignment and taught so as to promote understanding would lead to higher achievement and deeper approaches to studying. All the scales derived from the two questionnaires were included, with the addition of two items to cover a vocational extrinsic orientation and a feeling of a lack of purpose in being on the course. Two additional scales were created by subtracting the score on the deep approach prior to the beginning of the unit from the deep approach adopted during the unit itself.

The first factor has an identical pattern for both the total sample and electronic engineering. It describes positive perceptions of the teaching and learning experienced on the unit with increases in deep approach and decreases in surface approach. It also shows substantial loadings on the self-ratings on knowledge, skills and doing well on the unit. The second factor is defined in the total sample almost entirely in terms of organised studying together with effort and concentration. In the engineering sample, however, the factor also shows substantial loadings on self-ratings on skills and doing well both before and during the unit. It also suggested links with perceived easiness of the demands made by the course, as well as an increase in deep approach and support by other students. The final two factors describe deep

Table 1. Factor analysis of scales from the two questionnaires for total and engineering samples

Scales / Factor	Total sample I	II	III	IV	Engineering sample I	II	III	IV
Entry characteristics								
Intrinsic orientation			.30				.60	
Extrinsic (vocational)								.23
Lack of purpose				.33				.44
Intrinsic reasons							.45	
Extrinsic reasons				.27				.32
Prior academic progress								
Self-rating on doing well previously	.22		-.25		.41			-.25
Prior approaches to studying								
Deep approach			.96				.77	
Monitoring studying		.28	.52				.68	
Organised studying		.73				.53	.28	
Effort management		.71				.52	.27	
Surface approach				.98				.97
Easiness of perceived demands								
Knowledge requirements	.42				.26	.36		
Skill requirements	.42				.29	.42		
Experiences of teaching								
Course organisation	.78				.89			
Teaching for deep learning	.83				.80		.21	
Interest and relevance	.72				.68			
Staff support for leaning	.68				.70			
Student support	.35				.28	.20		
Changes in approaches								
Increase in deep approach	.39	-.53			.23	.22	-.47	
Increase in surface approach	-.33			-.54	-.38			-.56
Changes in achievements								
Increase in knowledge	.64				.59			
Increase in skills	.52				.30	.33		
Academic progress in course unit								
Self-rating on doing well on unit	.41				.28	.51		
Inter-correlation between factors	I	II	III	IV	I	II	III	IV
I *Experiences and outcomes*	•	.29	.19	-.13	•	.29	.00	.00
II *Organisation and effort*		•	.22	-.11		•	.17	.00
III *Deep approach*			•	-.27			•	-.22
IV *Surface approach*				•				•

Note. N = 1970 undergraduate students for all subject areas; 365 electronic engineering students The four factors extracted 47.5% and 49.7% of the variance respectively. Loadings > .40 are highlighted; < .20 omitted.

and surface approaches linked to intrinsic and extrinsic reasons for being in higher education, with surface also being quite strongly linked to a feeling of a lack of purpose among the engineering students. The negative relationships with changes in the approach suggest that students with high scores on either deep or surface are more likely to decrease their scores, but this is presumably an artefact created by regression to the mean.

Having looked at overall relationships, the next step is to look at teaching and learning in five of the settings in which we have been working. The first two are essentially case studies, using mainly the interview data to describe the context and the experiences of students. In the space available, it is impossible to explain the way in which these main findings were rooted in the qualitative analyses. The first of the case studies looks at a city college in which electronics is taught at an introductory level. All the other settings involve the teaching of a specific aspect of the degree course – analogue electronics – and so, before looking at the second case study, we need to discover what staff and students said about the ways of thinking that are required in that sub-area of the subject. After describing the second case study, analyses of the three of the remaining settings, taken together, are presented, making use of the inventory data, as well as the interviews.

2.2 Introduction to microprocessors in a city college

The first case study is a summary of an earlier publication (Bromage & Whitaker, 2005). It describes work which looked at a first year module of an electronic engineering on a course leading to a pre-degree level award (HNC). The module tutor characterises its main focus as using microprocessors in problem-solving systems. During the first "baseline" year, a cohort of ten students were aged between 17-19, most on "day release" from electrical maintenance in industrial settings and progressing from a two-year National Diploma. In the "follow-up" year, the cohort of eleven students was similar in character.

The module tutor's insight into "baseline" teaching and learning issues was sound; analysis of the data collected in the course of the ETL project tended to confirm and elaborate on them. The central issue, the module's "perceived relevance", cut across several, interrelated aspects, "teaching and learning activities", "ways of thinking and practising in the discipline", "core and threshold concepts", "set work and assessment strategies", "learning resources and support materials", "the influence of the academic community and validating bodies" and "students" perceptions of the learning environment. Two further issues, "learner independence" and "social relations and support" invoked relationships between "student engagement", "student independence" and "tutor feedback".

The central issue was traced to the equipment deployed in the module and it's alignment with technologies visible in the students' occupational milieu. Arguably, a precipitating factor was their colleagues' minimal understanding of what the students had learned or why. The influence of this "community of practice" (Wenger, 1999) apparently precipitated a "crisis of confidence" or "intellectual isolation" in the "baseline" students. Their occupational milieu emphasises the practicalities of "engineering technologists", whereas the occupational model built into the module is arguably of the "holistic professional engineer" (Robinson & Bramhall, 2001).

2.2.1 The agreed intervention

In the "baseline" year, learning activities featured the obsolete Z80 microchip, which has similar architecture to recent chips, and a BECCA-plus single-board computer, which lacks user-friendliness. The students consequently expended much time and energy mastering the equipment, a "core concept" aspect, and this arguably sapped their enthusiasm and confused them as to the module aims.

Their perceptions influenced the tutor, who decided to introduce the Programmable Interface Controller (PIC), a user-friendly update on the Z80 featuring enhanced functionality. The students were expected to master the equipment faster, facilitating a shift in emphasis from "core concepts" towards "ways of thinking and practising", using microprocessors to solve problems, through project-based learning. The approach was expected to foster independent learning. The "baseline" module was largely tutor-led, albeit with some hands-on programming. Project work in the "collaborative year shifted the balance towards student-centred working, with "tutor-led" provision of background resources.

The baseline year assessment, undertaken during the module's second half, comprised two reports on "peripheral equipment" and a three-hour written exam. The follow-up session featured project-based assessment with timetabled formative feedback, and in-class discussions on learning activities with tutor feedback. However, the follow-up cohort called for a "whole class" approach, as individual student's problems tended to dominate the sessions.

2.2.2 Responses to the collaborative initiative

The changes made in the follow-up session depended upon replacing the Z80 with the PIC processor system. This highlights how available facilities tend to condition and constrain teaching and learning possibilities. The baseline cohort had complained about BECCA-plus from the start, and saw the module as "too theoretical". The follow-up cohort had no complaints about the PIC-based single board computer. The follow-up year featured greater alignment between the visible technologies deployed in the module and those in the in students' workplaces. However, several students expressed similar reservations to their predecessors. It is arguable that is the role of abstract theory in the working practices of the "holistic professional" may be the main problem. Introducing the PIC processor enabled the tutor to "network" with the academic community, as suggested in particular by Smith (2002), who has developed a PIC-based computer and associated learning activities. Wider possibilities include using the PIC in distance learning, as discussed by Hett and Schubert (2003).

2.3 Ways of thinking in analogue electronics

In our initial discussions with staff and interviews with students, we began by exploring the nature of topics within analogue electronic engineering. Previous research had suggested that one of the specific difficulties students encounter in electronics is that they are faced with contrasting representations or models of a circuit – the actual circuit, the circuit diagram, simplifying transforms of it, algebraic solutions, and computer simulations (Entwistle et al., 1989). Students have to move between these different representations in solving problems or designing circuits and they also need to understand the function of a circuit in both practical and theoretical ways – the engineering applications and the physics of how it behaves.

In analogue electronics, one additional difficulty seems to be that understanding involves both analytic skills and an "intuitive" grasp of circuit characteristics – intuitive in the sense that the characteristics of analogue circuits are less transparent and predictable than digital ones. Students thus have to build up substantial experience of the properties of many different kinds of circuit before they can "see" what lies behind any new circuit diagram they meet or can decide what type of circuit will be required in a design problem.

Understanding electronic circuits thus involves a combination of intuition derived from experience, detailed analysis using problem-solving skills that involve algebraic knowledge and dexterity, and imagination in designing new circuits. This combination of skills, not surprisingly, creates more difficulty than other areas of the curriculum. Staff and students alike explained that a rather different way of thinking was required for analogue compared with digital, one which many students initially found it more difficult to acquire. As one undergraduate student commented:

> I think it requires a different kind of mindset than digital, which seems to be more to do with computer science. For analogue, I think it is much more mathematical and analytical. Even just a little difference in a circuit can make a big difference to how it operates, so you have to realise that and go back to first principles and work out how it works again.

2.4 Final-year analogue electronics in a new university

The main focus here is on staff and student perceptions of the teaching-learning environment in a final-year unit (Nisbet, Entwistle, Robinson, & McQuillin, 2005). Unusually, all of the teaching is delivered by one lecturer with responsibility for analogue electronics throughout the three years of the degree. Analysis of students' responses to our second questionnaire (ETLQ) indicated a high level of satisfaction with their experience of teaching and learning in the unit. The lecturer was perceived as having made the subject more interesting and having provided more examples than was the case in other units. The assessment had been made clearer, with good feedback on set work. Students also felt more confident about their knowledge and understanding. Interviews were also carried out with the lecturer and two groups of students, to explore their perspectives in greater detail.

2.4.1 The lecturer's perspective

The lecturer had considerable experience both in HE teaching and in industry. In his interview comments he emphasised the practical nature of the degree, together with the coherence, continuity and increasing complexity of the teaching and learning over the three years. Asked what he wanted the students to get out of the course, he emphasised the importance of teaching for understanding. He described how he tried to keep things simple, particularly with the maths, using repetition to promote understanding and drawing on a mixture of methods to encourage active participation, including gapped notes and diagrams. Above all, he emphasised the importance of hard work for the achievement of real understanding. He actively looked out for evidence of understanding, for example from his continuous assessment of laboratory work. He openly acknowledged that his approach was determined both by the changing nature of the student intake and a reduction in class contact time. He described his approach as one that started where the students were and led them gradually towards increasing confidence and self reliance. He also highlighted the influence of the lecturer in the encouragement of student learning by his own approach and behaviour towards students: conveying his own enthusiasm; being approachable and available outside timetabled classes; and being well organised and prepared.

2.4.2 The students' perspective

As already indicated, frequency distributions of items from the second questionnaire showed a high level of satisfaction with the experiences of this course unit, and this was supported by the student interview data. Those interviewed were particularly appreciative of the lecturer's organisation, approachability, availability, patient explanation and general supportiveness, all of which were perceived as having positive benefits for learning. Asked how they went about learning analogue electronics, students described a particular way of thinking that depended on memorisation for understanding, especially with regard to mathematical equations. In terms of doing well in analogue, they demonstrated awareness of their own responsibilities as learners in terms of maintaining interest and enthusiasm and putting in the work. This, they felt, was particularly important given that analogue continued throughout the three years of the degree, unlike other one-semester units where "you never look at it again".

The students also talked about the incremental nature of the subject, how it built on learning and knowledge from previous years and the importance of mastering the "building blocks" and keeping up with the work. Another aspect referred specifically to the importance of learning how to apply the theory; demonstrating applications to the world of work; and learning to think like a professional engineer. Some would have liked even more in the way of practical application, seeing the skills they were developing as related mainly to academic theory rather than to professional practice. Students who had done a placement year were enthusiastic about their experience of placement and emphatic that the course theory and concepts should be even more closely linked to applications met in industry, with more practical, hands-on experience. They also referred specifically to the benefits of the placement experience when tackling their final year project and to the positive motivational impact of the placement on their approach to their final year studies.

To sum up, both lecturer and students commented on the perceived advantages of continuity, coherence and connectedness over the degree programme as a whole. While this stemmed here from the unusual situation of having one lecturer teaching analogue electronics throughout the degree course, it does at least raise the issue of how best to ensure such coherence, given the growing recognition of the difficulties which students experience within a modular system without built-in connections between modules.

2.5 Analogue electronics in the two research-intensive universities

The next step is to look at the two research-intensive universities, starting with the methods of teaching and learning that were used across all the course units. We then draw mainly on the questionnaire data to examine differences between the three of the units in which collaborative initiatives were carried out, considering items which brought out these differences most clearly and, in particular, the approaches to studying that students reported carrying out before the unit started and during the analogue unit. We then consider the teaching-learning activities which students mentioned as being most helpful in their learning in these units, or making it more difficult. These analyses formed the basis of suggestions for the collaborative initiatives carried out, with the reasons for them being explained. Finally, we shall examine the way the initiatives were implemented and how students reacted to them.

2.5.1 Teaching and learning in the three settings

There was substantial similarity between the two departments in how the skills in thinking about analogue circuits were developed. Lectures introduced the theoretical ideas underlying various types of analogue circuits, their functions, and the analytic procedures involved in calculating the expected outputs from those circuits. Students were expected to work through a substantial number of circuit problems to build up the ability to recognise the component parts of circuits which combine to produce effects on the input to the circuit. Work on these examples was done partly by the students independently and partly during group tutorials or "examples classes" where help was provided by the lecturer or tutor. Assessment was based entirely on end-of-unit examination, except in one unit where some course work also counted. Students obtained rather little individual feedback on work handed in, although general pointers were provided on performance in class tests and all course units offered some worked examples through which students could check their own solutions. Laboratory experience was provided within a separate unit in the second-year courses, but it covered all the course units being taught at that time, with no direct match possible with topics being taught in the lectures. It was intended that students who attended the classes and completed the work would have a sufficient grasp of the topics to be successful in the end-of-unit examinations, but failure rates proved disappointingly high at the first sitting in all three units during the first phase of the project.

Although the types of teaching and the assignments were very similar across the three units, interviews with the staff suggested that there were marked differences in the way they thought about the subject, and those were, to some extent, reflected in the teaching. Staff who had substantial experience of working in industry were more likely to explain circuits in a functional manner, emphasising design aspects, while other lecturers brought the logical structure of the topic area to the fore, stressing the physical and analytic aspects more strongly. Thus, the teaching of analogue electronics varied in the relative prominence given to analysing existing circuits in mathematical detail and to considering how circuits could be designed to achieve required outputs. There seemed to be no disagreement about the need for both ways of thinking, but the balance between the analytic and the functional does seem to affect how students perceive the subject.

> When you're sitting and learning in class you tend to be doing circuit analysis and looking at equations whereas when you do anything in the real world or in the lab, you want to go in exactly the reverse direction. You want to take an idea and figure out how to implement it rather than have an implementation and figure out how it works... It's in the final stage, when you've already put all this effort and all this design and time into a circuit, you know that the analysis, no matter how hard it is, has to be done.

During the first year of our collaboration with departments, we sought to discover which aspects of the teaching students found most helpful, and which learning had proved most difficult for them. Students generally appreciated the overall quality of the *teaching* and the efforts that staff were making to help them to understand. Although students expected to find analogue interesting, they did not expect it to be easy; and that was their subsequent experience. In both second-year course units, a substantial proportion of the students reported aspects of analogue to be difficult to understand and suggested ways in which they might be given more support through the teaching arrangements. There was also a more general feeling about the "sameness" of their learning experience that became de-motivating over time.

> [In the learning, you're repeatedly] reading it, hearing it, talking about it, doing it, doing it, doing it... Personally for me that system doesn't work. And I don't know, I guess that's probably why, for first, second and part of third year, it was a case of scraping by. Except for in the case of projects, I've tried to go through the motions; it's the sameness. It's [the same] pattern, and each day is that pattern.

2.5.2 Comparisons between course units

Besides knowing how the items and scales interrelate, it was also important to consider differences between the three units on all the main aspects included in the first year of the work with departments. To make clearer what students were actually rating, individual items have been used throughout Table 2 which presents two kinds of comparison. For most of the items, straight comparisons are made between the three courses – two second-year courses and a smaller third-year unit. But the items describing approaches to studying introduce comparisons between the ways students said they were studying *before* starting the analogue unit and how they studied *during* that unit. (As these items are derived from well-established general scales, the wordings do not necessarily fit ideally with specific study activities undertaken in electronic engineering, but students do seem to be able to interpret them within that context.)

Looking at the ways students described how they were studying before and during the unit, we find that in Courses A and B the students' approaches *during* the unit were less deep, less organised and more surface, than their general approaches reported at the beginning of the unit. In Course C, however, the first deep item (which provides the clearest indication of a deep approach) suggests a deeper approach in the unit than beforehand in one item, and that is reinforced by a reduced level of surface approach in both those items.

In all three course units, students reported putting in less effort than in other units and, from the frequency distributions of individual questionnaire items, it seemed that about a quarter of students in each of the second-year classes had probably failed to put in the time and effort required to master the techniques. Some of the students indicated in the interviews that they had been deterred by the initial difficulty and so adopted "surface" coping strategies, rather than engaging with the problems in ways that would lead to understanding. As one student commented:

> You work through the tutorial problems and, for the analogue ones, you don't get any answers out of them. You ... sit down and work through the problems and realise you've done all of them wrong ... and you can't see how in the world you got from point "a" to point "b"... I tended to [work] blindly. I knew if I [just] followed these steps,

> then I could come to an answer... We can teach ourselves ... to do an example and have no idea what to do and we scrape by. But we probably would have got great marks had we actually understood what we were doing.

Students need to be convinced that the effort they have to put in is worthwhile and that they will be able to reach solutions to a reasonable proportion of the examples set.

In other research on electronic engineering students, Scheja (2002) suggested that they had experienced *delayed understanding*, as a result of which they felt they were falling behind in their studies and used a variety of coping ploys to try to catch up. Students in our own study made comments that suggest a similar experience. Of course, some delay in understanding is to be expected, but in this subject area it seems to be substantial. One second-year student commented:

> In second year I got a better understanding of what I learnt in first year. Now in third year I've kind of learnt what I was supposed to know in second year. It's a shame that I've never felt that I've learned it in the actual year [it was taught]...When you're being taught something, you're just desperately trying to learn it, and there's not necessarily a whole lot of interest. You're scrambling back to notes [in preparing for the exams], trying to understand the course. [Later on], you do get interested and [then] things start to fall into place.

2.5.3 Approaches to problem solving

Students interviewed generally agreed that they were, at first, not at all clear how to solve tutorial problems. They were looking for clear strategies to be offered within the lectures that would guide them more easily towards the solutions. They also wanted more worked examples to be provided to offer additional guidance. Although recognising that worked examples could be helpful, staff were wary of too much "spoon-feeding" in case it encouraged the mindless following of routines. As we have seen, both staff and students agreed that there was a way of thinking associated with the analysis of analogue circuits that had to be mastered, but achieving this competence proved difficult for a substantial proportion of the students. The marked tendency for surface approaches to be adopted made understanding less likely. It therefore seemed sensible to concentrate our collaborative initiatives on helping to make students more consciously alert to the ways of thinking that were involved, and to explore the reasons for the difficulty experienced more fully in the second year of the work with departments. The initiative agreed was based thus based on the evidence collected in the first year of the collaboration, but also on the more general research on student learning and psychology.

Table 2. Percentage agreement with items by questionnaire and course unit.

Scales and items Number of students competing first/both/second questionnaires		Second year Course A (N = 94/68/75)		Second year Course B (N = 68/40/49)		Third year Course C (N = 54/32/40)	
Attitudes towards the degree course							
I want to study the subject in depth		87.2		77.9		61.1	
I sometimes wonder why I ever decided to come here		5.2		14.7		29.6	
Relative easiness of demands made by course unit							
What I was expected to know to begin with.		65.3		71.4		62.5	
The rate at which new material was introduced		25.3		46.9		72.5	
The amount of work I was expected to do		33.3		34.7		52.5	
Approaches to studying		before	during	before	during	before	during
I usually set out to understand what we had to learn	deep	95.6	72.1	87.5	82.5	81.2	75.0
I look at evidence carefully to reach my own conclusion	deep	75.0	57.4	67.5	50.0	31.2	43.7
I've often had trouble in making sense of the things	surface	25.0	61.8	40.0	55.0	43.7	34.4
What I've learned seems unrelated bits and pieces…	surface	11.8	23.5	25.0	32.5	40.6	9.4
I have generally put a lot of effort into my studying	effort	60.3	51.5	77.5	60.0	53.1	40.6
I'm quite systematic and organised in my studying	organisation	65.9	44.1	62.5	47.5	46.9	50.0
Experiences of the teaching provided in the course unit							
How this unit was taught fitted in with what we were supposed to learn.		72.0		67.3		97.5	
I could see the relevance of most of what we were taught in this unit.		78.7		79.6		95.0	
I found most of what I learned in this course unit really interesting		45.3		34.7		82.5	
Plenty of examples illustrations were given to help us to grasp things		66.7		51.0		95.0	
Staff tried to share their enthusiasm about the subject with us.		89.3		91.8		100.0	
Staff were patient in explaining things which seemed difficult to grasp.		81.3		81.6		92.5	
Staff gave me the support I needed to help me complete the set work		69.3		51.0		75.0	
The feedback given on my set work helped to clarify things		63.7		30.6		47.5	
Talking with other students helped me to develop my understanding		81.3		71.4		72.5	
Students supported each other & tried to give help when it was needed		81.3		73.5		85.0	
Self-ratings of learning outcomes							
Knowledge and understanding about the topics covered		73.3		69.4		92.5	
Ability to think about ideas or to solve problems		77.3		71.4		92.5	
Skills or technical procedures specific to the subject		70.7		61.2		95.0	

2.5.4 Expert and novice learning

There is a substantial research literature in psychology on how novices differ from experts in the problem-solving skills required in employment settings, and how such skills can best be developed (Sternberg, Grigorenko, & Ferrari, 2002). Although problem-solving in electronic engineering clearly has aspects which are specific, there should still be elements in common with professional contexts. The main features highlighted in this psychological research were found in the teaching of analogue electronics, although not always in a fully developed form.

All the units gave students a large number of examples chosen to cover the most salient differences in the problems, but novices also have to be encouraged to look for recurring patterns and to develop systematic strategies. While students asked to be given clear guidelines for solution strategies, lecturers were aware of possible pitfalls. They wanted students to realise that mindless following of such guidelines would not get them very far in analogue electronics. The psychological research suggests that, in the early stages, novices do need the "scaffolding" provided by set routines or strategies, with that support gradually being removed as students develop in experience and confidence. The metaphor of scaffolding is appropriate because scaffolding is an external structure that supports another structure under construction. As the new structure is completed and capable of standing on its own, the scaffolding is removed (McCormick & Pressley, 1997, p. 15).

Hearing experts solve problems out loud is also important for novices, as it makes explicit the ways of thinking used by them in reaching solutions: staff did this quite regularly but students wanted rather more of this activity. And discussions about problem-solving processes and more generally in learning, have proved effective both in engineering (Nicol & Boyle, 2003) and in other subject areas (Biggs, 2003). Students we interviewed had generally not been given such opportunities in class, although some of them had formed self-help groups in their own time. Finally, the research suggests ways of encouraging novices to internalise their reasoning processes, for example, by making notes about mistakes made and better ways of tackling the problems. Some students seemed to be doing this, but others were not working so systematically.

2.5.5 The collaborative initiatives

All the teaching staff agreed to explore ways of encouraging more students to use a deep approach by focusing explicitly on the processes and strategies of problem-solving. Besides putting a strong emphasis on explaining the processes in lectures and tutorials (as was already happening), it was decided to introduce other student activities during the second year of the collaboration.

As a way of encouraging students to think more consciously about problem solving, students were asked to carry out their work on problems in a tutorial "log-book" which staff could look at during tutorials. They were encouraged to note down corrections to their attempted solutions in ways that would draw attention to where they had gone wrong, and what they should have done. Besides making their thinking explicit, the log-book also drew their attention to the need to build up a substantial number of solutions there. It was also agreed, where possible, also to get students to work together in small groups to discuss the problem-solving processes both in classes and in their own time.

2.5.6 Implementing the initiatives

In the event unexpected difficulties prevented a full implementation of the initiative in two of the units. The start was substantially delayed in Course A due to a prolonged illness of the lead lecturer, and was only used for a short time in Course B; however, it was fully implemented in Course

C. Questionnaires given at the end of each unit contained additional questions specifically about how much the students believed that the various teaching-learning activities on the unit had contributed to their learning and understanding. In addition, students were asked to add their own comments about what helped and hindered, and these will contribute to the eventual conclusions.

Table 3. Mean scores of ratings of relative helpfulness of teaching-learning activities

Teaching-learning activity	Mean scores on a 1 – 7 scale		
	Course A	Course B	Course C
	Mean (SD)	Mean (SD)	Mean (SD)
	N = 59	N = 73	N = 27
The way diagrams presented	5.0 (1.3)	5.3 (1.2)	5.9 (0.6)
The way ideas explained in lectures	4.3 (1.6)	5.6 (1.2)	5.2 (0.8)
Lecture explanations of problems	4.2 (1.8)	5.8 (1.3)	4.9 (1.1)
Worked examples provided	5.0 (1.4)	3.6 (2.1)	5.7 (1.1)
Working on problems on own	5.2 (1.3)	4.6 (1.5)	5.3 (0.9)
Using the log-book	4.2 (1.7)	4.3 (1.5)	5.1 (0.9)
Staff help in tutorials	5.0 (1.7)	4.0 (2.3)	5.9 (1.1)
Discussions with other students	4.8 (2.1)	4.7 (2.0)	5.0 (2.0)
Feedback on work submitted	3.5 (2.1)	3.6 (2.2)	2.6 (2.4)
Class tests and the results	4.3 (1.8)	4.2 (1.9)	not given

Table 3 shows the mean and standard deviations on seven-point scales for the samples obtained in the collaborative phase of the project, indicating how much each of the aspects was believed to contribute. The data were collected within lecture periods with inevitable variations in the nature of the samples obtained. There seemed little point, therefore, in carrying out tests of significance. The differences have thus to be seen as simply indicative, and used in conjunction with open-ended written comments and interview data to draw tentative conclusions.

Unit A was perceived by the students responding as being very strong in the provision of worked examples and in enabling students to work on problems on their own, supported by effective help in tutorials, although the explanations in lectures were rated less highly. Unit B was almost the converse, with the explanations appreciated, but worked examples and the tutorial help less highly regarded. There was considerable variation in the rating of tutorials in this unit, however, as students from different degree courses (such as mechanical engineering and computing) reported contrasting experiences. In neither unit was the feedback on work submitted felt to be very helpful, and that seems to have been a general reaction from students across most of the units we have looked at. These views were also expressed in the interviews.

The use of log-books was the main innovation in the teaching in all three units and it was hardly surprising that students rated that activity highly only where it had been fully implemented. In the interviews, reactions to the log-books varied. Initial reservations about an additional task were expected, and found, but there were also positive comments. Students appreciated having all their workings together and found their own comments helpful when reviewing their workings.

Some students also found that they had become more aware of the need to keep up with their work in preparing for the tutorials. A typical comment was:

> I got used to writing down all the problems in the log-book and then you can sort of look back and read through it and understand what you have done... At first I'd just look at a couple of tutorial questions and write down what I thought. But now I've got, like, pages of stuff written down, so I think the log-book now is really important to my understanding.

It was clear, however, that students did not appreciate being told precisely how they should use the log-books, as they develop a way of using them that is coherent with their established ways of studying. And some students had found it difficult to know what type of comments to make: reflection on learning processes does not come naturally and so requires a thorough introduction and substantial help until the idea has been fully grasped.

2.6 Teaching to enhance learning

The final analysis to date brings us more directly to the main aim of the project – to identify ways of enhancing the quality of student learning. This analysis has brought together all the items in the second questionnaire used to report students' experiences of the teaching with the additional items specific to electronic engineering (N = 129). Three of seven factors extracted described the main differences among the specific items, and these were linked to a sub-set of the general items. The combination of the two groups of items within each factor helps to suggest what aspects of the teaching-learning environment in analogue electronics students found most helpful in supporting their learning. The items picked out by these three factors are shown in Table 4. The first group of items describes teaching that is perceived by the students to be coherently organised and which is seen as providing good explanations and examples, emphasising the need to think more deeply about the subject. The second group indicates the types of support that students appreciated in working on the examples, while the third suggested the ways in which collaborating with other students had helped.

A tentative suggestion emerging from an overview of the analyses to date is that there are some aspects of the teaching and learning that are more directly, even logically and inevitably, related to the nature of the subject bring taught, while others derive from more general pedagogic considera-

Table 4. Items defining factors related to aspects helpful in learning analogue

Items are presented in the order of the size (above 0.35) of factor loadings in each set of items

Well-organised teaching providing good explanations, examples, emphasising thinking

Items on what helped in learning analogue
The way the lecturer(s) explained how to think about problems
The way ideas and concepts were explained in the lectures
The way diagrams were presented and used in lectures

General items relating to experiences of teaching and learning
Staff helped us to see how you are supposed to think and reach conclusions in this subject
Staff tried to share their enthusiasm about the subject with us
We weren't just given information; staff explained how knowledge is developed in this subject
The course unit was well organised and ran smoothly
The teaching encouraged me to rethink my understanding of some aspects of the subject
We were given a good deal of choice over how we went about learning
How this unit was taught fitted in well with what we were supposed to learn
Plenty of examples and illustrations were given to help us grasp things better

Supporting students' work on tutorial examples

Items on what helped in learning analogue
The help give by staff as you worked on tutorial problems
Feedback and comments from staff on the work submitted
Worked examples provided in handouts or on the web
The class tests and the results you were given
Working on the tutorial problems on your own

General items relating to experiences of teaching and learning
The feedback given on my work helped me to improve my ways of learning and studying
Staff gave me the support I needed to help me complete the set work for this unit
The feedback given on my set work helped to clarify things I hadn't fully understood
The different types of teaching (lectures, tutorials, labs., etc.) supported each other well
On this unit, I was prompted to think about how well I was learning and how I might improve
Doing the set work helped me to think about how evidence is used in this subject
I was encouraged to think about how best to tackle the set work

Working collaboratively with other students

Items on what helped in learning analogue
Group discussions with other students on doing the problems

General items relating to experiences of teaching and learning
Talking with other students helped me to develop my understanding
Students supported each other and tried to give help when it was needed
I found I could generally work comfortably with other students on this unit

tions. While this analytic separation seems worth exploring further, the reality is unlikely to allow clear-cut divisions and may well differ between contexts. At the current stage of our analysis certain aspects do seem to be logically essential for students to develop an understanding of analogue circuits, while others play a more supportive role in making the students' work easier and more enjoyable. Only if the logically necessary components are well developed, and sufficient of the supportive elements are present, will students report substantial satisfaction with their experience and find it relatively easy to develop their understanding. And, if substantiated, this conclusion will probably apply generally in the teaching of electronics, and possibly in other disciplines.

Looking, finally, at the project as a whole, it is demonstrating the value of using detailed feedback questionnaires, together with group interviews, to describe students' experiences of teaching. In this way it becomes much clearer which aspects of the teaching-learning activities are most appreciated by students as supporting their learning, and interpreting those findings in relation to the explanations provided by staff suggests ways in which current provision may be strengthened. At this stage of the project, these elements in teaching and learning electronics are only gradually becoming clear through the ongoing analyses of interview transcripts. Bringing together the whole set of analyses, and looking at these in relation to the other subject areas, should enable us to describe more clearly what is specific to teaching and learning in those disciplines and professional areas.

References

Beaty, E., Gibbs, G., & Morgan, A. (1997). Learning orientations and study contracts. In F. Marton, D. J. Hounsell, & N. J. Entwistle (Eds.), *The experience of learning* (2nd ed.) (pp. 72-88). Edinburgh: Scottish Academic Press.

Biggs, J. B. (2003). *Teaching for quality at university* (2nd ed.). Buckingham: SRHE & Open University.

Bromage, A., & Whitaker, P. (2005). Frission chips: Perceived relevance and microprocessor systems. *International Journal of Electrical Engineering Education, 42,* 21-29.

Entwistle, N. J. (2003). *Concepts and conceptual frameworks underpinning the ETL project* (ETL Occasional Reports, no. 3). Universities of Edinburgh, Durham and Coventry, ETL Project.

Entwistle, N. J., Hounsell, D. J., Macaulay, C., Situnayake, G., & Tait, H. (1989). *The performance of electrical engineering students in Scottish higher education.* Edinburgh: Scottish Education Department.

Entwistle, N.J., & Ramsden, P. (1983). *Understanding student learning.* London: Croom Helm.

Hett, A., & Schubert, T. (2003, September). *The mobile hardware lab.* Paper presented at the 2nd Global Virtual Learning and Higher Education Conference, Mansfield College, Oxford. (Abstract accessed at http://www.inter-disciplinary.net/vlhe03s5.htm August 2004).

McCormick, C., & Pressley, M. (1997). *Educational psychology: Learning, instruction, assessment.* New York: Longman.

Meyer, J. H. F. (1991). Study orchestration: The manifestation, interpretation and consequences of contextualised approaches to studying. *Higher Education, 22,* 297-316.

Meyer, J. H. F. (2000). Variation in contrasting forms of 'memorising' and associated observables. *British Journal of Educational Psychology, 70,* 163-176.

Nicol, D. J., & Boyle, J. T. (2003). Peer instruction versus class-wide discussion in large classes: A comparison of two interaction methods in the wired classroom. *Studies in Higher Education, 28*, 457-473.

Nisbet, J. B., Entwistle, N. J., Robinson, I. M., & McQuillin, B. (2005). Staff and student perceptions of the teaching-learning environment: A case study. *International Journal of Electrical Engineering Education, 42*, 30-40.

Pask, G. (1976). Styles and strategies of learning. *British Journal of Educational Psychology, 46*, 128-148.

Phillips, D. C. (Ed.). (2000). *Constructivism in education.* Chicago, IL: National Society for the Study of Education.

Robinson, I., & Bramhall, M. (2001, December). *The engineering professional: Education or formation?* Joint inaugural lecture, Sheffield Hallam University.

Scheja, M (2002). *Contextualising studies in higher education: First-year experiences of studying and learning in engineering.* Published Ph.D. thesis, Stockholm University Stockholm, Department of Education.

Smith, D. W. (2002). *PIC in practice: An introduction to the PIC microcontroller.* London: Butterworth-Heinemann.

Sternberg, R. J., Grigorenko, E. L., & Ferrari, M. (2002). Fostering intellectual excellence through developing expertise. In M. Ferrari (Ed.), *The pursuit of excellence through education* (pp. 57-84). Mahwah, NJ: Lawrence Erlbaum.

Tait, H., Entwistle, N. J., & McCune, V. (1998). ASSIST: A reconceptualisation of the *Approaches to Studying Inventory.* In C. Rust (Ed.), *Improving student learning: Improving students as learners* (pp. 262-271). Oxford: Oxford Centre for Staff and Learning Development.

Vermunt, J. D. (1998). The regulation of constructive learning processes. *British Journal of Educational Psychology ,68,* 149-171.

Wenger, E. (1999). *Communities of practice: Learning, meaning and identity.* Cambridge: Cambridge University Press.

Wiske, M. S. (Ed.) (1998). *Teaching for understanding: Linking research with practice.* San Francisco: Jossey-Bass.

Chapter 11

Learner control over information presentation in powerful electronic learning environments used in physics education

*Liesbeth Kester, Paul Kirschner,
and Gemma Corbalán-Pérez*

1 Introduction

Modern curricula are increasingly making use of powerful electronic learning environments (pELEs) to facilitate complex cognitive skill acquisition. Such environments stimulate active learning – knowledge construction by learners based on their cognitive and social activities in meaningful contexts (Salomon, 1998; Brown, Collins & Duguid, 1989) – by giving learners control over an environment containing realistic practice problems such as simulations and games (Merrill, 2002; Reigeluth, 1999; van Merriënboer & Kirschner, 2001) and varied information resources such as texts, auditory fragments, and animations. PELEs enable a qualitatively different way of learning compared to traditional learning environments (i.e., traditional classes and textbooks) in that they allow for learning in a non-linear fashion by giving learners more control over the instructional material. In these environments learners are allowed to select information, tasks, instructional formats (e.g., video, audio, graphic, or text), interface properties, and content (e.g., examples, analogies) in their preferred order and at their own pace (Merrill & David, 1994). The realistic practice problems in pELEs help learners (1) master complex skills that require integration of the knowledge, skills and attitudes necessary for effective performance, (2) learn to coordinate sub-skills that make up the complex skill, and, eventually, (3) transfer what is learned to situations outside school.

This chapter zooms in on learner control over information presentation and the acquisition of complex cognitive skills during problem solving in pELEs. The following sections will discuss the information that plays a role during complex cognitive skill acquisition and learner control over information presentation in pELEs and its effects on learning.

2 Information

Through the years many different terms have been used to distinguish between knowledge and accompanying information types that enable learners to perform complex skills and solve problems. In this contribution, the terms declarative and procedural are used to describe the knowledge learners need in order to perform complex skills and the terms theoretical and practical are used to describe the information necessary to help learners acquire these knowledge and skills during learning.

Declarative knowledge refers to the representations people have of objects and events in the outside world which is organized in what cognitive-psychological models refer to as *cognitive schemata*. In high school electronics, for instance, knowledge about the flow of current in an electrical circuit, strategies that can be used for troubleshooting a failed electrical circuit and knowledge about possible causes of the problem are considered declarative knowledge. This knowledge stored in cognitive schemata enables a person to exhibit schema-based behavior, that is, it allows her/him to apply general domain knowledge to domain-specific situations. This behavior requires conscious processing on part of the learner.

Schema-based behavior relies on skills that reflect understanding of the domain and they have to be mastered during practice. Such skills allow one to actually interpret and use the cognitive schemata to deal with or understand new (problem) situations in a particular domain. In high school electronics, for example, a skill that reflects understanding is reasoning about the differences between various connections (e.g., series or parallel) in electrical circuits and their influence on the circuit.

In order to master these skills, theoretical information, such as a conceptual model of how a domain is organized, is necessary. This information enables learners to construct the cognitive schemata through *elaboration* (Reigeluth & Stein, 1983; Reigeluth, 1999). The theoretical information is gradually coupled to already existing, relevant cognitive schemata in long term memory. During practice these cognitive schemata are modified and refined, resulting in more appropriate schemata given the experiences. This process is called *induction* (Proctor & Reeve, 1988; Holland, Holyoak, Nisbett, & Thagard, 1986). Elaboration of theoretical information and induction yields cognitive schemata that contain domain-general knowledge which is particularly useful when learners have to deal with unfamiliar problem situations. These situations require interpretation of cognitive schemata, that is, a different use of the same domain-general knowledge.

Procedural knowledge refers to operations carried out on the declarative knowledge. Automated cognitive schemata or productions are considered to be the cognitive units of this knowledge. Productions consist of a condition and an action. *If* the condition is met *then* the action takes place. For example, if current is to flow through a circuit, then the switch must be thrown or if a voltmeter has been connected in series then this must be changed and connected in parallel since current cannot flow through a voltmeter. The procedural knowledge stored in the productions enables the exhibition of *rule-based behavior*, that is, it allows the application of specific domain knowledge (i.e., rules) to domain-specific situations. This behavior does not require conscious processing on the part of the learner but is executed automatically (i.e., without thinking). This rule-based behavior relies on execution skills that also have to be mastered during practice. Execution skills allow the application of cognitive rules to new problem situations in a domain. In high school electronics, for instance, they allow the recognition of a switch and the need to push it or the recognition of a short circuit and how to fix it.

Mastery of execution skills requires the availability of practical information, such as task specific rules along with the facts, principles, or concepts needed to correctly apply these rules. This information enables learners to form productions through *knowledge compilation* (Anderson, 1993), that is, the compilation of declarative knowledge from long-term memory into procedural knowledge. After compilation, further practice causes the productions to gain strength every time they are successfully applied during practice. This process is called *strengthening* (Anderson, 1996; Anderson, 1982). Knowledge compilation of practical information and strengthening yield productions that contain domain-specific knowledge which is particularly useful when learners have to deal with familiar problem situations because these situations require the same use of the same domain-specific knowledge.

To sum up, cognitive skill acquisition requires learners to transform theoretical information into declarative knowledge and practical information into procedural knowledge. In pELEs learners are responsible for this process themselves. They are allowed to select and learn form these information sources in their own order and at their own pace. In the next sections, issues related to this learner control over information presentation are discussed but first, the concept of learner control is briefly introduced.

3 Learner control

Allowing learners to control their own learning facilitates perseverance and improves motivation (Reeve, Hamm, & Nix, 2003). Conventional wisdom says that the more the learner controls his/her own learning, the more rewarding the experience will be. Kinzie, Sullivan, and Berdel (1988) found that by transferring the locus of control from the teacher to the learner, intrinsic motivation to learn increased and more satisfaction was derived from the learning experience, ultimately leading to improved academic performance. This has been backed up by other researchers who have determined learner control to be an essential aspect of effective learning (Gary, 1987; Kohn, 1993; Lawless & Brown, 1997; Lou, Abrami, & d'Apollonia, 2001). However, Fry (1972) showed that learners with the highest degree of learner control learned the least. So, although learner control has undeniable positive effects on motivation, its effect on learning outcomes is equivocal.

Researchers hold that as levels of expertise increase through experience, teacher control should be decreased and learner control should be increased (see Niemiec, Sikorski, & Walberg, 1996 for a review). They assume that novice learners lack adequate domain-specific cognitive schemata to judge and thus control their own instruction which predisposes them to make ineffective instructional decisions. For example, novices tended to focus more on features of multimedia learning environments (e.g., sound effects) that were irrelevant for learning at the cost of presented text that was relevant for learning (Lawless & Brown, 1997). More experienced learners who do possess adequate cognitive schemata are less apt to make ineffective instructional decisions and therefore are capable of controlling their own learning. To conclude, although learner control has beneficial effects on perseverance and motivation, it does have equivocal effects on learning and learning outcomes. In general, Merrill (1975) suggested that learner control enables learners to learn how to adapt to new and unfamiliar educational situations but this is not unambiguously confirmed in research. It appears that novices and experts flourish by different amounts of learner control. In other words, expertise is an important factor in determining the amount of learner control in a pELE.

4 Learner control over information presentation

The pELEs discussed earlier contain realistic problems and rich information resources to help learners solve these problems. The amount of learner control over these information resources in the pELEs can be varied depending on the level of expertise of the learners. Learners can be given complete control over the information resources in the pELE, they can be given limited control or they can be given complete control with additional support. In the next sections these three forms of learner control and their effects on learning and acquiring complex skills mediated by level of expertise will be discussed.

4.1 Complete learner control over information presentation

Characteristic of complete learner control over information presentation is that all information resources are simultaneously available before and/or during problem solving. This optimally allows for active learning since all of the information is available and it is up to the learner to decide when to access what.

When confronted with a learning or practice problem, all learners need certain information to help them construct their own knowledge. To then solve the problem, learners need to determine and act upon their information requirements by choosing and using the right information at the right time. However, novices in a domain do not have a good impression of what there is to know about a particular problem (Ormrod, 2004) and therefore cannot determine which information might help them to solve it. The decisions made by learners on what information to use can result in misconceptions especially when dealing with more complex problems or tasks (Hannafin, Land, & Oliver, 1999). In addition, research shows that properly perceiving the problem demands is often problematic for domain-novices (see Broekkamp, van Hout-Wolters, van den Bergh, & Rijlaarsdam, 2004 and Broekkamp, van Hout-Wolters, Rijlaarsdam, & van den Bergh, 2002 for task demands in relation to test expectations; Luyten, Lowyck, & Tuerlinckx, 2001 for task perception; and Zumbach & Reimann, 2001 for goal orientation). This impedes novices in acting upon their information requirements.

Domain experts or more experienced learners more acquainted with the problem domain as well as the problems that can arise in it are better able to determine their own information requirements as well as to act upon them. In their case, complete learner control is the preferable option. Since, learner control has beneficial effects on motivation and active learning has beneficial effects on learning outcomes.

To conclude, giving learners complete control over information presentation is problematic for domain novices because these learners have difficulty determining their own information requirements and acting upon them. For domain experts or more experienced learners, however, complete learner control over information presentation is to be preferred over system controlled information presentation because this allows for active learning. The next sections discuss how domain novices could be supported (i.e., by limited learner control or by external support) during interaction with the information resources in pELEs so as to help them become more experienced and able to control their own learning processes in these environments.

4.2 Limited learner control over information presentation

Limited learner control, as opposed to complete learner control, pre-structures and pre-orders the information availability by making the theoretical or the practical information resources only available at times that will optimally support the learning processes involved in complex skill acquisition. In order to support elaboration, the theoretical information should be available *before* practice starts and *before* learners start problem solving. In this way domain novices have a framework in which to work and can use all their available information processing capacity for elaboration. The cognitive schemata constructed through this process optimally prepare the learners for the practice that is about to come (Kester, Kirschner, van Merriënboer, & Bäumer, 2001). During practice the cognitive schemata are refined and/or enriched based on experience (i.e., induction).

In order to support knowledge compilation, the practical information should be available *during* practice and even *during* problem solving. In this way all relevant information is active in working memory at the time it needs to be applied for problem solving, which is necessary for knowledge compilation to occur (Kester et al., 2001). Further practice enables strengthening of the productions that were formed after compilation. Furthermore, the compilation of declarative knowledge or practical information into productions frees up information processing capacity (after all, no conscious processing is required for applying productions) that can be used for induction during problem solving.

Kester and colleagues studied the just-in-time approach to information availability in a physics practical (Kester, Kirschner, & van Merriënboer 2004a; Kester, Kirschner, & van Merriënboer, in press) and in an electronic statistics course (Kester, Kirschner, & van Merriënboer, 2004b). They pre-structured and pre-ordered the information according to the just-in-time approach. Learners could determine themselves to use the pre-selected information or not. The results of these studies indicated that pre-structuring the information resources led to more effective (i.e., higher test performance scores) and more efficient (i.e., high test performance scores with low investment of cognitive capacity during practice) learning outcomes compared with simultaneous availability of the information resources before or during problem solving. However, no effects were found for pre-ordering the information. Availability of the theoretical information during problem solving and the practical information before problem solving yielded the same learning outcomes as the just-in-time availability of the information. Apparently in these contexts, pre-structuring the information by type has beneficial effects on learning, but the order in which the information types are presented does not seem to matter.

To conclude, limited learner control allows domain novices to allocate their cognitive capacity to the learning processes involved in complex skill acquisition. This has beneficial effects on learning. However, pre-structuring the information by type and making it available piecemeal during practice seems to account for this effect. A specific presentation order of the information types (i.e., theoretical information before problem solving and practical information during problem solving) does not have a surplus value.

A potential pitfall of this *just-in-time approach* is that the pre-structured and pre-ordered presentation of information does not always fit the information requirements of a particular learner. The information available at a specific time during practice might not be the information needed by the learner at that time and might, therefore, interfere with learning and thus, skill acquisition. To alleviate this, a second form of support is discussed in the next section. Learner control is not limited to helping domain novices gain experience, but is directly supported by specific support tools that enable domain novices to determine and act upon their information requirements during practice. This way, the risk of presenting the wrong information at the wrong time is avoided and the features of complete learner control that are beneficial for learning (i.e., active learning) are preserved.

4.3 Supported learner control over information presentation

Characteristic of supported learner control is that (1) all information resources are simultaneously available during the practical, (2) they are pre-structured with regard to type and (3) specific support is added in the learning environment to help learners use the available theoretical information and practical information.

As discussed earlier, two specific problems exist when domain novices have complete control over the use of available information sources. Novices either have difficulty (1) defining their information requirements in relation to a problem and/or (2) acting upon their information requirements (i.e., choosing and using the right information at the right time). In a pELE using supported learner control over information presentation, specific support is added in the form of (1) *conceptual support* to help domain novices form an impression of the available information in the problem domain and thus to help them determine their information requirements and (2) *procedural support* to help domain novices properly perceive the problem demands and thus to help them act upon their information requirements.

Hannafin et al. (1999) propose support in the form of *graphic organizers* (i.e., figural organizations of text information, Robinson, 1998). Graphic organizer is an umbrella term. Specific graphic organizers vary on a number of dimensions (Dunston, 1992), namely: type (i.e., concept maps, flow charts, tree diagrams or matrices), timing (i.e., pre-reading or post-reading), developer (i.e., teacher-constructed or learner-constructed), and user (i.e., elementary, secondary or post-secondary levels) of the organizer. In this chapter two graphic organizers are discussed, namely a teacher-constructed concept map (i.e., conceptual support) and a teacher-constructed flow chart (i.e., procedural support), both intended to help domain novices determine and act upon their information requirements. Concept maps have been successfully used for both knowledge acquisition (e.g., as communication tools for organizing concepts) and cognitive processing support (e.g., by providing multiple retrieval paths for accessing knowledge) (O'Donnell, Dansereau & Hall, 2002). Flow charts are an effective means to describe a process flow. These graphic organizers which both are static and descriptive are presented or available on-demand during problem solving in the pELE. *Conceptual support* is an aid in helping learners *determine* their information requirements. In order to do this, learners need an accurate impression of the problem domain. The decisions made by domain novices on what information to consider can result in misconceptions especially when dealing with more complex problems (Hannafin et al., 1999). Therefore, it is important that the graphic organizer directs learner attention to important concepts in the problem domain. Generally, the most suitable type of organizer for this is a concept map (see Figure 1) which depicts concepts in nodes which are connected to other concepts by labeled links (e.g., arrows).

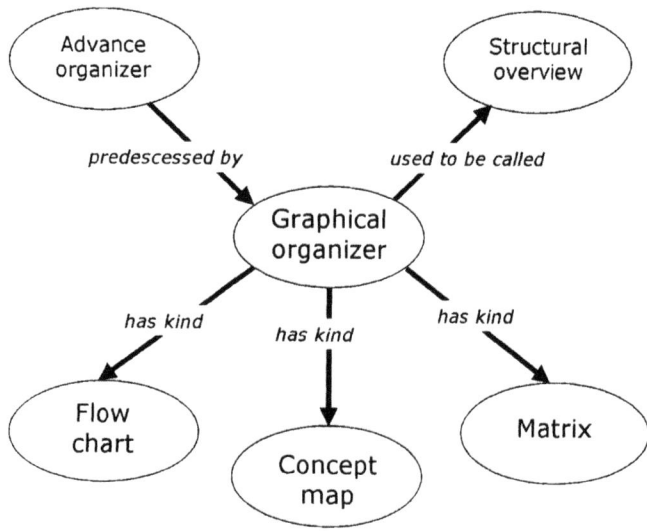

Fig. 1. Example of a concept map (adapted from Robinson, 1993).

Procedural support is an aid in helping learners *act* upon their information requirements. In order to choose and use the right information at the right time learners need an overview of the sequence of steps that enables them to proceed from the given state of a problem to a solution. Thus, acting upon their information requirements is very much guided by the problem demands. The graphic organizer should direct learner attention to the steps that will lead to a solution. The most suitable type of organizer for this is a flow chart (see Figure 2) which depicts a goal, linked to actions connected by arrows that indicate the sequence of these actions to reach the goal. Having established what support *could* be implemented in a pELE to help domain novices determine and act upon their information requirements, the next step is to define *how* this support could best be implemented. Should the support be present at the start and gradually faded during practice or should it always be present? Should the support be available on-demand or should it be presented? The answers to these questions

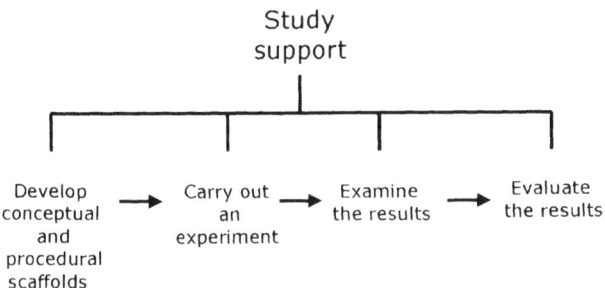

Fig. 2. Example of a flow chart.

depend on two learner characteristics, namely: expertise within a domain and domain-related learning and processing abilities.

As it is discussed earlier, expertise is acquired through experiences (Ericsson & Lehmann, 1996) that enable learners to acquire the knowledge necessary to perform a (complex) skill (Voss, Greene, Post, & Penner, 1983). Learner control should increase as expertise increases and during the process that helps domain novices to become domain experts support is provided to facilitate knowledge and skill acquisition. But all of this extra help does not come without a cost. Van Bruggen, Kirschner, and Jochems (2000) have shown that such support, though expected to facilitate learning and cause cognitive off-loading actually can cause an increase in cognitive load. The expertise reversal effect (Kalyuga, Ayres, & Chandler, 2003) is responsible for this increase. The effect arises when support, necessary for domain novices is also presented to more experienced learners who no longer need this support (Kalyuga, et al., 2003). For the more experienced learners the support is redundant and presenting redundant information during practice impedes learning (Sweller, van Merriënboer, & Paas, 1998). To avoid this effect, learner support should – according to these premises – be diminished as expertise increases (i.e., fading), enabling learners to allocate all of their available cognitive capacity to processes and information relevant for that learning which will have beneficial effects on learning outcomes. So, just as the pELE should allow for more learner control directly proportional to increasing expertise, the support within the pELE should diminish as expertise increases. For the graphic organizers this means that they become gradually less detailed as expertise increases.

Domain-related learning and processing abilities refer to the extent to which learners are capable of controlling their own learning in a specific domain. Shute and Gluck (1996) report positive effects, predominantly on motivation, for learner-controlled support as opposed to system-controlled presentation of support for both high-ability and low-ability learners. More recent research by Schnackenberg and Sullivan (2000), however, points out that low-ability learners choose fewer available support options in the learning environment than do high-ability learners. In addition, other research (O'Donnell et al., 2002) reveals that low-ability learners benefit more from graphic organizers than do high-ability learners who also appear to need this cognitive processing-support less. Thus, though low-ability learners need the support most, they do not appear to be capable of using it on-demand while high-ability learners, needing the support less, appear capable of using it on-demand. Finally, making support available to high-ability learners on-demand prevents redundant information being presented to them, thus avoiding possible learning impediment (Sweller et al., 1998). This has consequences for the implementation of the support. Low domain-related ability learners are probably better helped when system controlled support is presented to them while high domain-related ability learners are better off with learner controlled support which is available on-demand.

To conclude, supported control over information presentation enables domain novices to be active learners and helps them to make proper use of the information resources during problem solving. Fading the support as expertise increases and augmenting the control over this support as learner-ability is higher allows learners to adequately allocate their cognitive capacity to activities relevant for learning (i.e., elaboration and knowledge compilation) and thus complex skill acquisition.

5 Discussion

In this contribution three forms of learner control in pELEs wherein learners have to acquire complex skills through problem solving are discussed. Giving learners complete learner control in the pELE allows them to control their learning through unrestricted interactions with the realistic learning tasks and the information resources. Although learner control has beneficial effects on learning and learning outcomes, it has been shown that domain novices often lack two specific abilities for interacting with available information resources, namely (1) they are not adequately able to determine their information requirements and (2) they are not adequately able to act upon them. Therefore, support is necessary to help learners (especially domain novices) to be active learners in pELEs.

Domain novices could be supported by limiting their control over information presentation in a pELE. Limited learner control pre-structures (i.e., theoretical and practical information) and pre-orders (i.e., theoretical before and practical information during problem solving) the information available in the learning environment. Limited learner control has beneficial effects on learning processes and outcomes, although these effects primarily can be attributed to pre-structuring the information. However, this approach limits active learning and a potential pitfall could be that the pre-structured, pre-ordered information availability does not always fit the information needs of a particular learner. The information available at a specific time during problem solving might not be the information needed by the learner at that time and might, therefore, interfere with learning and thus, complex skill acquisition.

Lastly, supported learner control over information presentation combines the beneficial effects on learning processes and outcomes of both the complete learner control and limited learner control by allowing active learning (i.e., as with complete learner control), by providing support for active learning by pre-structuring the information resources (i.e., as with limited learner control), and by adding conceptual and procedural support to the pELE. It was argued that adding conceptual support (i.e., a concept map) to the learning environment enables learners to form an impression of the problem domain and thus to determine their information requirements. In addition, it was argued that adding procedural support (i.e., a flow chart) to the learning environment enables learners to properly perceive the problem demands and thus to act upon their information requirements. This support is believed to facilitate learning provided that it is faded as expertise increases and the control over this support is augmented as learner-ability is higher. In other words, the pELE should adapt to the learners level of expertise and ability.

An adaptive pELE requires the dynamic assessment of expertise and ability which is typically done by taking the learner's performance (i.e., the number of correctly answered test items, the number of errors, or the time on task) into account. However, the amount of invested mental effort could also indicate the level of expertise and domain-specific ability. For instance, two learners attained the same performance level, one learner had to work laboriously through an effortful process to arrive at the correct answers, while the other learner reaches the same answers with a minimum of mental effort. Both learners perform equally well but expertise and ability are presumably higher for the learner who performed the task with a minimum of mental effort. So, an appropriate assessment of expertise and domain-specific ability should thus at least include measures of mental effort and performance (Van Merriënboer, Salden, Corbalán-Pérez, de Croock, Kester, & Paas, 2004).

To conclude, future research should focus on ways to support learners to become active learners in pELE's. Such environments are often too complex to leave learners to their own fate. It was shown that simplifying these environments by limiting learner control did help learners to achieve higher learning outcomes but at cost of learners autonomy. So, to facilitate both higher learning outcomes and autonomy, external support in the form of graphic organizers was proposed. This seems a promising direction for future research especially when this research aims at dynamically adapting the support to expertise and learner-ability.

References

Anderson, J. R. (1982). Acquisition of cognitive skill. *Psychological Review, 89*, 369-406.
Anderson, J. R. (1993). *Rules of the mind*. Hillsdale, NJ: Erlbaum.
Anderson, J. R. (1996). ACT: A simple theory of complex cognition. *American Psychologist, 51*, 355-365.
Brown, J.S., Collins, A., & Duguid, P. (1989). Situated cognition and the culture of learning. *Educational Researcher, 18*, 32-42.
Broekkamp, H., van Hout-Wolters, B. H. A. M., Rijlaarsdam, G., & van den Bergh, H. (2002). Importance in instructional text: Teachers' and students' perceptions of task demands. *Journal of Educational Psychology, 94*, 260-271.
Broekkamp, H., van Hout-Wolters, B. H. A. M., van den Bergh, H., & Rijlaarsdam, G. (2004). Teacher's task demands, students' test expectations and actual test content. *British Journal of Educational Psychology, 74*, 205-220.
Dunston, P. J. (1992). A critique of graphic organizer research. *Reading Research & Instruction, 31*, 57-65.
Ericsson, K. A., & Lehmann, A. C. (1996). Expert and exceptional performance: Evidence for maximal adaptation to task constraints. *Annual Review of Psychology, 47*, 273-305.
Fry, J. P. (1972). Interactive relationship between inquisitiveness and student control of instruction. *Journal of Educational Psychology, 63*, 459-465.
Hannafin, M., Land, S., & Oliver, K. (1999). Open learning environments: Foundation, methods, and models. In C.M. Reigeluth, (Ed.), *Instructional-design theories and models: A new paradigm of instructional theory* (Vol. 2, pp. 115-140). Mahwah, NJ: Erlbaum.
Holland, J.H., Holyoak, K.J., Nisbett, R.E., & Thagard, P.R. (1986). *Induction: Processes of inference, learning and discovery*. Cambridge, MA: MIT Press.
Kalyuga, S., Ayres, P., & Chandler, P. (2003). The expertise reversal effect. *Educational Psychologist, 38*, 23-31.
Kester, L., Kirschner, P. A., & van Merriënboer, J. J. G. (in press). The management of cognitive load during complex cognitive skill acquisition by means of computer simulated problem solving. *British Journal of Educational Psychology*.
Kester, L., Kirschner, P. A., & Van Merriënboer, J. J. G. (2004a). The optimal timing of information presentation during mastering a complex skill in science. *International Journal of Science Education, 26*, 239-256.
Kester, L., Kirschner, P. A., van Merriënboer, J. J. G. (2004b). Just in time presentation of different types of information in learning statistics. *Instructional Science, 32*, 233-252.
Kester, L., Kirschner, P. A., van Merriënboer, J. J. G., & Bäumer, A. (2001). Just-in-time information presentation and the acquisition of complex cognitive skills. *Computers in Human Behavior, 17*, 373-391.
Kinzie, M. B., Sullivan, H.J., & Berdel, R. L. (1988). Learner control and achievement in science computer-assisted instruction. *Journal of Educational Psychology, 80*, 299-303.
Lawless, K.A., & Brown, S.W. (1997). Multimedia learning environments: Issues of learner control and navigation. *Instructional Science, 25*, 117-131.
Lou, Y., Abrami, P. C., & d'Apollonia, S. (2001). Small group and individual learning with technology: A meta-analysis. *Review of Educational Research, 71*, 449-521.
Luyten, L., Lowyck, J., & Tuerlinckx, F. (2001). Task perception as a mediating variable: A contribution to the validation of instructional knowledge. *British Journal of Educational Psychology, 71*, 203-223.

Merrill, M.D. (1975). Learner control: Beyond aptitude-treatment interactions. *AV Communication Review, 23*, 217-226.
Merrill, M. D., & David, G. T. (1994) *Instructional design theory.* Englewood Cliffs, NJ: Educational Technology Publications.
Merrill, M. D. (2002). First principles of instruction. *Educational Technology, Research and Development, 50*(3), 43-59.
Niemiec, P., Sikorski, C., & Walberg, H. (1996). Learner-control effects: A review of reviews and a meta-analysis. *Journal of Educational Computing Research, 15,* 157-174.
O'Donnell, A. M., Dansereau, D. F., & Hall, R. H. (2002). Knowledge maps as scaffolds for cognitive processing. *Educational Psychology Review, 14,* 71-86.
Ormrod, J. E. (2004). *Human learning* (4th ed.). Upper Saddle River, NJ: Pearson Education.
Proctor, R. W., & Reeve, T. G. (1988). The acquisition of task-specific productions and modification of declarative representations in spatial-precueing tasks. *Journal of Experimental Psychology: General, 117,* 182-196.
Reeve, J., Hamm, D., & Nix, G. (2003). Testing models of the experience of self-determination in intrinsic motivation and the conundrum of choice. *Journal of Educational Psychology, 95,* 375-392.
Reigeluth, C. M., & Stein, F. S. (1983). The elaboration theory of instruction. In C. M. Reigeluth (Ed.), *Instructional-design theories and models: An overview of their current status* (pp. 335-381). Hillsdale, NJ: Erlbaum.
Reigeluth, C. M. (Ed.). (1999). *Instructional design theories and models: A new paradigm of instructional theory.* Mahwah, NJ: Erlbaum.
Robinson, D. H. (1998). Graphic organizers as aids to text learning. *Reading Research & Instruction, 37,* 85-105.
Salomon, G. (1998). Novel constructivist learning environments and novel technologies: Some issues to be concerned with. *Research Dialogue, 1*(1), 3-12.
Schnackenberg, H. L., & Sullivan, H.J. (2000). Learner control over full and lean computer-based instruction under differing ability levels. *Educational Technology Research and Development, 48*(2), 19-35.
Shute, V. J., & Gluck, K. A. (1996). Individual differences in patterns of spontaneous online tool use. *The Journal of the Learning Sciences, 5,* 329-355.
Sweller, J., Van Merriënboer, J. J. G., & Paas, F. (1998). Cognitive architecture and instructional design. *Educational Psychology Review, 10,* 251-296.
Van Bruggen, J. M., Kirschner, P. A., & Jochems, W. (2000). External representation of argumentation in CSCL and the management of cognitive load. *Learning & Instruction, 12,* 121-138.
Van Merriënboer, J. J. G., & Kirschner, P. A. (2001). Three worlds of instructional design: State of the art and future directions. *Instructional Science, 29,* 429-441.
Van Merriënboer, J. J. G., Salden, R. J. C. M., Corbalán-Pérez, G., de Croock, M. B. M., Kester, L., & Paas, F. (2004). *Dynamic selection of learning tasks according to the 4C/ID-Model.* Paper presented at the AECT convention, October 20-25, 2004, Chicago, USA.
Voss, J. F., Greene, T. R., Post, T. A., & Penner, B. C. (1983). Problem-solving skill in the social sciences. In G. H. Bower, (Ed.) *The psychology of learning and motivation: Advances in research and theory* (pp. 165-213). New York: Academic.
Zumbach, J., & Reimann, P. (2001). Enhancing learning from hypertext by inducing a goal orientation: Comparing different approaches. *Instructional Science, 30,* 243-267.

Chapter 12

The impact of external graphical representations in different knowledge domains: Is there a domain effect?

Katrien De Westelinck and Martin Valcke[1]

1 Multimedia learning in social sciences: Impact of the knowledge domain

The Cognitive Theory of Multimedia Learning (CTML), put forward by Mayer (2001a), presents a clear framework to direct instructional design of both printed and interactive multimedia materials. Despite the theoretical and practical appeal of the theory for instructional designers, daily teaching experience of the authors of the present chapter, responsible for freshman courses in the knowledge domain of educational sciences, is not always in line with the CTML. It appears that students cope with external graphical representations such as schemas, tables and graphs added to learning materials. And, as will be discussed in the next sections, recent research is not always able to replicate the positive findings that have been reported in earlier CTML-studies in other knowledge domains. The authors suggest that the nature of the knowledge domain and the nature of the external graphical representations interact with the validity of the CTML-design principles. By testing the original CTML-design principles in another knowledge domain questions about extending and/or generalizing the cognitive theory of multimedia learning are raised.

2 Basic assumptions and design guidelines of CTML

Cognitive processing of information is the concept from which Mayer (2001a, 2003) starts to formulate three central assumptions of the Cognitive Theory of Multimedia Learning (CTML): the dual channel assumption (Baddeley, 1992; Broadbent, 1956; Chandler & Sweller, 1991; Mayer, 2001a; Mayer, 2003; Moore, Burton, & Myers, 1996; Nelson, 1979; Paivio, 1978; Paivio, 1991; Shannon & Weaver, 1949), the active processing assumption (Mayer, 2001a; Mayer, 2003; Wittrock, 1989) and the limited capacity assumption (Mayer, 2001a; Mayer, 2003; Sweller, 1988; Sweller, 1989; Sweller, 1994).

---

[1] This study was partially funded by the Flemish Government under the BOF program, nr. 011D00103.

This leads to the following design principles (Mayer, 2001a; Mayer 2001b; Mayer, 2003): (a) the *multimedia principle*: learners benefit more from printed text enriched with pictures than from printed text alone, (b) the *temporal contiguity principle*: learners perform better when corresponding printed text and pictures are presented simultaneously instead of successively, (c) the *spatial contiguity principle*: learning is fostered when printed text and pictures are presented close to one another on a page or on screen, (d) the *coherence principle*: learning performance is higher when extraneous sounds, words, pictures are excluded, (e) the *modality principle*: learners learn more from animation enriched with audio (narration) than from animation enriched with printed text, (f) the *redundancy principle*: learners perform better when presented with animation and narration instead of animation and narration combined with printed text matching the narration, and (g) the *individual differences principle*: all design principles have a stronger impact with low prior knowledge learners and learners with higher spatial abilities (see Mayer, 2001a, 2001b and 2003 for an overview). The generic nature of these design principles for all knowledge domains and types of external graphical representations is stressed by Mayer (2001a), but is questioned in this chapter.

3 External graphical representations

First generation research focused on generic principles to understand consistencies in the processing of verbal and visual information (Anglin, Towers, & Levie, 1996; Goldman, 2003). Second generation research focuses rather on the affordances and acquaintance of the students with iconic sign system as reflected in external graphical representations and this in relation with the nature of the knowledge domain.

Verbal and pictorial representations behold a clear difference subscribed by Mayer. Verbal representations such as text (descriptive) require more mental effort to be processed by the learner and pictorial representations (depictive) are considered as being more original modes of knowledge representation and are more intuitive, closer to visual experience (Mayer; 2001a, p. 68).

Being acquainted with descriptive and depictive representations can influence the processing of the representations by the learners. As to the depictive representations, the question is raised whether the learners have sufficient and adequate prior knowledge that directs their understanding of these representations. Prior knowledge related to the mastery of the iconic sign system that is at the base of the external graphical representations is needed. When learners are confronted with new or unknown iconic sign systems, it is expected to result in learner difficulties (e.g., weaker processing and/or more processing time needed). It points at a mismatch between the iconic sign system of a learner and the one used in the external graphical representations (De Westelinck, Valcke, De Craene, & Kirschner, 2005). The same idea has been put forward by other authors in the literature, but has yet not been related to CTML (Dobson, 1995; Goldman, 2003; Goodman, 1976; Lewalter, 2003; Stenning, 1999).

Considering the issue of familiarity with the iconic sign system, the *activation principle* is introduced in this chapter. According to this principle, learners are invited to develop their own external graphical representation; thereby building on an iconic sign system they are familiar with. By developing a personal external graphical representation, learners are forced to process the new knowledge elements and to construct a visual mental model, next to the model based on text. This process also reinforces the familiarity with the personal iconic sign system. Several authors promote this *activation principle* (Marzono, Pickering, & Pollock, 2001; Wileman, 1993).

4 The first study: CTML in the social sciences

4.1 Hypotheses

The central hypothesis put forward in this first research is that learners in the social sciences knowledge domain will experience difficulties with external graphical representations; thus resulting in non-confirmation of the original CTML-hypotheses. The unfamiliarity with the iconic sign system used to develop the external graphical representations can have an influence on the selection, processing and organisation processes of mental models. Students are e.g., expected to experience cognitive load due to being unfamiliar with the iconic sign system. Confirmation of this overall hypothesis implies that the CTML-design guidelines are to be extended by a supplementary design principle that considers the mastery of the iconic sign system by the learner and the nature of the knowledge domain. The theoretical position about the nature of external graphical representations is applicable to both static (e.g., graphs) and dynamic (e.g., animations) external depictive representations.

In the first study, hypotheses related to five CTML-design principles were tested: the multimedia, spatial contiguity, coherence, modality and redundancy principle. In addition a sub-hypothesis was tested, in relation to each of the former hypotheses, whether application of the principles did lead to higher or lower levels of cognitive load as reported by the subjects.

4.2 Research method

4.2.1 Participants
In total 190 freshmen, the entire first year student population studying educational sciences, participated in this study (academic year 2002-2003).

Participation was a formal part of the course "Instructional Sciences". Informed consent was obtained from all students prior to experimentation.

4.2.2 Procedure

Three to six experiments were set up during two consecutive weeks in relation to each of the five CTML-design principles. Students were randomly assigned to the experimental conditions. Each experimental package consisted of (a) a prior knowledge test consisting of a retention and transfer test, (b) a specific elaboration of the learning materials to be studied, and (c) a post-test to test the mastery of the complex knowledge elaborated in the learning materials (retention and transfer questions). Twice, the students were asked to estimate their perceived *mental effort*. Literature and research confirm the validity and reliability of this approach to determine cognitive load (Gopher & Braune, 1984; Paas, 1992; Paas, van Merriënboer, & Adam, 1994; Van Gerven, Paas, van Merriënboer, & Schmidt, 2002). No time limit was set to study the materials and/or to fill out the tests. The answers to the retention and transfer questions were scored by three independent researchers based on a scoring checklist. Scores for the tests were standardized.

4.2.3 Materials

The content of the learning materials was both complex and new to the students: an introduction to the learning styles literature (the learning content). Nine themes were outlined to be presented to the students. Mayer's recommendations were taken into account when developing the external graphical representations. Figure 1 depicts a sample page of printed learning materials with integrated external graphical representations about Kolb's learning style approach. It is clear from the example that the external graphical representations do not build on a formal and/or existing iconic sign system. Moreover, the approach is similar to the typical external graphical representations found in most psychology and educational sciences textbooks.

4.3 Result and discussion

4.3.1 Multimedia principle

Students studying learning materials with no external graphical representations always attain higher mean post-test scores. Analysis of variance reveals (see Table 1) that these differences are significant for the second experiment with very large to large effect sizes ($d = 1.12$ for the transfer test and $d = .95$ for the total post test score). This suggests that the original CTML-hypothesis can not be confirmed for any of the six experiments related to this principle. This might confirm that learners have problems when studying from external graphical representations because of inadequate

Type 1 Accomodator

A hands-on learner. This learner learns/works especially through intuition. Applying in a realistic environment is what he/she wants. There is a sensibility for feelings and interpersonal aspects.

Type 2 Diverger

Problems will be looked at from different points. Observing is chosen above active participating. Information is gathered and arranged. Imagination is the base for problem solving.

Type 3 Converger

Problem solving and finding practical solutions has the first choice. Technical problems are chosen above social or interpersonal subjects.

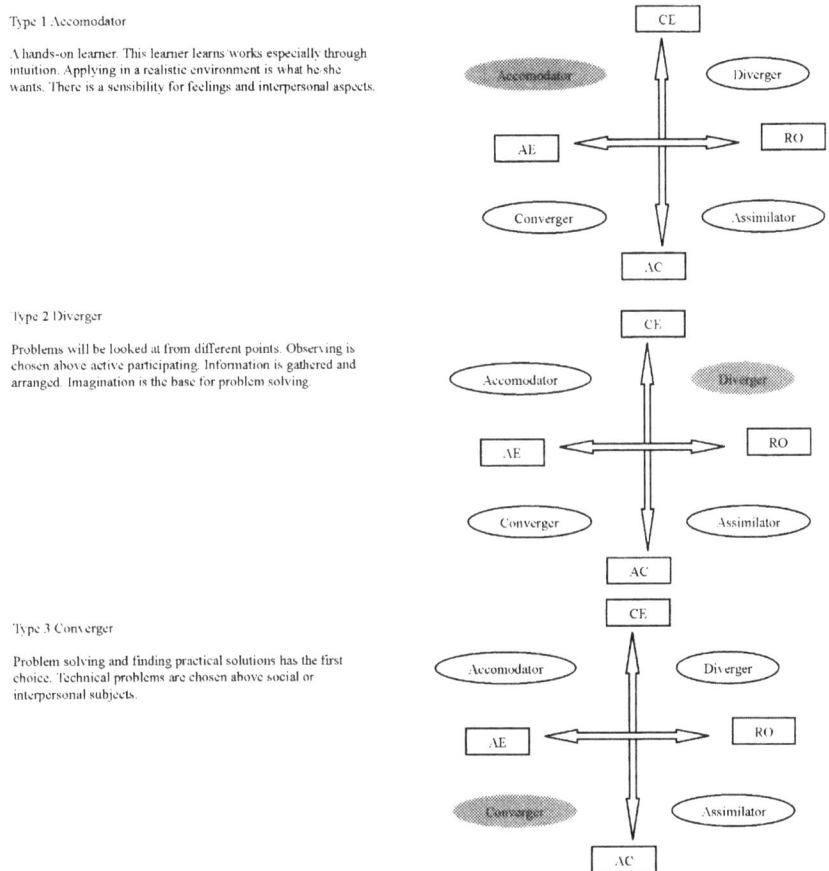

Fig. 1. Example of learning materials related to the coherence principle building on the learning style model of Kolb.

experience with or knowledge of the iconic sign system used. These results are consistent with Cox (1999), Lowe (2003) and Schnotz and Bannert (2003), and Dobson (1999).

4.3.2 Spatial contiguity

In 2 of the three experiments that helped to test this hypothesis, students obtain higher post-test scores when illustrations are not integrated into the text. These differences are significant in the first experiment, reflecting a medium effect size of $d = .72$. These results are not surprising in the light of the discussion of the first principle.

Table 1. Summary of ANOVA results in study 1

Session 1		Multimedia		Spatial contiguity		Coherence		Modality		Redundancy	
		$F_{(1,69)}$	p	$F_{(1,67)}$	p^c	na^a		$F_{(1,49)}$	p	na^a	
Sub 1	Retention	4.09	.05	8.74	.004			2.07	.16		
	Transfer	.69	.42	8.74	.004			.11	.74		
	Total	2.73	.10	.09	.76			.02	.88		
Sub 2	Retention	.87	.35	.13	.72			.12	.73		
	Transfer	21.56	.00	.18	.67			.41	.53		
	Total	15.49	.00	.08	.77			.10	.75		
Sub 3	Retention	.91	.34	.19	.66			.62	.43		
	Transfer	.21	.65	.02	.88			1.90	.17		
	Total	.93	.34	1.60	.21			.13	.72		
	Cognitive load	$-^b$	$-^b$					.28	.60		

Session 2		$F_{(1,48)}$	p	na^a		$F_{(185)}$	p	na^a		$F_{(1,49)}$	p
Sub 4	Retention	.20	.66			6.60	.02			1.17	.28
	Transfer	.93	.34			1.52	.22			1.01	.32
	Total	.73	.40			5.70	.02			.00	.98
Sub 5	Retention	2.92	.09			3.13	.08			.06	.80
	Transfer	.21	.65			.03	.86			2.52	.12
	Total	2.60	.11			2.38	.13			3.17	.08
Sub 6	Retention	3.71	.06			.11	.74			0.2	.90
	Transfer	.14	.71			2.36	.13			.01	.94
	Total	2.18	.15			1.49	.23			.00	.98
	Cognitive load	1.40	.24			7.99	.006			.01	.91

^{a}Not applicable. No experiments were set up to test this specific hypothesis during this session. ^{b}Due to a layout error in the package of the students for the condition with external representations, an insufficient number replied to the question to estimate their cognitive load. ^{c}Since students in both conditions obtain the maximum score for the retention question in relation to this first sub study, no F-value can be calculated.

4.3.3 Coherence principle

In 2 of the three experiments to test the hypothesis about the impact of the coherence principle, students studying learning materials that consist of summaries with external graphical representations perform better on post test questions. But none of these differences are significant. This questions the generic nature of the coherence design principle when external graphical representations are used that are depictive and that are not based on a previously acquired iconic sign system.

4.3.4 Modality principle

In the three experiments, inconsistent results were observed in student performance. The condition where animations were enriched with audio did not consistently lead to higher performance as compared to conditions where the animations were enriched with text. Moreover, none of the differences in performance were significant. Also Tabbers, Martens and van Merriënboer (in press-b, 2001) could not replicate the CTML-findings in their studies. Of particular importance is the fact that in their study they also focused on less formal symbolic icon systems, used in the knowledge domain "research methodologies in social sciences".

4.3.5 Redundancy principle

The post test scores of students studying non-redundant learning materials; i.e., animation with narration and without additional text, were mostly higher. But the differences are not significant.

4.3.6 Cognitive load

The impact on cognitive load was tested in relation to each of the former five hypotheses. At a descriptive level, minor differences in cognitive load could be observed, but most differences are not significant. Only in the experiments related to the coherence principle, a significantly higher cognitive load was reported, reflecting a medium effect size of $d = .72$. But this significant effect is not in line with the CTML. Materials building on summaries with external graphical representations are – contrary to the CTML-assumptions – invoking higher cognitive load than expanded versions with external graphical representations. This is in line with the research of Tabbers et al. (in press-b). They also report inconsistent results as to the impact of external graphical representations on cognitive load.

The discussion in relation to the five experiments leads to rather consistent conclusions. In relation to each experiment, the analysis results do not confirm or reject the CTML-hypothesis. The practical implications of these findings are that instructional designers are expected to pay additional attention to the nature of the knowledge domain when developing external graphical representations. The results suggest that this is especially the case when students are not acquainted with the iconic sign system used to develop the representations.

5 The second research: The activation principle

5.1 Background and hypotheses

The results of the first study revealed that the positive findings of Mayer could not be replicated in the social sciences. It was hypothesized that in the social science domain there is not an established iconic sign system shared by instructional designers, experts and novices to develop external graphical representations. From this hypothesis follows that students will not benefit from external graphical representations and that the CTML-design principles would not hold. In a second study, this hypothesis was tested in an alternative way by adding a new design principle to Mayer's list: the *activation principle*. The central hypothesis for this second study is stated as follows: learners that are actively engaged in designing and developing their personal external graphical representations will perform better on post tests than learners studying learning materials with external graphical representations developed by others.

The *activation principle* can be readily linked to the CTML when focusing on the active processing assumption that founds this theory (2003). The selection, organisation and integration processes that foster the development of mental models presuppose that the learners are active. Developing personal external graphical representations is in the context of the present study put forward as a catalyst to promote these internal cognitive processes. Also other authors have suggested ways to foster the active processing (Burton, Moore, & Magliaro, 1996; Driscoll, 2004; Seels, Berry, Fullerton, & Horn, 1996; Van Hout-Wolters, Simons, & Volet, 2000). The *activation* principle can also be linked to the approach proposed by Novak (1998) and the theoretical base he puts forward to ground the use of concept maps.

But it might also be hypothesized that asking learners to develop external graphical representations might invoke cognitive load (Sweller, 1988). Next to processing new complex knowledge, students are asked to develop external graphical representations. This extra process might hinder the construction of schemas in working memory and confront learners even faster with the limited capacity of their working memory; thus invoking a higher level of intrinsic cognitive load. In the literature, there is plenty of reference to the relationship between cognitive load and prior knowledge (Kirschner, 2002). Several authors have made suggestions to cope with cognitive load and to reduce extraneous cognitive load. They put forward a variety of instructional design ideas and there is empirical evidence to support the positive impact of such measures (Paas, 1992; Stark et al., 2002; Sweller, 1999; Sweller et al., 1998):

- Worked examples: learners work with exemplary partially solved problems.
- Goal-free problems: this helps learners to redirect their attention from a means-end strategy to a strategy in which they are invited to work forward from the given information.
- Hierarchical approach: this implies that based on a task analysis, learners tackle first the sub-components of the knowledge base before working on the more complex knowledge elements.
- Emphasis-manipulation approach: In the context of a problem, students are invited to tackle a specific sub-part of the problem.
- Completion strategy: students complete incomplete solutions. The next time they are expected to work on a larger incomplete problem.
- Expert-like problem analysis: students follow a specific set of questions that replicate the type of approach adopted by an expert.

In the present study, we take into account the potential negative impact on cognitive load and add an experimental condition in which students are presented with pre-worked external graphical representations. If the traditional CTML-principles hold, the presentation of pre-worked representations is expected to require lower levels of mental effort from the learners. If the alternative hypothesis holds – the assumption that representations has to build on familiar iconic sign systems – presenting learners with these pre-worked representations will still require more mental effort; thus reflecting more cognitive load.

5.2 Research method

5.2.1 Participants

The entire population of freshmen, studying educational sciences ($N=217$) participated in this study (2003-2004). Participation was a formal part of the course "Instructional Sciences". Informed consent was obtained prior to experimentation.

5.2.2 Procedure

Students were randomly assigned to one of the four experimental conditions: (1) studying printed learning materials with no external graphical representations, (2) learning materials with ready-made external graphical representations, (3) learning materials to which the students were invited to add their personal external graphical representations, and (4) learning materials with pre-worked external graphical representations.

In each condition, the students studied the learning materials that focused at content level on complex and new knowledge about theories and models of *Instructional Design (ID)*. Three ID-sub themes were presented to the students in one single two hour session.

The three sub themes were presented in three subsequent experimental packages consisting of (a) a prior knowledge test consisting of a retention test, (b) a specific presentation of the learning materials to be studied, and (c) a post-test to test the mastery of the complex knowledge elaborated in the learning materials (retention and transfer questions). Comparable to the first study, the students were asked twice to estimate their perceived *mental effort*. Again no time limit was set to study the materials and/or to fill out the tests. The answers to the retention and transfer questions were scored by three independent researchers based on a scoring checklist.

5.3. Results and discussion

Table 2 presents a summary of the descriptive results. Analyses of variances, with the pretest results as the co-variable were carried out to compare post test results and measures of cognitive load. In case of statistically significant differences, Cohen's d was calculated to determine the effect size (Talheimer & Cook, 2002).

Table 3 gives an overview of the significant F-values when comparing the performance and cognitive load measures in the different conditions. The third experiment did not result in significant differences. This might be due to fatigue, given the duration of the study. But the results in relation to the first two experiments are clear. Students who are actively engaged in developing personal external graphical representations score higher on the retention and transfer tests (effect size $d = .66$ for the first experiment and $d = .54$ for the second experiment). These results suggest that the activation principle leads to better performance, but the results also confirm the CTML *multimedia principle*.

Significant differences are found in experiment two when comparing the group receiving learning materials with external graphical representations and the group developing personal external graphical representations, in favour of the latter (medium effect size $d = .63$). These results suggest that the *activation principle* is confirmed in this knowledge domain and when no formal iconic sign system is available. The result in the other experiments show a comparable trend, but the differences are not significant.

Completing pre-worked external graphical representations versus developing personal external graphical representations results in significant differences with a large effect size ($d = .86$) in the second experiment. Students who develop personal representations show superior performance. The same trend is seen in the other experiments, but it is yet not significant. These results are in line with the outcomes of other studies where activation was built in the learning materials. But the way *activation* is introduced is sometimes different. Lowe (2003), e.g., reports the positive impact of adding cues to focus the learners' attention to particular aspect of the representation, especially for learners with limited prior knowledge. A more

Table 2. Mean scores and standard deviation for performance measures and cognitive load in the second study

		Text without representations		Text with representations		Completing pre-worked representations		Developing representations	
		M^a	SD	M^b	SD	M^c	SD	M^d	SD
Sub 1	Retention	3.61	0.95	3.69	1.16	4.16	1.23	4.04	1.14
	Transfer	7.91	3.41	9.22	3.45	8.44	3.36	9.96	3.48
	Total	11.52	3.60	12.91	3.70	12.59	4.01	14.00	3.87
Sub 2	Retention	1.57	0.89	1.65	0.83	1.71	0.87	1.95	0.84
	Transfer	2.81	1.10	2.67	0.93	2.23	1.06	3.21	1.04
	Total	4.38	1.59	4.32	1.40	3.94	1.55	5.17	1.29
Sub 3	Retention	1.12	0.51	1.15	0.58	1.10	0.59	1.07	0.69
	Transfer	1.91	1.92	2.18	1.79	1.89	1.69	1.56	1.57
	Total	3.03	1.93	3.33	2.10	2.99	1.98	2.62	1.99
		M^a	SD	M^b	SD	M^c	SD	M^d	SD
	Cognitive load 1	5.41	1.47	4.81	1.60	4.67	1.60	4.17	1.42
	Cognitive load 2	7.00	1.30	6.24	1.43	6.17	1.71	5.83	1.69
	Total	12.43	2.34	11.07	2.69	10.35	2.99	9.94	2.59

$^a N = 54.$ $^b N = 55.$ $^c N = 54.$ $^d N = 54.$

Table 3. Overview of ANOVA results in study 2

		Text without representations vs Text with representations		Text without representations vs Completing pre-worked representations		Text without representations vs Developing representations		Text with representations vs Completing pre-worked representations		Text with representations vs Developing representations		Completing pre-worked representations vs Developing representations	
		$F(1, 107)$	p	$F(1, 106)$	p	$F(1, 106)$	p	$F(1, 107)$	p	$F(1, 107)$	p	$F(1, 106)$	p
Sub 1	Retention	0.15	0.70	6.69	0.01	4.45	0.04	4.16	0.04	2.47	0.12	0.28	0.60
	Transfer	3.99	0.05	0.66	0.42	9.61	0.00	1.44	0.23	1.26	0.26	5.38	0.02
	Total	3.96	0.05	2.14	0.15	11.89	0.00	0.18	0.70	2.27	0.14	3.44	0.07
Sub 2	Retention	0.19	0.67	0.68	0.41	5.23	0.02	0.17	0.70	3.72	0.06	2.16	0.15
	Transfer	0.46	0.50	7.57	0.01	3.88	0.05	5.33	0.02	8.15	0.01	23.43	0.00
	Total	0.06	0.82	2.07	0.15	7.97	0.01	1.76	0.19	10.87	0.00	19.90	0.00
		$F(1, 107)$	p	$F(1, 106)$	p	$F(1, 106)$	p	$F(1, 107)$	p	$F(1, 107)$	p	$F(1, 106)$	p
Cognitive load 1		4.00	0.05	6.26	0.01	19.80	0.00	0.23	0.63	4.94	0.03	2.94	0.09
Cognitive load 2		8.43	0.00	7.93	0.01	15.94	0.00	0.05	0.83	1.84	0.18	1.07	0.30
Total		7.79	0.01	9.23	0.00	26.73	0.00	0.17	0.68	4.87	0.03	2.75	1.00

direct activation was studied by Stern, Aprea and Ebner (2003) who also asked their students to construct external graphical representations, concluded that active construction of graphs by students improves significantly knowledge transfer. Their results also underscore that the *passive study* of available graphs leads to lower test performance.

The results in relation to cognitive load reveal significant differences. Consistently, students that have to develop their personal external representations report significantly lower levels of mental load. But there is no significant difference between conditions that ask to develop completely new representations or to further develop pre-worked representations. These results obviously underscore the importance of the *activation principle*.

6 The third research: The nature of developing personal external graphical representations

6.1 Background and hypotheses

Building on the results of the second study, a new study was set up that focused on the way students elaborate their personal external graphical representations. Students differ in the way they develop these external graphical representations. In this context we can refer to the concept of *visual thinking*, introduced by Wileman (1993). This is the ability to conceptualize and present thoughts, ideas and data as pictures and graphics, in order to replace much of the available verbal/textual representation. He distinguishes three overlapping strategies of thought: imaging, seeing and designing. The designing strategy is considered as a central element of activation. Wileman (1993) advocates that there are three types of symbols that can be used in visual thinking: pictures, verbal symbols and graphical symbols. The first category is not considered in the present study. The verbal symbols are defined as words. Graphical symbols consist of image-related graphics, concept-related graphics and relationship graphics. Image-related graphics are highly recognizable representations of an object or idea. Concept-related graphics remove as much detail as possible and make the knowledge object more abstract. Relationship graphics are abstract symbols conceived to show relationships between ideas. The *visual thinking* theory of Wileman was used to categorize the external graphical representations student had developed in their learning materials. In the context of the present study, the category "arbitrary" was re-labeled as "relationship graphics" to stress the structural nature of this type of representations.

This third study centres on the hypothesis that the nature of the external graphical representation will have a differential impact. The more elaborated the type of representation, the higher the activation of the cognitive processes (organisation and integration), resulting in more integrated andorganised mental models. In the present study, an extra condition was added to the experimental design. In this additional condition, students received training to develop external graphical representations. This extends the former hypothesis by stating that being more familiar with an iconic sign system will result in more elaborated graphical representations – reflecting more advanced cognitive processing - and resulting in better test performance.

6.2 Research method

6.2.1 Participants

Ninety students participated in this research. They were selected ad random from the total population of freshman studying educational sciences. Participation was a formal part of the course "Instructional Sciences". Informed consent was obtained prior to experimentation.

6.2.2 Procedure

Ninety students in the training condition received, prior to the experimentation a short introduction about how to develop external graphical representations. During the training the application and the use of external graphical representations were demonstrated. The training presented a variety of graphical representations that reflect clearly the typology of Wileman (1993).

When the study started, the students received materials comparable to those discussed in the second study. In relation to the three experiments, pre test and post test scores where obtained and twice the students were asked to estimate their perceived *mental effort* as a measure of cognitive load. A researcher, not involved in the research, coded the personal external graphical representations developed by the students. This coding was based on the categorization of Wileman (1993).

Table 4. Descriptive results (percentages)

	Without training (n=48)	With training (n=48)
Verbal symbols	64	56.4
Image-related graphics	1.80	4.44
Concept-related graphics	12.25	6.70
Relationship graphics	11.46	13.33
Verbal symbols and image-related graphics	2.37	3.11
Verbal symbols and concept-related graphics	7.51	15.11
Concept-related graphics and relationship graphics	0.40	0.88

6.3 Results and discussion

Table 4 shows that there is a difference in the frequency each category of external graphical representations appears in the two research conditions.

In both groups, verbal symbols are used to the highest extent but in different proportions (64% group without training and 56.4% group with training). The table also indicates that the following representation types are observed to a larger extent in the training condition: image-related, relationship graphics, the combination verbal symbols and image-related, the combination verbal symbols and concept-related, the combination concept-related and relationship graphics. The concept-related category decreases in this condition to 6.70%. The students are clearly unfamiliar with the iconic sign system used in the social sciences as discussed earlier. This leads to a very large use of verbal symbols. Giving students training resulted in the adoption of a larger variety of representation categories. This explains the expectations that the usage of verbal symbols decreases and the use of concept-related graphics and relationship graphics will increase. The fact that the concept-related category decreased was not expected.

Part of the explanation for the unexpected results might be related to the position of the training in the learning process. In this experiment, students were expected to apply the typology immediately after the training. This expectation might have been wrong. There has been hardly time for exercising and developing a rather automated approach to developing the different types of representations. Students already using "concept-related graphics" might even have been inhibited in using them because of the training that "forced" them to adopt the wider variety of representations.

Next to a hypothesis about the impact of the training, we can also study the impact of high usage levels of types of representations on cognitive processing and on performance. This hypothesis demands to study whether the specific iconic sign system used by the students is a predictor for higher or lower results on the retention and transfer test. Therefore a linear regression was performed. High usage levels of concept-related graphics and relationship graphics are considered as predictors for higher levels of cognitive processing and consequently better performance. The students were subdivided into two groups based on the usage level of these representation types.

The results of the analyses are not significant. A high usage level of complex external graphical representations does not predict the results on the retention and transfer tests and does not have a significant impact on cognitive load indicators in the present study. This can be due to the small number of cases. But again, the (un)familiarity with the iconic sign system might have played a role. We expected that the concept-related graphics and relationship graphics would have invoked higher levels of cognitive processing takes place. But, the training was organised too close in time to the experimentation; thus inhibiting exercising the 'newer' types of representation and thus not advancing the automatic use of these representations. This suggests that more training should be organised and that the training should be spread over a longer period of time.

7 Methodological discussion of the three studies

A number of methodological questions can be raised in relation to the studies and experiments in this research. A first question focuses on the quality of the external graphical representations. Are the results not the outcome of less effective external graphical representations? As explained, much time and effort was invested in the design of the representations, and this by a large team. Secondly, the representations are typical for the approach found in textbooks in the field of psychology and educational sciences. Thirdly, both the static and dynamic representations were designed taking into account the task demands for the students. The inherent structure of the themes were clearly and explicitly depicted or animated in the representations. The retention and transfer question in the post tests also focused on these features. The latter is important since recent studies (see e.g., Schnotz & Bannert, 2003) have proven that non task-appropriate representations do not foster comprehension and mental model construction. Questions about the selection and difficulty level of the specific content of the learning packages can also be put forward. But it was not the first academic year that these contents, although complex in nature, were part of the freshman curriculum in the study programme of the educational sciences.
A typical quality of the CTML-studies of Mayer and his colleagues is the very short duration of the studies. Learning processes limited to 180 seconds are no exception. In the present studies, larger chunks of learning content had to be processed by the students, during a longer period of time. It is possible that the study tasks in the current studies were more demanding than in Mayer's original studies. This could e.g., have affected the results in the third experiment of the second study. Tabbers et al. (in press-a) also mention this particular divergence between their studies and these by Mayer as a potential source of inconsistent results.

A critical issue is the fact that individual differences were not taken into account. Since the research population was rather homogeneous in terms of their prior knowledge (freshman), it seemed not useful to take this into account. This might be an issue for future research since Mayer's seventh principle (2001a) refers to the impact of prior knowledge and spatial abilities. He also concludes that external graphical representations might serve different cognitive functions for different subjects. Next to prior knowledge other variables, such as differences in learning styles or spatial abilities, can help to explain the actual research results.

Time on task is an important factor in a lot of researches and analyses.

The first research had, as said in the part materials, no time limit. The students could work as long as they wanted on their material. The variable time was not manipulated in the studies, but could play an important role in real life learning situations.

Next, in the three studies the students studied only materials related to the social sciences. This questions whether the findings do not reflect the specific background of these students in this knowledge domain. Future research should consider to present learning materials from different knowledge domains to these students and/or to set up studies involving students of other knowledge domains.

A last remark is about the way the *activation principle* has been operationalized. Students were invited to develop their personal external graphical representations. This is only one way to foster activation as was suggested in the discussion section of study 2. Alternative approaches can be studied, such as collaboration, explaining to others, writing comments next to the learning materials, etc.

8   Implications for instructional design and future research

The central research hypothesis of this study questions the generic nature of the CTML-design guidelines. The results suggest that instructional designers ought to consider more carefully the nature of knowledge domain. Depending on the knowledge domain there are/are not formal iconic sign systems available to develop external graphical representations. This affects the extent to which students are familiar with these systems. In the present studies learning materials from the educational sciences have been studied. This knowledge domain clearly differs from e.g., the natural sciences when it comes to the availability of an iconic sign system to develop (depictive/descriptive) external graphical representations. In the natural sciences it is easier to use depictive representations (derived from real life objects, subjects, situations) and specific sign sets (e.g., to represent molecule structure, chemical structures).

The results of the present studies suggest that developers of learning materials should pay explicit attention to the nature of the iconic sign systems in a knowledge domain. As suggested in the three studies, learners could be helped to understand this iconic sign system, develop pre-worked representations or they could be asked to develop representations themselves. Van der Pal and Eysinck (1999) suggest a comparable approach by building up a specific formal language that learners have to master in order to build up graphical representations in the domain of logics.

Building on the methodological remarks about the three studies, characteristics of future research can be outlined. Future research should take into account variables related to individual differences between learners and the knowledge domain in which they study. Alternative activation approaches could be tested; among them research conditions that build on collaborative learning when studying with or without external graphical representations and when developing external representations.

9   Conclusions

Although the cognitive theory of multimedia learning is supported by a large number of empirical studies, the results of the studies discussed in the present chapter question the extent to which the CTML-design guidelines are applicable in all knowledge domains. The chapter stresses the importance of the nature of the external graphical representations added to learning materials in the social sciences knowledge domain. Depictive external graphical representations not based on a formal iconic sign system, seem to present learners with difficulties when processing information. The results challenge the CTML but do not question the CTML. The outcomes of the present research rather present extensions to this theory and extra design guidelines to be taken into account. The results also confirm that more *second generation* CTML-research is needed that considers the unique affordances of external graphical representations in close relation to the active cognitive processing of learners.

References

Anglin, G., Towers, R., & Levie, W. (1996). Visual message design and learning: The role of static and dynamic illustrations. In D. Jonassen (Ed.), *Handbook of research for educational communications and technology*, pp. 755-794. London: Macmillan.
Baddeley, A. D. (1992). Working memory. *Science, 255*, 556-559.
Broadbent, D. (1956). Successive responses to simultaneous stimuli. *Quarterly Journal of Experimental Psychology, 8*, 145-152.
Chandler, P., & Sweller, J. (1991). Cognitive load theory and the format of instruction. *Cognition and Instruction, 8*, 293-332.
Cox, R. (1999). Representation construction, externalised cognition and individual differences. *Learning and Instruction, 9*, 343-363.
Dobson, M. (1995). *Predicting learning outcomes through prior quantitative and post qualitative analysis of interactive graphical representation systems*. Paper presented at the Conference of the European Association for Research on Learning and Instruction, Nijmegen.
Dobson, M. (1999). Information enforcement and learning with interactive graphical systems. *Learning and Instruction, 9*, 365-390.
De Westelinck, K., & Valcke, M. *Extending the Cognitive Theory of Multimedia Learning with the Activation Principle*. Manuscript submitted for publication.
De Westelinck, K., Valcke, M., De Craene, B., & Kirschner, P. (2005). Multimedia learning in social sciences: Limitations of external graphical representations. *Computers in Human Behavior, 21*, 555-573.
Goldman, S. (2003). Learning in complex domains: When and why do multiple representations help? *Learning and Instruction, 13*, 239-244.
Goodman, N. (1976). *Languages of art: An approach to a theory of symbols*. Indianapolis: Hacket.

Gopher, D., & Braune, R. (1984). On the psychophysics of workload: Why bother with subjective measures? *Human Factors, 26,* 519-532.

Lewalter, D. (2003). Cognitive strategies for learning from static and dynamic visuals. *Learning and Instruction, 13,* 177-189.

Lowe, R. K. (2003). Animation and learning: Selective processing of information in dynamic graphics. *Learning and Instruction, 13,* 157-176.

Mayer, R. E. (2001a). *Multimedia learning.* Cambridge: Cambridge University Press.

Mayer, R. E. (2001b). Cognitive, metacognitive and motivational aspects of problem solving. In H. Hartman (Ed.), *Metacognition in learning and instruction* (pp. 87-102), Dordrecht, The Netherlands: Kluwer Academic Press.

Mayer, R. E. (2003). The promise of multimedia learning: Using the same instructional design methods across different media. *Learning and Instruction, 13,* 125-139.

Moore, D. M., Burton, J. K., & Myers, R. J. (1996). Multiple channel communication: The theoretical foundations of multimedia. In D. H. Jonassen (Ed.), *Handbook of research for educational communications and technology* (pp. 851-878). New York: Macmillan.

Nelson, D. L. (1979) Remembering pictures and words: Appearance, significance and name. In L. S. Cernack & F. Craik (Eds.), *Levels of processing in human memory* (pp. 45-76). Hillsdale, NJ: Erlbaum.

Paas, F. (1992). Training strategies for attaining transfer of problem-solving skill in statistics: A cognitive load approach. *Journal of Educational Psychology, 84,* 429-434.

Paas, F., van Merrienboer, J., & Adam, J. (1994). Measurement of cognitive load in instructional research. *Perceptual and Motor Skills, 79,* 419-430.

Paivio, A. (1978). A dual coding approach to perception and cognition. In J. Pick, H. Pick, & E. Saltzman (Eds.), *Modes of perceiving and processing information* (pp. 39-51). Hillsdale, NJ: Erlbaum.

Paivio, A. (1991). Dual coding theory: Retrospect and current status. *Canadian Journal of Psychology, 45,* 255-287.

Schnotz, W., & Bannert, M. (2003). Construction and interference in learning from multiple representations. *Learning and Instruction, 13,* 141-156.

Shannon, C. E., & Weaver, W. (1949). *The mathematical theory of communication.* Urbana, IL: University of Illinois Press.

Stenning, K. (1999). The cognitive consequences of modality assignment for educational communication: The picture in logic teaching. *Learning and Instruction, 9,* 391-410.

Stern, E., Aprea, C., & Ebner, H. G. (2003). Improving cross-content transfer in text processing by means of active graphical representation. *Learning and Instruction, 13,* 191-203.

Sweller, J. (1988). Cognitive load during problem solving: Effects on learning. *Cognitive Science, 2,* 257-285.

Sweller, J. (1989). Cognitive technology: Some procedures for facilitating learning and problem solving in mathematics and science. *Journal of Educational Psychology, 81,* 463-474.

Sweller, J. (1994). Cognitive load theory, learning difficulty and instructional design. *Learning and Instruction, 4,* 295-312.

Tabbers, H., Martens, R., & van Merriënboer, J. (in press-a). The interaction of modality with pacing in multimedia learning. *British Journal of Educational Psychology.*

Tabbers, H., Martens, R., & van Merriënboer, J. (in press-b). Multimedia instructions and cognitive load theory: Effects of modality and cueing. *British Journal of Educational Psychology.*

Tabbers, H., Martens, R., & van Merriënboer, J. (2001). The modality effect in multimedia instructions. In J.D. Moore & K. Stenning (Eds.), *Proceedings of the 23rd annu-*

al conference of the Cognitive Science Society (pp. 1024-1029). Mahwah, NJ: Erlbaum.

Thalheimer, W., & Cook, S. (2002, August). *How to calculate effect sizes from published research articles: A simplified methodology.* Retrieved August 18, 2003, from http://work-learning.com/effect_sizes.htm

Van der Pal, J., & Eysink, T. (1999). Balancing situativity and formality: The importance of relating a formal language to interactive graphics in logic instruction. *Learning and Instruction, 9*, 327-341.

Van Gerven, P., Paas, F., van Merrienboer, J., & Schmidt, H. (2002). Cognitive load theory and aging: Effects of worked examples on training efficiency. *Learning & Instruction, 12*, 87-105.

Wileman (1993). *Visual communicating.* Englewood Cliffs, NJ: Educational Technology Publications Inc.

Wittrock, M. C. (1989). Generative processes of comprehension. *Educational Psychologist, 24*, 345-376.

Chapter 13

Using representational tools to support historical reasoning in CSCL

Gellof Kanselaar, Carla van Boxtel, and Jannet van Drie

1 Introduction

1.1 Collaborative knowledge construction in a CSCL environment

Current trends in the field of learning and instruction stress the importance of active knowledge construction and collaborative learning. Technology can play a major role in implementing these new trends in education, for it can support the construction of knowledge by representing learners' ideas and understandings and for it can function as a social medium to support learning by dialogue (Kanselaar, de Jong, Andriessen, & Goodyear, 2000). Computer-supported collaborative learning aims at enhancing and supporting peer interaction and the joint construction of products by the use of technology (Lipponen, 2002). The key factor that determines the success of CSCL can be found in the quality of the interaction processes students engage in. After all, meaningful learning in collaborative learning is related to the quality of the interaction processes (Van der Linden, Erkens, Schmidt, & Renshaw, 2000). Although research in the field of CSCL has resulted in positive learning outcomes (Lethinen, Hakkarainen, Lipponen, Rahikainen, & Muukonen, 2001), the use of CSCL is no guarantee for a productive dialogue (see also Kirschner, 2002; Stahl, 2002; Veldhuis-Diermanse, 2002). More research is needed to reveal under which conditions computer-supported collaborative learning can lead to the intended knowledge construction.

An important question is what *kind* of interaction processes promote collaborative knowledge construction and *how* such interaction can be provoked and supported. Studies on collaborative learning processes are conducted from different perspectives. A distinction can be made between a domain-specific, an elaboration, and a co-construction perspective (Van Boxtel, 2004). The main focus of the domain-specific perspective is on the propositional content and quality of the discourse. From this perspective an important question is whether the students make progress from their everyday reasoning towards a deeper understanding and the more scientific ways of reasoning on the topic at hand. Types of talk that are of interest from a domain-specific perspective are the explication of ones own conceptions, the comparison of own conceptions with new information and interpretations of others, and the search for meaningful relations.

The main focus of the elaboration perspective is on the types and quality of the cognitive processes during group work. Elaborative activities, such as the verbalization of prior knowledge, questioning and the creation of meaningful relations by giving examples, using analogies, reformulating or referring to previous experiences are considered important ingredients of a productive student interaction. From this perspective, in a collaborative learning situation, it is important to promote elaborative talk. Elaborative talk is often constituted by the asking and answering of questions and through the elaboration of controversy by providing justification and argumentation.

The co-construction perspective puts the contingencies of the actions of both partners and the mediational role of tools in the centre. From this perspective an important question is whether knowledge is really shared and co-constructed. In many groups the participants do not equally contribute. Sometimes one of the participants does almost all of the talking and work. Kumpulainen and Mutanen (1999) distinguished different modes of social processing. The individualistic mode implies that students work individually in the group and do not share ideas or try to co-construct meanings. The dominative mode reflects unequal participation and the collaborative mode reflects joint meaning making. Co-construction of knowledge implies that meanings are extended, deepened or transformed because participants build on each others contributions (Van Boxtel & Van Drie, 2003). Joint meaning making and co-construction of knowledge requires a shared focus and coordination on the task content level, the meta-cognitive level and the socio-communicative level (Erkens, Jaspers, & Prangsma, 2001).

In many studies one of the perspectives prevails, whereas a multi-perspective approach may have advantages when we want to make progress in the design of collaborative learning environments. In the study that is reported in this chapter we adopt such a multi-perspective approach. The study is about the use of representational tools to support historical reasoning in a computer-based collaborative inquiry and writing environment.

1.2 The potential of external representations

As has been stated before, using a CSCL-environment does not automatically result in knowledge construction. This was confirmed by a first study we conducted. In this study we used a CSCL-environment that enables students to collaboratively engage in a historical inquiry task and the collaborative writing of an essay (Van Drie, Van Boxtel, & Van der Linden, in press). Students used a shared text processor, a private notepad and had access to information sources. All communication between the collaborating students took place by an integrated chat facility. We used a writing task, because previous research has shown that a writing task can deepen students' knowledge and understanding (Boscolo & Mason, 2001;

Klein, 1999; Tynjälä, Mason, & Lonka, 2001). Furthermore, research has shown that writing tasks may result in deeper historical understanding (Boscolo & Mason, 2001; Voss & Wiley, 1997). Collaborative writing can trigger critical reflection, externalisation of thinking and immediate feedback (Gere & Stevens, 1985). Moreover, in writing an argumentative text, learners may have different views or use different arguments, which may result in a productive discussion (Veerman, 2000). Furthermore, a small group inquiry task in which students jointly write an essay is a task that is more and more used in current Dutch history classes.

The results of this study showed that although the students learned from the task and were engaged in historical reasoning in their chat-discussions, the reasoning episodes were often very short, and of poor quality. Furthermore, the collaboratively written essays did not show the quality we had hoped for.

Based on these results, we thought about ways to promote and raise the level of historical reasoning both in the chat and in the essay. We decided to study the possibilities of adding representational tools. In the following sections, we consider the potential of asking students to construct an external representation when they collaborate on an historical inquiry task and write a common essay in a CSCL-environment. In line with the domain-specific, elaboration and co-construction perspectives described above, we focus on the way the construction of an external representation may support historical reasoning, elaboration and co-construction.

Supporting historical reasoning. From a domain-specific perspective it is important to know whether tools in a CSCL environment can promote thinking and reasoning within the domain at hand. In our study the focus is on the domain of history. We consider historical reasoning as a key aspect of building historical knowledge. A historical reasoning is always constructed in relation to a historical question or hypothesis and implies that the learner situates historical phenomena in time, uses historical concepts, organizes information to describe processes of change and continuity, explain a historical phenomenon or to compare historical phenomena, supports claims with arguments making use of historical sources and takes into consideration the trustworthiness, representativeness and usefulness of the sources. Historical events, processes, and structures need to be organized to build an interpretative historical case (Leinhardt, Stainton, Virji, & Odoroff, 1994).

An important dimension of external representations is the format that is used to display information (De Jong, Ainsworth, Dobson, Van der Hulst, Levonen, Reimann, Sime, Van Someren, Spada, & Swaak, 1998). The construction of a particular type of external representations may support particular components of historical reasoning. For example, construction of a causal diagram may provide guidance when learners are asked to explain a historical phenomenon, whereas a matrix can be a useful format to organize aspects of change and continuity. Furthermore, the representational artifact that is constructed in a representational tool can function as a writing aid. Experimental studies of Suthers and Hundhausen (2002) showed that representational notations can have significant effects on learners' discourse (both verbal and written) during the collaborative construction of external representations in the area of science. Suthers and Hundhausen compared the construction of three types of external representations: text, matrix and diagram. In their study, students worked together at one computer. The matrix group represented significantly more evidential relations. The empty cells in a matrix seemed to have prompted users to fill in all available evidential relations.

Supporting elaboration. From an elaboration perspective it is important that students are stimulated to engage in elaborate activities. Zhang and Norman (1994) state that external representations guide, constrain or determine cognitive behavior. Much research on the use of external representation focused on the (individual) use of *presented* external representations. However, in a CSCL environment students are supposed to be actively engaged in the construction of their own knowledge. Cox (1999) states that *self-constructed* external representations may help to translate information from one type of representation to another, thus supporting deeper understanding of the underlying concepts and situations. The construction of an external representation can promote verbalization of own conceptions, the (re-)ordering of information in useful ways and can provide perceptual assistance. A graphical representation, for example, can make information explicit and can direct attention to central problems and relations and help to distinguish core issues from more peripheral ones (Suthers & Hundhausen, 2001).

Supporting co-construction. An important condition for the co-construction of knowledge is that group members participate and contribute more or less equally and that they coordinate their activities. In face-to-face collaboration coordination is partly constituted by gesturing and using facial expressions (Schegloff, 1991), whereas the lack of these impose certain constraints on the coordination processes in electronic communication. In an electronic discourse via a chat facility it is important to coordinate and keep focus on the main issues (Veerman, 2000). From a co-construction perspective the question is whether external representations can contribute to the construction and maintenance of a shared understanding and a joint problem space between co-learners (Crook, 1998; Veerman & Treasure-Jones, 1999). According to Suthers and Hundhausen (2002) an external representation can increase the conceptual complexity that can be handled in group interactions and facilitate elaboration on previously represented information.

Of course, reasoning within a domain, elaboration and co-construction are intertwined. Collaboration can stimulate the articulation of task-related knowledge and information. This verbalization makes it possible for ideas to be questioned, criticized and elaborated, and thus generates explanations, justifications and a search for new relations, which are important aspects of elaboration, historical reasoning and co-construction of knowledge.

1.3 Aim of the study

External representations may support collaborative knowledge construction in a group-ware environment through the facilitation of desired (domain-specific) cognitive and communicative processes. Moreover, external representations may be helpful to organize available information in the preparation of the co-authoring of an essay. In this study we studied the influence of the construction of three different kinds of external representations: a diagram, a list and a matrix. The main question is whether and how the construction of different representations influences the collaborative process and the learning outcomes. More particularly, we are interested in the appearance and quality of domain-specific reasoning, elaboration and co-construction, for especially these processes are believed to constitute positive learning outcomes of collaborative learning.

2 Method

2.1 Design

The study consists of a pre-test post-test design with four conditions. In the experimental groups the students were asked to co-construct an argumentative diagram with arguments pro and contra (Diagram condition), a list of arguments pro and contra (List condition) or a matrix in which changes can be described and characterized (Matrix condition). In the control condition no representational tool was available and students did not receive the instruction to co-construct an external representation. The experiment was conducted in two phases: the first year the experiment was conducted for the Diagram and List condition, in the next year for the Matrix and Control condition.

2.2 Participants

Subjects were 157 students from three history classes in secondary (pre-university) education, aged 16-17. The experiment took place at school, during their history lessons and lasted for six lessons in two weeks time. The students worked in pairs behind their own computer and the pairs were divided over two computer labs. We excluded the pairs in which one of the students missed more than one lesson. Our analyses include 65 pairs (130 students). Within their class, the students were randomly assigned to pairs and to one of the two conditions. In the first year of the experiment 16 student pairs participated in the Diagram condition and 14 in the List condition. In the second year 18 in the Matrix condition and 17 in the Control condition. In both years (different) students from the same schools (and the same teachers) participated.

2.3 Task and learning environment

The subjects were asked to perform a historical inquiry task, which involved studying historical sources (such as texts from textbooks, different interpretations of historians, photos, tables and interviews) and writing an essay of approximately 1,000 words. The task was about the question whether the changes in the behavior of the Dutch youth in the sixties of the twentieth century were revolutionary or not. The students worked six lessons (of 50 minutes) on the task and did not receive instruction on the subject in advance. In the experimental conditions the students were instructed to collaboratively construct an external representation, for which they could use the historical sources. After finishing the construction of the representation they could start writing the text, for which they could use the constructed representation and the sources. In a control condition, the students performed the same task, without the instruction to construct an external representation.

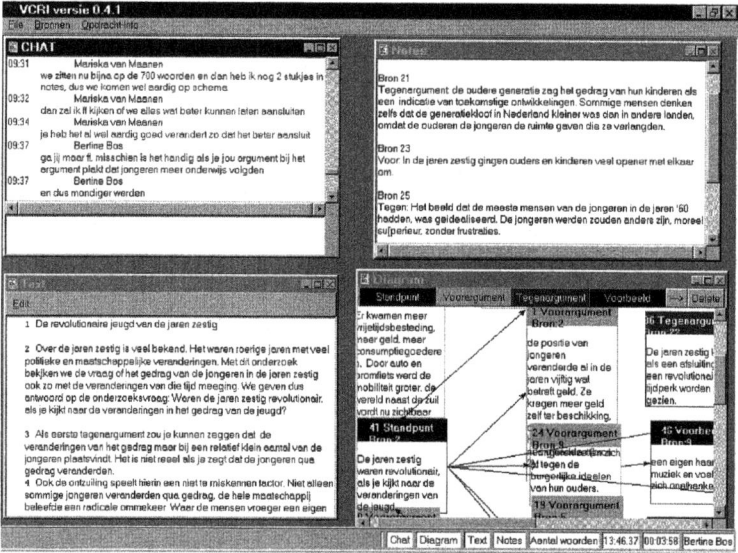

Fig. 1. The main screen of VCRI for the diagram condition.

The students worked in a computer-supported learning environment called Virtual Collaborative Research Institute (see http://edugate.fss.uu.nl/-vcri; Jaspers & Erkens, 2002). VCRI is a groupware program that enables students to work collaboratively on an inquiry task and essay writing. Each student works at one computer, physically separated from the partner. Communication takes place by means of chat. Figure 1 shows the main screen of VCRI in the diagram condition. Information about the task and relevant historical sources can be found in the database menu. The upper left window contains a chat facility and the chat history. The lower left window contains a shared text processor that can be used by taking turns. The upper right window contains a private notepad. In the lower right window the representational tool is shown (in this case the diagram). The different representational tools are all shared tools. In the control condition no such tool was added.

Below we describe the representational tools that were used in the experimental conditions.

Argumentative diagram. The task asks students to take a point of view and support it with arguments. An argumentative diagram can represent a point of view and arguments pro and contra. Figure 2 shows the diagram tool that we used in our study. Arguments pro, arguments contra and examples can be represented in text-boxes (each with their own color). The arguments can be linked to a box in which students could write down their

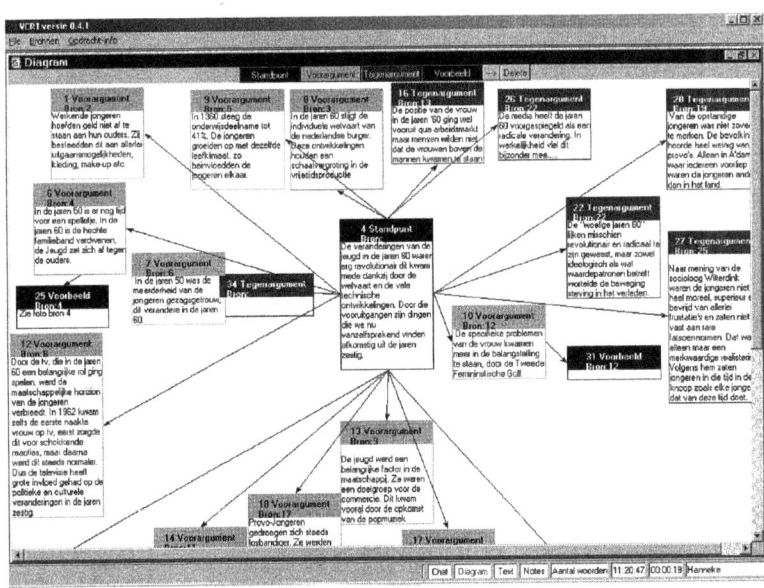

Fig. 2. Example of a diagram constructed by one of the dyads (in Dutch).

viewpoint. All text-boxes can be linked to each other by arrows. Furthermore, in each box students can refer to the source from which the argument or the example derives.

List. Whereas an argumentative diagram organizes arguments in a graphical way and arguments can be linked to each other and to a point of view, arguments can also be organized in a linear way. In the List condition we used a list tool. In this window students can list arguments pro and arguments contra.

Matrix. The argumentative diagram and list do not pay explicit attention to more domain-specific aspects of the argumentation process that is required by the task. The task is about historical change. Historical change can occur in very different areas, for instance beliefs or family life. In describing and evaluating processes of change, historians often make a distinction between political, economical, social and cultural changes. Furthermore, they characterize changes according to their tempo and impact. A matrix is a format in which changes can be characterized using several columns. The matrix that was used in the matrix tool consists of a table format, which can be filled by the students. In the source column the number of the source can be put down, in the column description of changes, students can describe the historical changes (but also things that stay the same). In the next column they can answer the question whether they think the change can be defined as revolutionary or not (yes or no). The last column contains a sort function. Students can categorize the changes in the way they choose. When they push on the sort button, all the changes are sorted. For example, students categorize the changes as cultural, political and economical. After sorting, all the changes with the same label are listed below each other.

2.4 Instruments and analyses

Our analyses focused on the process as well as the products of the collaboration on the historical task. All actions during working on the task were logged. We analyzed the interaction processes in the chat protocols, the jointly constructed representations, the collaboratively written essays and the results of the individual post-test. In our analyses of the processes we focused on historical reasoning, elaboration and co-construction.

Chat protocols. The interaction processes in the chat protocols were coded by using MEPA, a computer program for Multiple Episode Protocol Analysis (Erkens, 2002, see http://edugate.fss.uu.nl/mepa). The interaction processes were coded on the level of utterances and were first analyzed on the dimension of Task Acts. Five main categories were distinguished:

utterances related to the content of the task at hand (coded Task), to procedures to perform the task (coded Procedure), talk about the technical functioning of the computer-program (Program), social talk (Social), and greetings at the start or ending of a working period (Greetings).

We coded historical reasoning on an episodic level. We distinguished historical reasoning episodes and episodes in which no historical reasoning occurred. Historical reasoning episodes are episodes consisting of Task utterances in which students say something about the past, give an interpretation of the past or of the value of sources. Six types of historical reasoning were discerned: situating historical phenomenon in time, describing the past, describing changes (or continuity), explaining the past, discussing the sources and taking a point of view and support this with argumentation.

We also analyzed the historical reasoning episodes on the appearance and type of elaboration. We discerned three types of elaboration: question, conflict and reasoning (Van Boxtel, 2000). Furthermore, we analyzed the amount of co-construction in the historical reasoning episodes. Inspired by the modes of social processing of Kumpulainen and Mutanen (1999) we made the following distinction: individual reasoning (only propositional contributions of one student), reasoning dominated by one of the students, and co-construction (both students equally contribute to the reasoning).

We coded historical reasoning episodes as *co-elaborated historical reasoning* whenever the reasoning reflected both elaboration and co-construction. The fragment below shows an example of co-elaborated historical reasoning. In this example Paula and Wendy discuss their point of view on the question whether the sixties were revolutionary or not. Paula and Wendy co-construct their meaning on this subject. First, they talk about which point of view they are taking, and whether they both agree on this. They ask questions which elicit elaboration, such as "What is our opinion?"; "Why?" and "Which arguments pro are we going to use?". They both, in turn, add arguments to support their meaning, and they elaborate upon the reasoning of the partner, as is shown in line 16 and 17.

Interrater reliability for the different categories mentioned was satisfactory and ranged from .69 to .95 (Cohen's kappa).

Next to the degree of co-construction in historical reasoning, we used a second indicator for the co-construction of knowledge, namely the equality in participation. We measured the asymmetry in participation as the mean percentages deviation from an equal distribution of chat, representational tool and essay contributions in the dyads.

Scoring of the external representations. The external representations that the students produced were scored on the number of arguments pro and contra that were represented. The interrater reliability (Cohen's kappa) was

Example 1:

Co-elaborated historical reasoning (fragment of chat protocol, translated from Dutch)

1	Paula	*But what is our opinion?*
2	Wendy	*To start with, what is your opinion?*
3	Paula	*The sixties were revolutionary.*
4	Wendy	*Why?*
5	Paula	*Because the consequences are still noticeable now.*
6	Wendy	*Okay, that is true.*
7	Paula	*But it already started in '50.*
8	Wendy	*That's true too, but that's got little to do with the revolutionariousness, so the sixties were indeed revolutionary!?*
9	Paula	*If you think so too.*
10	Wendy	*Yes, sure I do too.*
11	Paula	*Okay.*
12	Wendy	*Which arguments pro are we going to use?*
13	Paula	*That young people became a group, and that they had their own opinion.*
14	Wendy	*The depillarization* went on strongly.*
15	Paula	*Yes, and the consumptive society arose.*
16	Wendy	*People started to think more flexible about sex, which meant greater freedom for young people.*
17	Paula	*Yes, young people had more freedom anyway, because of their being financially independent they were able to leave their parents more early and they were independent of their parents.*
18	Wendy	*Exactly.*
19	Paula	*Okay.*

* Depillarization refers to the breakdown of the strict division in socio-religious groups or pillars (Protestants, Catholics, Socialists, and Liberalists) that existed in Dutch society since the beginning of the twentieth century

.89 for the arguments pro and .78 for the arguments contra. We also scored the number of sources referred to in the representation; the total number of arguments used (arguments pro plus arguments contra) and the balance of arguments pro and contra. The balance refers to the difference between the number of arguments pro and the arguments contra. So, a higher score means less balance. We have to take into account that based upon the sources that were provided, more arguments pro could be identified compared to arguments contra. In sum, sixteen arguments pro could be identified from the sources and ten arguments contra.

Scoring of the essays. The essays were scored on six aspects of historical reasoning: time references, changes and continuity, explanations, use of sources, argumentation, and the use of historical concepts. The scoring took into account both amount and quality. For example, the number of explanations given, as well as the quality of the explanations given. Furthermore, a score was given for the structure of the complete essay. The maximum score on the essay was 60 points. The essays were independently judged by two researchers and differences were discussed until agreement was reached.

Pre-test and post-test. The pre- and post-test focused on subject knowledge about the sixties, for the aim of the task was to improve subject-matter knowledge. The test contained seven open answer questions and one multiple choice question. The items were constructed in line with the different aspects of historical reasoning (see Table 1).

Table 1. Description of the items of the tests.

Item	Description	Components of historical reasoning	Max score
1a	Associations fifties*		7
1b	Associations sixties*		7
2	Situating historical phenomena in time**	Time	10
3	Giving a definition of four concepts	Concepts	8
4	Giving examples of four concepts	Concepts	8
5a	Giving characteristics of the youth in the fifties	Changes	4
5b	Describing changes in the behavior of the youth in the sixties		4
6a	Giving causes for the changes in the behavior of the youth in the sixties	Explanation	10
6b	Indicating the most important cause		2
7a	Giving arguments pro the given statement	Viewpoint	6
7b	Giving arguments contra the given statement		6
8a	Interpretation of a source	Source	2
8b	Interpretation of a source		2
8c	Evaluating the trustworthiness of both sources		3

* association item: item in which students are asked to give associations on the fifties and the sixties in a mindmap.
** Multiple choice items. The answers were correct or false.

The pre- and post-test consisted of the same questions; only for some items different historical sources (for example a different picture or text) were used. The maximum score on both tests was 79. The interrater reliability of the scoring, on ten randomly chosen tests, varied between .70 and 1.00 (Cohen's kappa). After excluding item 1a, in which the students had to give associations on the fifties, the item homogeneity (Cronbach's alpha) turned out to be acceptable (pre-test .72; post-test .64).

Questionnaires. After finishing the assignment the students were asked to fill out a questionnaire that contained evaluative questions about the task and the computer environment.

2.5 Hypotheses and statistical analyses

We expected that in the CSCL-environment that we used, tools for the joint construction of an external representation would be helpful for the organization of the available information and writing an essay together. The main question of this study is whether and how the construction of an external representation in a CSCL-environment influences the collaborative processes and the learning outcomes. We expected that the experimental conditions (Diagram, List and Matrix) would show more co-elaborated historical reasoning, better essays and higher scores on the post-test than the control group. Based upon the characteristics of the different forms of representation used, we were interested in differences in the collaborative processes, the constructed representations and the written essays. We also had some explicit expectations. We expected that a graphical form would have more potential to promote balance in the representation of arguments pro and contra than a linear format, because in a diagram the balance is more salient. In a diagram one can easily see whether the balance between arguments pro and contra is uneven. We expected that, compared to the Diagram and the List, the Matrix would have more potential to support important components of historical reasoning in both chat and essay and would therefore result in more historical reasoning in the chat, better essays and consequently higher scores on the individual post-test.

To test whether students learned from the task, we performed a paired sample T-test. To test whether there were significant differences between the conditions we conducted analyses of variance: One-way ANOVA, as well as MANOVA and MANCOVA. First, however, we checked whether the assumptions for analyses of variances were met. Because the demand of homogeneity of variance was not met for all the variables, we used Dunnett's C post hoc test. When a different post hoc test is used, this will be mentioned. Furthermore, we used correlational analyses to verify our assumption that the amount of co-elaborated historical reasoning, the quality of the constructed representation, the quality of the essay and the scores on the post-test are positively related.

3 Results

In this section we present the results of the analyses of the chat protocols, the quality of the constructed representation in the tool, the essays, and the results on the pre- and post-test. Finally, we will present the results of the correlational analyses.

3.1 Chat protocols

The mean length of the protocols was 361.4 utterances (SD 171.5). Only a small part of the utterances was given the code historical reasoning: a mean of 26.7 utterances (a mean of 7.4% of the total number of utterances). Table 2 shows the mean frequencies of utterances that are part of different types of historical reasoning episodes.

With respect to the number of historical reasoning utterances Table 2 shows that students in the Matrix and Control Condition showed more his-

Table 2. Mean frequencies and standard deviations of historical reasoning in the chat protocols for the four conditions (N=65)

Historical reasoning	Diagram (N = 16)	List (N = 14)	Matrix (N = 18)	Control (N = 17)
Time	0.4 (1.1)	1.3 (2.8)	1.2 (3.0)	5.1 (6.5)
Description	3.4 (4.9)	2.3 (3.2)	5.2 (5.9)	6.8 (11.1)
Change	3.4 (5.0)	2.9 (4.2)	14.1 (15.4)	6.1 (11.8)
Explanation	0.4 (1.3)	0.9 (2.7)	1.2 (3.5)	0.8 (2.9)
Source	0.7 (1.8)	0.1 (0.5)	1.4 (5.2)	0.9 (3.0)
Standpoint	8.4 (6.6)	10.1 (7.1)	11.2 (11.5)	15.5 (17.1)
Total	16.7 (14.8)	17.6 (11.0)	34.3 (23.4)	35.2 (35.3)

torical reasoning, compared to the List and Diagram condition. A One-way ANOVA revealed a significant difference between the conditions on the amount of historical reasoning ($F(3, 61) = 3.056; p \leq .05$), however the post hoc tests did not yield any differences between conditions. With respect to the types of historical reasoning, Table 2 shows that much historical reasoning was about the point of view the students would take and about the historical changes in the sixties. Both aspects were central to the task. A MANOVA on the components of historical reasoning revealed an overall effect ($F(18, 164) = 1.840; p \leq .05$). Significant differences between the conditions were found for the categories Time ($F(3, 61) = 4.745; p \leq .01$) and Change ($F(3, 61) = 4.004; p \leq .05$). A Dunnett's C post hoc test revealed that students in the Matrix condition talked significantly more about historical changes compared to the students in the List condition. This is in line with our expectations. Furthermore, the students in the Control condition made more time references compared to the students in the Diagram condition.

We were also interested in the amount of elaboration in the chat protocols and distinguished three types of elaboration. The mean frequencies of utterances that were part of an *elaborated* historical reasoning episode are given in Table 3. Most elaboration was related to the asking and answering of a question. The analyses of variance showed no significant differences in amount and type of elaboration between the conditions.

Table 3. Mean frequencies and standard deviations of elaboration in the chat protocols for the four conditions and the results of analyses of variance (N = 65)

	Diagram (N = 16)	List (N = 14)	Matrix (N = 18)	Control (N = 17)	F	p
Elaboration	12.2 (12.7)	11.8 (10.4)	20.9 (18.2)	27.1 (32.4)	2.047	.117
-question	6.1 (9.1)	7.2 (8.4)	10.5 (9.0)	13.2 (12.2)	1.730	.170
-conflict	0.9 (3.0)	1.4 (4.0)	2.0 (6.1)	0.9 (2.7)	0.265	.850
-reasoning	5.1 (5.3)	3.1 (4.3)	8.4 (11.7)	13.0 (21.7)	1.707	.175
No elaboration	4.6 (4.8)	5.9 (6.1)	13.4 (16.8)	8.1 (5.5)	2.580	.062

Did the conditions show differences in the degree of co-construction? Table 4 shows three indicators of co-construction: the degree of co-construction in historical reasoning (frequency of utterances that are part of co-constructed, dominated and individual historical reasoning episodes), the amount of co-elaboration (frequency of utterances that are part of reasoning episodes that are both co-constructed and elaborated), and the equality of participation in the chat.

Table 4. Mean frequencies and standard deviations of co-construction in the chat protocols for the four conditions and the results of analyses of variance (N = 65)

	Diagram (N = 16)	List (N = 14)	Matrix (N = 18)	Control (N = 17)	F	p
Degree of co-construction						
-Co-construction	7.6 (10.5)	10.3 (9.8)	22.8 (20.0)	28.4 (31.1)	3.884	.013
-Domination	3.4 (5.1)	2.2 (4.1)	4.2 (7.1)	3.3 (4.2)	0.371	.774
-Individual	5.8 (4.9)	5.0 (5.9)	7.3 (7.4)	3.5 (4.1)	0.969	.413
Co-elaboration	6.7 (10.0)	9.6 (10.3)	13.4 (13.7)	23.9 (30.4)	2.727	.052
Equality chat Participation	8.8 (8.4)	18.1 (8.2)	10.3 (7.0)	11.8 (9.4)	3.574	.019

The results of a one-way ANOVA (Table 4) with co-construction as a dependent variable revealed a significant effect. However the post hoc tests did not show any significant differences. We expected that the conditions with a representational tool would showed more co-elaborated historical reasoning than the control group. With respect to the amount of co-elaboration, the Control and Matrix conditions showed the largest amount of co-elaboration. Although the ANOVA resulted in a marginally significant difference, the post hoc tests did not yield any significant difference between the conditions.

Furthermore, Table 4 shows that the asymmetry in chat participation was quite low, so both students contributed equally in the chat. A One-way ANOVA revealed a significant difference between the conditions. Tukey HSD showed that this difference existed between the List and Matrix and between the List and the Diagram. In the Diagram and the Matrix condition the participation in the chat was more equal than in the List condition.

3.2 Constructed representations

In the experimental conditions the students collaboratively constructed a representation. Did the three experimental conditions differ in the number of represented arguments, the balance between arguments pro and contra, the number of sources used and the equality of participation in the construction of the representation?

ANOVA's were conducted to test whether there were differences between the conditions. The results showed an overall effect of the conditions on the total number of arguments ($F(2, 45) = 13.191; p \leq .00$), arguments pro ($F(2, 45) = 17.279; p \leq .00$), as well as arguments contra ($F(2, 45) = 4.281; p \leq .05$). The post hoc tests revealed that both in the List and in the Matrix condition more arguments were used compared to the Diagram condition. In the Matrix most arguments pro were used, next to the List and the Diagram. The post hoc tests did not show any significant differences on the number of arguments contra.

Additionally, we looked at the balance between the arguments pro and contra. The balance was computed as the difference between the number of arguments pro and the number of arguments contra. So, a larger score means less balance. A one-way ANOVA revealed a significant difference between the conditions ($F(2, 45) = 4.916; p \leq .05$). This difference was found between the Diagram and Matrix condition. In line with our expectations, the diagrams showed more balance than the matrices.

Table 5 also shows the number of sources used in the representations. In sum, 26 sources were available. In the Matrix condition almost all sources were used (a mean of 25), in the List condition the mean number of used sources was 21 and in the Diagram condition students used the least sources. A one-way ANOVA revealed a significant difference between the conditions ($F(2, 45) = 36.155; p \leq .00$), and the post hoc tests showed that this difference was between all three conditions. No difference in symmetry of participation during the construction of the tool was found.

Table 5. Mean scores and standard deviations of representation scores for the diagram, list and matrix and the results of analysis of variance (N = 48)

	Diagram (N = 16)	List (N = 14)	Matrix (N = 18)	F	p
Total arguments	13.5 (3.7)	17.6 (3.1)	18.6 (2.0)	13.191	.000
-Arguments pro	8.9 (2.4)	10.9 (1.6)	12.5 (1.2)	17.279	.000
-Arguments contra	4.6 (1.9)	6.7 (2.5)	6.1 (1.7)	4.281	.020
Balance pro and contra	4.3 (2.3)	4.2 (2.8)	6.4 (2.1)	4.916	.012
Sources used	14.3 (4.8)	20.9 (4.5)	25.1 (0.7)	36.155	.000
Equality in participation	27.1 (17.0)	27.7 (19.4)	31.2 (21.7)	.219	.804

In the questionnaire the students were asked to give their opinion about working with the representational tool. About 80% of the students who worked with one of the representational tools ($N = 96$) thought it a useful way of working. Reasons that they gave were that the tool helped them to select important information for the essay, and to structure this information. About 15% (5% was missing) was not that positive and considered the construction of the representation as extra work, or preferred their own way of working. The students who worked in the Control group were asked whether they preferred the way they worked, or the way the other group of students in their class worked (they used the Matrix). One third of the 30 students who filled out the questionnaire did actually prefer to work with the matrix tool, for they thought it to be a useful way to select and organize the information.

3.3. Learning outcomes

3.3.1 Essays

Did the construction of different representations result in differences in learning outcomes? First, we examine the results of the collaboratively written essays. In Table 6 we have presented the scores for the categories that we used to describe the quality of the essays.

Table 6. Mean scores and standard deviations and maximum scores for the essays in four conditions (N = 65)

	Diagram ($N = 16$)	List ($N = 14$)	Matrix ($N = 18$)	Control ($N = 17$)	Maximum score
Time	4.8 (0.8)	5.4 (0.7)	5.0 (0.8)	5.4 (0.9)	6
Concept	6.9 (1.2)	6.4 (1.1)	6.9 (1.3)	7.3 (1.6)	12
Change	6.1 (1.1)	6.5 (0.9)	6.8 (1.2)	6.6 (1.1)	9
Explanation	4.4 (0.8)	4.1 (1.6)	4.6 (1.3)	4.4 (0.9)	9
Standpoint	8.5 (2.5)	10.2 (2.0)	8.8 (2.2)	9.2 (2.2)	15
Source	3.9 (1.1)	4.1 (1.0)	3.9 (1.1)	4.4 (1.2)	6
Structure	1.9 (0.8)	1.9 (0.7)	1.9 (0.7)	1.9 (0.6)	3
Total	*36.7 (5.1)*	*38.6 (4.9)*	*38.1 (5.3)*	*39.2 (4.6)*	*60*
Equality in participation	41.8 (34.2)	37.1 (27.4)	44.6 (27.5)	34.7 (25.7)	

A MANOVA was conducted on the essay scores, which did not result in significant differences between the conditions ($F(21, 161) = 1.070$; $p = .39$) Next, we looked at the equality in participation in the construction of the essay. The high mean scores show that, compared to the equality of participation in the chat and in the construction of the representation, there was relatively less symmetry in the contribution of the two partners during the writing of the essay. No differences between the conditions were found. We expected that the conditions in which the students had constructed an external representation would show higher scores for the essays than the control group. One possible explanation for the fact that this expectation was not met could be that the students who did not have to construct a representation could spend more time on writing the essay. To check this assumption we distracted from the log files the time spend on the different tools in the CSCL-environment: the chat, the notes, the construction of the representation and the writing of the essay (see Table 7). If the aforementioned explanation is to be true, the control group should have spent significantly more time at the writing of the essay. Although the difference between the conditions turned out to be marginally significant, the post hoc test (Tukey HSD) did not yield any significant difference between the conditions. Thus, the students in the Control condition did not spend significantly more time on the writing of the essay, compared to the other conditions. However, they did spend significantly more time on writing in the notes. Tukey HSD post hoc test showed a significant difference between the Control condition and the other three conditions. In general the note window was used by the individual student (it was not a shared tool) to summarize important information from the sources. They also used the note window to write (parts of) paragraphs for the essay, when the partner was writing in the text editor (in which they could not work in at the same time). The fact that the students in the Control condition spent more time making notes, could actually mean that they spent more time on the writing of the essay, not in the shared text editor, but in their personal note window.

Table 7. Mean time (in minutes) and standard deviations spent on the different tools in the CSCL-environment for the four conditions (N = 65)and the results of a one-way ANOVA

	Diagram (N = 16)	List (N = 14)	Matrix (N = 18)	Control (N = 17)	F	p
Chat	76.3 (34.8)	71.9 (22.9)	80.5 (18.4)	85.2 (25.8)	.747	.529
Notes	43.4 (25.6)	61.0 (35.6)	55.6 (31.3)	93.2 (36.4)	6.280	.001
Representation	66.4 (21.1)	54.2 (16.0)	77.1 (33.6)	-	3.165	.052
Essay	49.0 (26.1)	47.1 (27.5)	55.6 (24.4)	68.8 (20.9)	2.553	.064

3.2.3 Pre- and post-test

In Table 8 the results of the pre- and post-test on the main items are presented, as well as the maximum scores. A paired samples T-test showed that the students improved on all items of the test ($p \geq .05$), the only exception was that the students in the List condition did not improve on their scores on the Source item.

The total score on the pre-test turned out to be different for the conditions ($F(3, 126) = 14.562; p = .000$). The post hoc test revealed that the score in the Diagram and List conditions was higher than the score in the Matrix and Control condition. We therefore used the score on the pre-test as a covariate in the analyses. A MANCOVA with the total pre-test score as a covariate showed a significant effect of the conditions on the post-test scores ($F (21, 353) = 1.763; p \geq .05$). Simple contrast analyses showed the following significant differences ($p \geq .05$) between the conditions:
- The Control condition scored higher than the Diagram condition on Explanation, Standpoint and Source;
- The Control condition scored higher than the List condition on Standpoint and Source;
- The Control condition scored higher than the Matrix condition on Concepts;
- The Diagram condition scored higher than the List condition on Associations;

- The List condition scored higher than the Matrix condition on Concepts. We expected the Matrix condition to score higher on the items about Change, because in this condition in the chat the students reasoned more about processes of change and continuity, but this expectation was not met.

Table 8. Mean scores and standard deviations of the pre-test and the post-test per condition, and maximum scores (N = 130)

	Diagram (N = 32)		List (N = 28)		Matrix (N = 36)		Control (N = 34)		Max. Score
	Pre-test	Post-test	Pre-test	Post-test	Pre-test	Post-test	Pre-test	Post-test	
Associations	3.1	5.9	3.1	5.3	2.6	5.4	2.0	5.5	7
	(1.4)	(1.0)	(1.6)	(1.4)	(1.9)	(1.1)	(1.3)	(1.2)	
Time	6.4	7.1	5.9	7.5	5.5	7.3	4.9	7.5	10
	(1.6)	(1.5)	(1.8)	(1.3)	(2.0)	(1.5)	(2.5)	(1.8)	
Concept	8.1	11.2	8.1	12.1	5.9	9.6	5.4	11.2	16
	(2.7)	(2.4)	(2.7)	(2.0)	(2.5)	(2.6)	(2.9)	(4.4)	
Change	2.5	4.3	2.6	4.6	1.9	4.2	1.9	4.5	8
	(1.3)	(1.4)	(1.5)	(1.5)	(1.4)	(1.3)	(1.3)	(1.3)	
Explanation	2.6	5.1	2.5	5.1	1.4	5.0	0.8	5.9	12
	(1.9)	(2.7)	(1.8)	(2.3)	(1.7)	(2.5)	(1.1)	(2.4)	
Standpoint	1.7	3.3	2.1	3.4	1.7	3.5	1.1	3.7	12
	(1.2)	(1.9)	(1.2)	(1.4)	(1.4)	(1.4)	(1.2)	(1.4)	
Source	3.4	4.2	3.6	4.1	3.0	4.4	2.7	4.6	7
	(1.7)	(1.7)	(1.7)	(1.6)	(1.8)	(1.7)	(1.8)	(1.9)	
Total	27.8	41.1	27.9	42.1	21.8	39.4	18.7	43.0	72
	(4.3)	(7.2)	(5.5)	(5.9)	(6.5)	(7.6)	(8.4)	(7.6)	

3.4 Correlational analyses

We were interested in the question whether more co-elaborated historical reasoning in the chat protocols went together with higher scores for the essay and higher scores on the post-test. Furthermore, we wanted to know whether the students who constructed a representation of higher quality also wrote a better essay and performed better on the post-test. We therefore carried out correlational analyses for the variables: co-elaborated historical reasoning, scores of the constructed representation, scores of the essay and the scores on the post-test. Notice that the scores on the test are individual scores, whereas the scores on the other three variables are group scores. To calculate the correlations between the test scores and the other variables, the pair score was subscribed to the individual students. This results in an enlargement of the N. In the Diagram condition there was a significant correlation between the number of arguments in the representation and the post-test scores ($r = .49$, $p = .005$, $N = 32$). Only in the Matrix condition the number of utterances that belonged to co-elaborated episodes correlated significantly with the score of the essay ($r = .66$, $p = .003$, $N = 18$). More co-elaboration went together with higher scores for the essay. However, in the other conditions this result was not found.

4 Discussion

We studied the effects of the construction of an external representation on the collaborative construction of historical knowledge in a CSCL-environment and on individual learning outcomes. We focused on historical reasoning, elaboration and co-construction. A general result was that the chat was hardly used for discussion of the content. In all conditions only a small part of all utterances was related to historical reasoning. We found the same result in a previous study. Perhaps because typewritten utterances involve more effort than speaking, students might confine themselves to what is minimal necessary for the coordination of the task. Furthermore, historical reasoning, elaboration and co-construction not only take place in the chat discussion but also *through* the use of the tools. If a student for example adds an argument in the diagram or puts some sentences in the shared text editor, he or she does not mention it in the chat. However, by adding it in the representational tool or text, the argument is in a way communicated to the other student and becomes part of the shared context. The fact that the argumentation in the tool and in the text is of reasonable quality, brings us to the conclusion that the tool does not only function as a cognitive tool which can elicit elaborative activities, but as a tool *through which* students communicate and elaborate. We did not analyse the amount of historical reasoning, elaboration and co-construction in this way.

We compared the effects of different representational tools. The results of our analyses show some important advantages and disadvantages of each form of representation. We expected the matrix to have more potential to support domain-specific reasoning. Our hypothesis was confirmed. The students in the Matrix condition talked most about historical changes, a component of historical reasoning that was most important for the task that we used. In the Matrix condition the students represented the most arguments and used almost all sources. This finding is in line with results of the study of Suthers and Hundhausen (2002) in which the matrix group represented the most evidential relations. In our study the matrix seems to have prompted students to fill in all available changes and continuities. However, the students who constructed a matrix did not produce a better essay, nor did they score higher on the post-test.

In the Diagram condition the jointly constructed representation contained significantly less arguments and references to sources than the Matrix and List condition. The students were provided with a lot of sources which they could use to answer the historical question and to write the essay. A diagram might be less suited for representing a lot of information. An advantage of an argumentative diagram lies in the fact that it is possible to organize the arguments and to interrelate these with links. However, a diagram might become too complex and too hard to organize when a lot of information has to be organized. The results of our study also showed an advantage of constructing a diagram. In line with our expectations, in the diagrams students reached more balance between arguments pro and contra. Both a diagram and a matrix are graphical forms of representation. In one of the conditions we used a linear form of representation: a list. In the Diagram and Matrix condition the participation in the chat was more equal compared to the chat participation in the List condition. From a co-construction perspective, one might conclude that graphical forms of representation have more potential to provoke an equal participation of collaborating students. In general, the participation in the chat and in the construction of the external representation was reasonably equal, whereas the participation in the writing of the essay showed much more asymmetry. More research is needed to investigate how students can be promoted to contribute more equally in the co-authoring of an essay.

An important construct in our study is co-elaborated historical reasoning. It combines activities that can be considered important for collaborative learning: domain-specific reasoning, elaboration and co-construction. Contrary to our expectations, the conditions in which students constructed an external representation did not show more co-elaborated historical reasoning in the chat. Because students did not used the chat very intensively to discuss the content of the task, it is not so surprising that co-elaborated reasoning did not correlate with scores for the essay and with individual learning outcomes. Only in the Matrix condition the number of utterances that belonged to co-elaborated episodes correlated significantly with the score of the essay.

The students who constructed an external representation did not produce better essays than the students in the control group. Additional analyses suggest that the students in the control group spent more time on writing the essay which might have resulted in a comparable quality of the essay as in the experimental conditions. The students in the Control group spent more time making notes in which also parts of the essay were written when the other student was working in the text editor.

The collaborative construction of a representation did not result in the general positive effect that we expected. The Control group scored as well as, and sometimes even better than, the experimental groups. A possible explanation is that students had not enough experience with constructing an external representation, let alone how to use this representation for writing the essay. Especially the diagram was new, whereas the list and matrix were probably more familiar. Furthermore, a number of aspects is of influence on students' behavior and learning results, such as motivation, text writing skills and experience with CSCL. We conducted some exploratory analyses on the aspect of experience with CSCL. We did this, because some of the students who participated in the Control and Matrix condition had more experience with CSCL, for they had participated in other research with a similar kind of CSCL-environment. The students in these conditions showed higher scores on several aspects. We checked whether this experience was of influence on their chat discussions. We divided our participants in two new groups, the first group had experience with CSCL ($N = 23$) and the other did not ($N = 42$). We conducted a MANOVA on the level of Task acts, for we are interested whether the general pattern of the chat-discussion was influenced by experience. Our additional analyses suggest that experience with CSCL is of influence on how students interact with each other in chat discussions. More specifically, students with experience showed more historical reasoning in their chat discussions. When we excluded the experienced students, there turned out to be no effect of the conditions on the amount of historical reasoning.

In sum, our study shows that the representational tools that we used influenced some aspects of the collaborative learning process in a CSCL-environment, but did not have the expected positive effects on the learning outcomes (although all students learned from the task). Continued work in this area needs to give us more insight into the support that representational tools can give, especially with respect to the domain-specific reasoning that is asked for in the task. Furthermore, more research about the role of experience with a CSCL-environment and of experience with constructing and using external representations is needed.

References

Boscolo, P., & Mason, L. (2001). Writing to learn, writing to transfer. In P. Tynjälä, L. Mason, & K. Lonka (Eds.), *Writing as a learning tool. Integrating theory and practice* (pp. 83-104). Dordrecht: Kluwer Academic Publishers.

Cox, R. (1999). Representation construction, externalised cognition and individual differences. *Learning and Instruction, 9*, 343-363.

Crook, C. (1998). Children as computer users: The case of collaborative learning. *Computers and Education, 30*, 237-247.

De Jong, T., Ainsworth, S., Dobson, M., Van der Hulst, A., Levonen, J., Reimann, P., Sime, J., Van Someren, M.W., Spada, H., & Swaak, J. (1998). Acquiring knowledge in science and mathematics: The use of multiple representations in technology-based learning environments. In M.W. Van Someren, P. Reimann, H.P.A. Boshuizen, & T. de Jong (Eds.), *Learning with multiple representations* (pp. 9-40). Oxford: Pergamon.

Erkens, G. (2002, March). *MEPA. Multiple Episode Protocol Analysis (Version 4.8)* [Computer software]. Utrecht, The Netherlands: Utrecht University.

Erkens, G., Jaspers, J., & Prangsma, M. (2001). *Coordinated activity in collaborative learning*. Paper presented at the 9th European Conference on Learning and Instruction, August 28th – September 1st, Fribourg, Switzerland.

Gere, A.R., & Stevens, R.S. (1985). The language of writing groups: How oral response shapes revision. In S.W. Freedman (Ed.), *The acquisition of written language. Response and Revision* (pp. 85-105). Norwood, NJ: Ablex.

Jaspers, J., & Erkens, G. (2002, September). *VCRI. Virtual Collaborative Research Institute* (Version 1.0) [Computer software]. Utrecht, The Netherlands: Utrecht University.

Kanselaar, G., De Jong, T., Andriessen, J., & Goodyear, P. (2000). New Technologies. In

P.J.R. Simons, J.L. van der Linden, & T. Duffy (Eds.), *New learning* (pp. 55-82). Kluwer: Academic Press.

Kirschner, P. A. (2002). Can we support CSCL? Educational, social and technological affordances for learning [Inaugural Address]. In P.A. Kirschner, W. Jochems, P. Dillenbourg, & G. Kanselaar (Eds.), *Three worlds of CSCL: Can we support CSCL?* Heerlen: Open Universiteit Nederland.

Klein, P.D. (1999). Reopening inquiry into cognitive processes in writing-to-learn. *Educational Psychology Review, 11*, 203-270.

Kumpulainen, K., & Mutanen, M. (1999). The situated dynamics of peer group interaction: An introduction to an analytic framework. *Learning and Instruction, 9*, 449-473.

Leinhardt, G., Stainton, C., Virji, S.M., & Odoroff, E. (1994). Learning to reason in history: Mindlessness to mindfulness. In M. Carretero & J.F. Voss (Eds.), *Cognitive and instructional processes in history and the social sciences* (pp. 131-158). Hillsdale, NJ: Lawrence Erlbaum Associates.

Lethinen, E., Hakkarainen, K., Lipponen, L., Rahikainen, M., & Muukonen, H. (2001). *Computer supported collaborative learning: A review.* CL-Net Project. Available online at: http://www.kas.utu.fi/clnet/clnetreport.html [2001, September 4].

Lipponen, L. (2002). Exploring fundations for Computer-Supported Collaborative Learning. In *Computer Support for Collaborative Learning: Foundations for a CSCL Community*. Proceedings of CSCL 2002, January 7-11, Boulder, Colorado, USA.

Schegloff, E. (1991). Conversation analysis and socially shared cognition. In L.B. Resnick, J.M. Levine, & S.D. Teasley (Eds.), *Perspectives on socially shared cognition* (pp. 150-171). Washington: American Psychological Association.

Stahl, G. (2002). Contributions to a theoretical framework for CSCL. In *Computer Support for Collaborative Learning: Foundations for a CSCL Community*. Proceedings of CSCL 2002, January 7-11, 20002, Boulder, CO, USA.

Suthers, D.D., & Hundhausen, C.D. (2001) Learning by constructing collaborative representations: An empirical comparison of three alternatives. In P. Dillenbourg, A. Eurelings, & K. Hakkarainen (Eds.), *Proceedings European Perspectives on Computer-Supported Collaborative Learning* (pp. 577-584).. Maastricht: Universiteit Maastricht.

Suthers, D.D., & Hundhausen, C.D. (2002). The effects of representation on students' elaborations in collaborative inquiry. In *Computer Support for Collaborative Learning: Foundations for a CSCL Community*. Proceedings of CSCL 2002, January 7-11, 20002, Boulder, CO, USA.

Tynjälä. P., Mason, L., & Lonka, K. (2001). Writing as a learning tool: An introduction. In P. Tynjälä, L. Mason, & K. Lonka (Eds.), *Writing as a learning tool. Integrating theory and practice (pp. 7-22)..* Dordrecht: Kluwer Academic Publishers.

Van Boxtel, C. (2004). Dialogic physics learning: Studying student interaction from three different perspectives. In P. Renshaw & J.L. van der Linden (Eds.), *Dialogic learning* (pp. 125-144). Dordrecht: Kluwer Academic Publishers.

Van Boxtel, C. (2000) *Collaborative concept learning. Collaborative learning tasks, student interaction, and the learning of physics concepts.* Dissertation, Utrecht University, The Netherlands.

Van Boxtel, C., & Van Drie, J. (2003). *Collaborative reasoning as a key concept for analyzing classroom discourse.* Paper presented at the EARLI Conference, august 26th - 30th, Padova Italy.

Van der Linden, J.L., Erkens, G., Schmidt, H., & Renshaw, P. (2000). Collaborative learning. In P.R.J. Simons, J.L. van der Linden, & T. Duffy (Eds.), *New learning* (pp. 37-54). Dordrecht: Kluwer Academic Publishers.

Van Drie, J., Van Boxtel, C., & Van der Linden, J.L. (in press). Historical reasoning in a computer-supported collaborative learning environment. In A.M. O'Donnell, J.L. van der Linden, & C.E. Hmelo (Eds.), *Collaborative learning, reasoning and technology.* Hillsdale, NJ: Lawrence Erlbaum Associates.

Veerman, A. (2000). *Computer-supported collaborative learning through argumentation.* Dissertation, Utrecht University, The Netherlands.

Veerman, A., & Treasure-Jones, T. (1999). Software for problem solving through collaborative argumentation. In J. Andriessen & P. Courier (Eds.), *Foundations of argumentative text processing* (pp. 203-230). Amsterdam: University Press.

Veldhuis-Diermanse, E. (2002). *CSCLearning? Participation, learning activities and knowledge construction in computer-supported collaborative learning in higher education.* Dissertation, Wageningen University, The Netherlands.

Voss, J.F., & Wiley, J. (1997). Developing understanding while writing essays in history. *International Journal of Educational Research, 27*, 255-265.

Zhang, J., & Norman, D.A. (1994). Representations in distributed cognitive tasks. *Cognitive Science, 18*, 87-122.

List of contributors

Bromage, Adrian, Center for Higher Education Development, Coventry University, UK

Catrambone, Richard, School of Psychology, Georgia Institute of Technology, USA

Corbalán-Pérez, Gemma, Educational Technology Expertise Centre (OTEC), Open University of the Netherlands, The Netherlands

Crahay, Marcel, Service de Pédagogie Expérimentale, Université de Liège, Belgium

De Bock, Dirk, Centre for Instructional Psychology and Technology, University of Leuven, Belgium

De Corte, Erik, Centre for Instructional Psychology and Technology, University of Leuven, Belgium

de Jong, Ton, Department of Instructional Technology, University of Twente, The Netherlands

De Westelinck, Katrien, Department of Education, University of Ghent, Belgium

Depaepe, Fien, Centre for Instructional Psychology and Technology, University of Leuven, Belgium

Entwistle, Noel, Department of Higher and Further Education, University of Edinburgh, UK

Fagnant, Annick, Service de Pédagogie Expérimentale, Université de Liège, Belgium

Gerjets, Peter, Knowlegde Media Research Center, Tübingen, Germany

Hannula, Minna M., Centre for Learning Research, Turku, Finland

Hessels, An, Centre for Instructional Psychology and Technology, University of Leuven, Belgium

Hoek, Dirk, Faculty of Psychology, Open University of the Netherlands, The Netherlands

Janssens, Dirk, Centre for Instructional Psychology and Technology, University of Leuven, Belgium

Kanselaar, Gellof, Department of Educational Sciences, University of Utrecht, The Netherlands

Kester, Liesbeth, Educational Technology Expertise Centre (OTEC), Open University of the Netherlands, The Netherlands

Kirschner, Paul, Educational Technology Expertise Centre (OTEC), Open University of the Netherlands, The Netherlands

Lehtinen, Erno, Centre for Learning Research, University of Turku, Finland

Mattinen, Aino, Centre for Learning Research, University of Turku, Finland

Nisbet, Jennifer, Higher and Community Education, University of Edinburgh, UK

Scheiter, Katharina, Department of Applied Cognitive Psychology and Media Psychology, University of Tübingen, Germany

Schoenfeld, Alan, Graduate School of Education, University of California, Berkeley, USA

Seegers, Gerard, Department of Education, University of Leiden, The Netherlands

Valcke, Martin, Department of Education, University fo Ghent, Belgium

van Boxtel, Carla, Department of Educational Sciences, University of Utrecht, The Netherlands

Van Dooren, Wim, Centre for Instructional Psychology and Technology, University of Leuven, Belgium

van Drie, Jannet, Department of Educational Sciences, University of Utrecht, The Netherlands

Verschaffel, Lieven, Centre for Instructional Psychology and Technology, University of Leuven, Belgium

Vlassis, Joëlle, Service de Pédagogie Expérimentale, Université de Liège, Belgium

Vosniadou, Stella, Department of Philosophy and History of Science, University of Athens, Greece

www.ingramcontent.com/pod-product-compliance
Ingram Content Group UK Ltd.
Pitfield, Milton Keynes, MK11 3LW, UK
UKHW021835140426
5217IPUK00021B/1470